Perception and Basic Beliefs

Perception and Basic Beliefs

Zombies, Modules, and the Problem of the External World

JACK C. LYONS

OXFORD

UNIVERSITY PRESS

2009

OXFORD
UNIVERSITY PRESS

Oxford University Press, Inc., publishes works that further
Oxford University's objective of excellence
in research, scholarship, and education.

Oxford   New York
Auckland   Cape Town   Dar es Salaam   Hong Kong   Karachi
Kuala Lumpur   Madrid   Melbourne   Mexico City   Nairobi
New Delhi   Shanghai   Taipei   Toronto

With offices in
Argentina   Austria   Brazil   Chile   Czech Republic   France   Greece
Guatemala   Hungary   Italy   Japan   Poland   Portugal   Singapore
South Korea   Switzerland   Thailand   Turkey   Ukraine   Vietnam

Published by Oxford University Press, Inc.
198 Madison Avenue, New York, New York 10016

www.oup.com

Oxford is a registered trademark of Oxford University Press

Library of Congress Cataloging-in-Publication Data
Lyons, Jack C.
Perception and basic beliefs : zombies, modules, and the problem
of the external world / Jack C. Lyons.
p.   cm.
ISBN 978-0-19-537357-8
1. Knowledge, Theory of.   I. Title.
BD161.L96   2009
121'.34—dc22   2008021283

1 3 5 7 9 8 6 4 2
Printed in the United States of America
on acid-free paper

For Patricia Lyons Linder 1960–2005

This book offers solutions to two persistent and I believe closely related problems in epistemology. The first problem is that of drawing a principled distinction between perception and inference: what is the difference between seeing that something is the case and merely believing it on the basis of what we do see? The second problem is that of specifying which beliefs are epistemologically basic (i.e., directly, or noninferentially, justified) and which are not. In concert with a growing number of contemporary epistemologists, and in opposition to the historically dominant tradition that holds that only beliefs about our current sensory experiences are directly justified, I contend that perceptual beliefs (beliefs about external objects) are themselves basic. (Not all basic beliefs are perceptual beliefs, however.) In contrast with both the tradition and the current trend, I argue that what makes a belief a perceptual belief, or a basic belief, is not a matter of the subject's contemporaneous nondoxastic experiences, nor the content of the belief in question, nor the subject's auxiliary beliefs; what determines whether a belief is basic or perceptual is the nature of the cognitive system, or "module," that is causally responsible for the belief. The class of modules whose outputs are perceptual beliefs, I argue, is a subset of the class of modules whose outputs are basic beliefs. Thus, even zombies, who in the philosophical literature lack conscious experiences altogether, can have basic, justified, perceptual beliefs.

It is doubtful that a theory of either perceptual belief or basic belief can be cogently defended in an epistemological vacuum. The theories of perceptual and basic beliefs developed here are embedded in a larger reliabilist epistemology. Not only does the reliabilist background theory lend substance and credibility to the theories of perceptual and basic beliefs I defend but also these theories in turn make for a better fleshed-out, new and more tenable, version of reliabilism. It is clear that if reliability is sufficient for justification, then nothing that is not entailed by reliability is necessary. In particular, reliabilism implies that neither inferential support nor sensory experiential validation is needed for justified belief. Implicit awareness of this point has surely been responsible for a great deal of resistance to reliabilism, but the point is rarely or never made explicit. Having made it explicit, the nonnecessity of experience and inference is something the reliabilist must either avoid or embrace.

I embrace the nonnecessity of experiential states. One of the most salient and striking features of perception is its experiential component, and though perception does yield belief and knowledge, these are all but overshadowed by the rich experiential, phenomenological element. This nondoxastic ingredient is also philosophically interesting in its own right. However, I think that the distinctively epistemological role of nondoxastic experience has been generally overrated. I don't believe that experiential states are the epistemological prime movers they are standardly thought to be, and the theory I defend is explicitly nonexperientialist, in that it allows beliefs, even perceptual beliefs, to be justified in the absence of any experiential state whatsoever.

Regarding the nonnecessity of inferential support, I want to split the difference with the antireliabilist, and the distinction between basic and nonbasic beliefs makes this possible. Though I do not think that every belief can be noninferentially justified, I do insist that some can. I agree that inferential support is required for nonbasic beliefs, and unlike previous reliabilist theories, mine explicitly marks some beliefs as nonbasic. However, I insist that reliability is indeed sufficient for the justification of basic beliefs; these beliefs do not require inferential support. My theory of basic beliefs is an externalist theory (i.e., whether a particular belief is basic cannot be ascertained by the agent on the basis of mere reflection), but this theory of basic beliefs actually bolsters reliabilism against a famous class of objections usually thought to argue for a kind of internalism. Though reliabilist theories generally constitute versions of foundationalism, mine does so explicitly and transparently, drawing an express distinction between basic and nonbasic beliefs. The famous objections just mentioned neither impugn the very notion of noninferential justification nor show that reliability is never sufficient for justification; rather, they show merely that *some* beliefs are nonbasic. I develop a detailed reliabilist theory, using the general framework of my theory of basic beliefs to work out a reliabilist theory of inferential justification in order to account for the justification of these nonbasic beliefs.

The plan of the book is as follows: in chapter 1, I lay out the basic issues, explaining why one might be interested in a theory that allows beliefs about external objects to be basic. In chapter 2, I distinguish between two senses in which something might be thought to justify beliefs; this makes it possible to sharpen the standard taxonomy of doxastic and nondoxastic theories, invoking two orthogonal principles: the Belief Principle holds that only beliefs can serve as evidence for beliefs; the Grounds Principle holds that every justified belief is one that is based on evidence. Though the former principle is often cited as the central slogan of doxastic theories (the diametric opposite of externalist theories like my own), it is actually a principle that the externalist can embrace. In fact, insistence on this principle can serve as a premise in an argument in favor of a nonevidentialist epistemology. Chapter 3 consists of a lengthy and sustained attack on what I take to be the experientialist orthodoxy, which maintains that nondoxastic experiences serve as evidence to justify basic beliefs. I use a cognitive scientific approach and chapter 2's distinction between evidential and nonevidential justifiers to breathe new life into a—vaguely—Sellarsian argument against experientialism. Whether experiential states are conceived as low-level states (sensations) or high-level states (percepts), they cannot serve as justifying evidence for basic beliefs. I offer an independent argument for the thesis that only beliefs can serve as justifying evidence for beliefs. The purpose of all this is to argue that some kind of nonevidentialist theory is true.

In chapter 4, I explain and defend the view that a perceptual belief is a belief that is the output of a perceptual system, that is, a perceptual module, where the notion of a perceptual module can be characterized in nonepistemic and nonexperientialist terms. Not only does this give us a principled and naturalistic distinction between perceptual beliefs and other beliefs but also, I argue, it gives us an intuitively correct one. The theory has the result that zombies and other creatures utterly lacking in perceptual experiences can nonetheless have (justified) perceptual beliefs. In chapter 5, I argue that, by holding that reliability is sufficient for the justification of basic beliefs while insisting that some beliefs are nonbasic, the reliabilist is immune to famous counterexamples involving clairvoyance and similar odd cognitive capacities. The reliabilist theory developed thus far holds that perceptual beliefs are basic, and I argue that this theory does not invite clairvoyance-type objections. I argue that other influential reliabilist attempts to answer the clairvoyance objection ultimately fail, and so will any such attempt that does not explicitly appeal to the basic-nonbasic distinction and require inferential support for the nonbasic beliefs. In chapter 6, I extrapolate from my account of perceptual beliefs and propose a general theory of basic beliefs: a basic belief is one that is the result of the noninferential operation of a primal system, an inferentially opaque cognitive system that has resulted from an interplay of learning and innate constraints. I explain all this and argue that it gets the cases intuitively right. I go on to argue that we can transcend and improve on these naive intuitions by turning to the empirical sciences to correct our untutored assumptions about which cognitive systems there are, where they come from, and what their outputs are.

The final evaluation of a theory of basicality is best done in the context of a full theory of justification, and since the framework is already in place, I provide a sketch of a wholly general theory in chapter 7. The cognitive system approach to basic beliefs has a natural analogue in my notion of a basic inference, and the use of this notion makes it possible to flesh out an inferentialist version of reliabilism. Though reliabilists have had little to say about inferential justification, this is a subject we need not avoid. A fairly detailed version of reliabilism, I hope more plausible than its predecessors, emerges. Despite the role it reserves for inferential justification, I argue that the resulting theory is still wholly externalist, albeit in a way that avoids notorious problems for earlier externalist theories. I finish by returning to the epistemological problem of the external world and explaining how and in what sense my theory solves this problem.

This book is an exercise in naturalized epistemology. The last two decades have witnessed the growth of a whole literature arguing for the relevance of empirical concepts and findings to epistemological theory construction. Important though such abstract argumentation may be, the case for a thoroughgoingly naturalistic epistemology will rest ultimately on its fruits, rather than on in-principle arguments for its necessity. I hope the present work reflects positively on the larger enterprise.

I am well aware that not everyone has been convinced of the need for or even the coherence of a naturalistic approach to epistemological issues. While it will quickly become obvious to the reader that I do not wish simply to read an epistemological theory off the results of some empirical disciplines, it will also become obvious that I am accepting the basic conceptual framework of contemporary cognitive science as my own framework. Thus, for example, I think of mental states ultimately as representational states, and I think of such states as the outputs of computational mechanisms, which are realized in brain tissue (though presumably could be realized in other kinds of matter as well). The account of cognitive modules recently adverted to, and developed in more detail in chapter 4 and elsewhere (Lyons 2001, 2003), is explicitly intended to capture the conception of cognitive systems operative in the best contemporary work in cognitive neuroscience.

Because I will sometimes criticize other theories for appealing to vague metaphors when detailed theses are called for, it is imperative to point out that the contemporary cognitive scientific appeal to representations, computations, and the like—as well as my own appeal to the same—is intended literally. When I say that a piece of brain realizes a computational mechanism for extracting face information from edge representations (chapter 4), there is nothing metaphorical about this. Epistemologists unfamiliar with recent work in the cognitive sciences and the philosophy of mind will find helpful overviews in Block (1995a) and Harnish (2002), but I can't rehearse here the arguments for what I take to be the standard philosophical underpinning of current cognitive science.[1]

This empirically minded approach is not something for which I will apologize, nor do I intend to defend it except to note two points.

The first is that although science has gotten many things wrong in the past, our current science nevertheless remains our best present guess as to the nature of the world around us. Correlatively, our current cognitive science represents our best guess as to the ultimate nature of the cognitive mind. It may very well be fundamentally mistaken; if so, much will have to be rewritten, but I see in that no argument in favor of waiting for some bulletproof theory of mind before developing epistemological theories.

The second point is the all too often overlooked fact that there really is no such thing as neutrality here. Knowing and forming justified beliefs are things that minds do, and it is hardly likely that we will be able to say much about the former without making some assumptions about the latter. To take the basic mental operations to be, say, the grasping or apprehending of Fregean senses, rather than computational

---

1. Another, thorough but contentious, overview is offered by Pylyshyn (1984), whose understanding of computation is much narrower—and more classical—than I have in mind here.

operations over physically encoded representations, is to make strong ontological commitments about the nature of the mind. This is true despite the fact that such "clutching" metaphors are too obscure to know what exactly all these commitments are. Similarly, to insist that proper epistemological methodology maintains theoretical neutrality by relying only on our commonsense understanding of the mind and mental states is to make substantial, and in this case empirically testable, commitments. Among them are (a) that folk psychology is basically correct, (b) that introspection is a reasonably good source of information about the real nature of mentality, and furthermore, (c) that introspection and common sense give us a *better insight* into the real nature of the mind than the cognitive sciences and philosophy of mind. Though I am not an eliminativist—I am, after all, working hard to develop a theory of basic and perceptual *beliefs*—I think that all three of these assumptions are problematic. The constant flow of surprising findings from cognitive neuropsychology, the explanatory power of the highly theoretical (sometimes counterintuitive) posits of cognitive psychology, and the unificatory promise of physicalism itself, all conspire to suggest that there is something badly incomplete about folk psychology and its chief investigative tool, introspection. It would be fatuous for a philosopher to insist on commonsense grounds that space is infinite or that there could be no vacuum, despite the contrary consensus of professional physicists. And it would be disingenuous for such a philosopher to try to protect her theories by advocating "neutrality" and "agnosticism" on these issues. Similarly, if one is to deny the basic cognitive framework assumed by contemporary cognitive science, one would have to ground this denial in much more than just common sense. And if one is to avoid this framework, the avoidance must be grounded in genuine deficiencies of the framework, rather than mere overtures of ecumenicalism.

So I begin with the assumption that the mind is roughly how cognitive science reveals it as being, and to the extent that this conflicts with the mind's being roughly how folk psychology reveals it as being, so much the worse for the folk psychological picture. Again, though I won't defend this starting point, the reader will easily recognize where such theoretical assumptions are being made, and the present approach has the virtue of not masking theory-laden assumptions under the guise of ontological neutrality. Every argument contains unargued premises; mine (at least the psychological premises) will have the merit of being easily recognized as such.

There are a number of people without whose help and encouragement this book either would not have been written or would have been a much worse book. Starting more or less at the beginning, I'd like to thank my excellent undergraduate philosophy teachers from Valparaiso University, especially Thomas Kennedy, Kenneth Klein, and Jonathan Strand; their enthusiasm, intelligence, and patient encouragement had a lot to do with my going into this line of work. I started thinking in earnest about some of the epistemological and cognitive scientific issues that occupy this book when I wrote my doctoral dissertation (1999), and my dissertation committee, Alvin Goldman, John Pollock, and Keith Lehrer, shaped my thinking about material that appears here in chapters 5 and 6. All three of them taught me a great deal about epistemology and philosophy in general. Patrick Rysiew, Mark Wunderlich, and Aaron Champene took the time to read parts of the manuscript and offered detailed and helpful suggestions. Thanks to Chris Hill for useful discussions of many of these topics, as well as general guidance and moral support. Thanks also to two anonymous referees for Oxford University Press. Two people deserve special thanks. Tom Senor has supported this project from beginning to end, as fellow epistemologist, colleague, department chair, and friend. He has provided useful comments on several parts of the manuscripts, and I've benefited from many hours of discussion of these and related epistemological issues. For about a decade and a half now, Alvin Goldman has given expert and patient mentoring and support, including—though by no means limited to—reading parts of this manuscript and offering helpful suggestions. I have learned more about epistemology from him than from anyone else (as the reader will soon see). This book would not be in your hands right now were it not for him.

As for personal support, my whole family has also been very encouraging, especially my parents. Dad: I hope this book makes you proud. Mom: I'm sure your years of prayers to St. Jude on my behalf haven't done me any harm—so thanks! Finally, and closest to home, I'd like to thank Raina Smith for her patience with me and confidence in me, more of each, probably, than I deserve.

A research incentive grant from the University of Arkansas and a summer research stipend from the Fulbright College of Arts and Sciences at the University of Arkansas were invaluable. A version of chapter 4 was published as "Perceptual Belief and Nonexperiential Looks" in *Philosophical Perspectives* 19 (2005), 237–56. Some of the material from chapters 2 and 3 appear as "Experience, Evidence, and Externalism" in *Australasian Journal of Philosophy* 86 (2008), 461–79. Thanks to both journals for permission to reprint that material here.

CONTENTS

ABBREVIATIONS

ARP	Alternative reliable process theory of defeat
CT	Cartesian theory of evidential justification
EOF	External object foundationalism
ER	Early reliabilism
IR	Inferentialist reliabilism
IT	Intellectualist theory of evidential justification
KR	Kindergarten reliabilism
MSF	Mental state foundationalism
PE	Percept experientialism
PEJ	Principle of Evidential Justification
PIJ	Principle of Inferential Justification
PST	Perceptual system theory
SA	Supervenience argument
SE	Sensation experientialism
SR	Simple reliabilism
SRT	Straight reliabilist theory of evidential justification

Perception and Basic Beliefs

External Object Foundationalism

There are, as everyone knows, two kinds of foundationalism. Foundationalism is the view that (a) there is a privileged class of basic beliefs, that is, beliefs whose justification does not depend on inferential or evidential connections to other beliefs, and (b) all nonbasic beliefs, if justified, ultimately derive their justification from evidential relations to these basic beliefs. Foundationalism is thus committed to the existence of basic beliefs, but different versions of foundationalism disagree about the nature of these basic beliefs.

Mental state foundationalism (henceforth, MSF) is the more traditional view and is quite restrictive about which beliefs it allows as basic. Beliefs about one's current existence, the contents of one's mind, and certain a priori truths are basic, but this is where it ends. MSF holds that the only epistemologically basic beliefs especially relevant to perception are beliefs about the agent's own current mental states, especially beliefs about one's current sensory experiences. In particular, our perceptual beliefs about external objects are not themselves basic but derive their justification from beliefs about how we are appeared to. *External object foundationalism* (EOF), on the other hand, is an increasingly popular view, and it is far more liberal than MSF. While it accepts all the basic beliefs that MSF does, EOF claims in addition that at least some beliefs about external, physical objects are basic.

As everyone knows, there are more than just two kinds of foundationalism; we already had strong, weak, minimal, modest, modern, classical, neoclassical, Cartesian, doxastic, nondoxastic, formal, substantive, simple, and iterative, just to name a few. I divide the field where I do not because we need any more idiosyncratic jargon but because the distinction between MSF and EOF highlights an issue of central importance in recent epistemology and the overriding concern of the present work: the issue of which beliefs are basic.

Descartes ([1641] 1985) represents the paradigm mental state foundationalist. As is well known, Descartes held that our knowledge of the external world begins with knowledge of our own mental states; these introspective beliefs are basic, and our beliefs about external objects depend inferentially on them. In this way, he endorsed a kind of egoism about the sources of knowledge: all knowledge of other things depends on knowledge of ourselves. In the context of foundationalism, this egoism leads quite naturally to MSF. What is most distinctive and problematic about Descartes's particular version of MSF is his treatment of nonbasic beliefs. On the standard reading, Descartes thought that (some) beliefs about external objects could be deduced from beliefs about one's current mental states, but only via a circuitous route, involving the existence and goodness of God.[1] Although Descartes took other beliefs to be basic as well, for example, belief in one's own existence and certain a priori metaphysical principles, the basic empirical beliefs involved in perception were taken to be beliefs about one's present experiences. Beliefs about bodies, in particular, were explicitly held to be inferential and thus nonbasic. Locke ([1690] 1975) also endorsed a version of MSF where beliefs about external objects are inferentially supported by the basic beliefs about our sensory experiences—not in accordance with Cartesian deduction, however, but via inference to the best explanation. Beliefs about our sense experiences are basic, and certain facts about them—primarily their stability, coherence, and involuntariness—are best explained by the hypothesis that they are caused by external objects. More recently, Chisholm (e.g., 1966, 1977, 1982b, 1989) claimed that the inference to physical objects from the basic beliefs about how one is appeared to is neither deductive nor abductive, but a special, sui generis, kind of direct inference: there are fundamental epistemic principles licensing beliefs about physical objects on the basis of corresponding beliefs about one's own mental states.

Predictably, each of these three major branches of MSF is fairly controversial. Though some kind of abductivist theory currently seems to be the most popular version of MSF (see BonJour 1999, 2001, 2002; Fumerton 1985, 1995, 2001; Alan Goldman 1988), it has certainly had its share of critics (including Hume [1739] 1978; Chisholm 1977; Pollock 1986, 2001; Plantinga 2001).

Descartes seems to have held MSF on the assumption that basic beliefs must be infallible, indubitable, incorrigible, or the like, and beliefs about external objects are obviously none of these. For a long time, this general outlook constituted a kind of orthodoxy: though beliefs about one's own current mental states may be infallible or indubitable, beliefs about external objects are clearly not; thus, only the former beliefs might count as basic. However, most contemporary epistemologists now believe with good reason that (a) there need be no such restriction on basic beliefs (nothing like this follows, after all, from a characterization of basicality in terms of noninferential justification) and (b) if there were such a restriction, even beliefs about one's own current mental states would, most likely, fail to count as basic.

---

1. Although I am laying out what I think is the standard interpretation of Descartes, I don't necessarily mean to cosign. My aims here are to put the epistemological issues in appropriate context, not to engage in any kind of serious historical scholarship. For these purposes, the (perhaps fictional) Descartes of Intro to Philosophy fame will do.

If fallible, dubitable, and/or defeasible beliefs are allowed into the privileged base, however, the traditional Cartesian obstacle to countenancing basic beliefs about external objects falls away. External object foundationalism would avoid the major problems facing MSF by allowing perceptual beliefs—beliefs about physical objects—to be basic. EOF need not worry about what kind of inference would link beliefs about our mental states to beliefs about mind-independent objects or how to show that such an inference is cogent.

More importantly, EOF would offer a tidy solution to the famous problem of the external world.

1. The Problem of the External World

For much of the history of epistemology, a central issue—perhaps *the* central issue—has been the problem of the external world. Perception is, or so we think, a rich source of knowledge and justified belief about the world around us. Were it not for perception, we would probably have very little knowledge of any contingent facts. We believe in a world of external objects—tables, rocks, trees, other people, and so on—but how is it possible for such belief to be justified, for it to be reasonable, for it to count as knowledge?

As Montaigne and Descartes pointed out, it is possible to have a dream so vivid and coherent as to be indistinguishable from waking reality. A truly convincing dream, however, would be one where I believed more or less as I do now: that I am sitting at my desk, that there is a coffee cup to my left, and so forth. And, it seems, I would believe these things for more or less the same reasons as I do now: I'm having such-and-such visual, tactile, and other sensory experiences. But if such kinds of experience are compatible with my having a vivid dream, then I need some reason for thinking that these particular experiences are veridical, that they are caused from without rather than from within. And the difficulty is that I seem to have no non-question-begging reason to think that they are thus caused. I couldn't produce an a priori argument against the possibility of dreaming, since dreaming is clearly possible. And all a posteriori arguments have to take for granted the reliability of sense-perception, which is exactly what is currently in question. If all this is so, then my sensory experience as of a cup in front of me seems to offer me no adequate reason for believing that there really is a cup in front of me. A pervasive kind of skepticism seems to result. Thus the problem of the external world.

The problem in its modern formulation is due mainly to Descartes, and of course his own solution was to offer an a priori argument for the existence of God and deduce from God's goodness that a certain subset of sense perception was veridical. However, his arguments, both for the existence of God and for the claim that God's existence validates sense perception, have been notoriously unconvincing.[2]

---

2. These failures of the Cartesian project are quite independent of the infamous Cartesian circle, the charge being that Descartes illicitly helped himself to an assumption in favor of the legitimacy of reason in constructing his first argument for the existence of God, from which he inferred the legitimacy of reason. The complaint noted here is that even ignoring that circularity, his more modest project of securing the legitimacy of sense perception on the assumption of the legitimacy of reason still fails.

For more than half of the intervening history between Descartes and the present, the dominant solution to the problem of the external world was to endorse some kind of idealism or phenomenalism, the basic idea of which was to solve the problem of the external world by reducing the putatively external world to an essentially internal one. Berkeley ([1710] 1975) claimed that if tables and chairs and the like really are just collections of ideas, rather than mind-independent objects, the problem posed by representative realism would not even arise. Representative realism, typified by Descartes, is the view that perception (i.e., veridical perception) involves three elements: a mind; an external object; and a mental representation of the external object, that is, an idea, sensation, or experiential state. The mind has direct access to the mental representation but only indirect access to the external object. Because the mental representation is logically distinct from the external object, knowledge of the former does not guarantee knowledge of the latter, and this is what generates the problem of the external world.

Idealism and phenomenalism failed, in that they simply could not provide an adequate metaphysics or semantics. Furthermore, it was, or should have been, clear all along that a metaphysical theory was going to be at best a *part* of the solution to the problem. Skepticism concerning the external world is an epistemological problem, and it is highly unlikely that anything short of an epistemological solution was going to suffice. For instance, although Berkeley and his successors claimed that trees and rocks were mind-dependent, they still needed to insist that not all appearances were veridical. Though Berkeley may have had a different theory of hallucination and illusion than the realist, he insisted along with the realist, and took pains to make sense of the fact, that things are not always as they seem. Due to the uncontested fact that there is a distinction between appearance and reality, however, the claim that reality is itself mind-dependent does little to allay the central epistemological worries. My having a certain rocklike visual experience does not entail that there is a rock, for a rock is something more than a particular fleeting sensation. For there to be a rock in front of me is not merely for me to have a certain visual experience; it is also, minimally, for certain counterfactuals to be true, counterfactuals about what additional experiences I would have under certain conditions.

But now I am back in what is essentially the Cartesian predicament: I know I'm having a certain sensation right now, but I need some non-question-begging reason for thinking this sensation indicates the existence of a real object. Though the sensation might be, loosely speaking, a part of the rock, it is nonetheless possible for me to have a qualitatively identical sensation without there being a real rock (i.e., without the relevant counterfactuals being true). Because the sensation is logically distinct from the rock, knowledge of the former does not guarantee knowledge of the latter. Even idealists dream, and I might be dreaming right now, even on the assumption that idealism is true. If so, I am not perceiving a real rock after all. According to Descartes's *epistemological* principles, for me to be justified in believing that this is a real rock, I would need to have some reason to think I am not dreaming. The rest of the argument follows the familiar Cartesian pattern.

An idealist metaphysics would perhaps have the result that objects like rocks and chairs, as collections of mental states, are not utterly foreign to the mind. This may have epistemological consequences, but it is nowhere close to providing a solution to the central skeptical problems. For that, we will need a specification of conditions that are sufficient for justification and knowledge. Once that epistemological theory is in place, it is far from clear how much the independently inadequate idealist metaphysics really had to contribute. Epistemological problems, it seems, require epistemological solutions.

Since an epistemological solution is going to be needed anyhow, a more promising approach to the problem of the external world has been to grant that there really are external, mind-independent objects and to focus on constructing an epistemology that can explain how justified perceptual belief might be possible. The idea is not to refute the skeptic but merely to undermine the skeptical arguments. Descartes's problem hinges on the claim that we are justified in our external object beliefs only if we are justified in thinking that our sensory experiences are reliable indicators of the truth. This is an epistemological claim and it, or something like it, is an essential premise in most arguments for skepticism about the external world. A plausible epistemology that refutes this claim, or is at least compatible with its denial, provides one important way of avoiding the skeptical conclusion, even if not a way of proving the antiskeptical conclusion.

This is where external object foundationalism comes in. The problem of the external world, at least in its traditional guise, is precisely the problem of explaining whether and how we can legitimately infer beliefs about the external world from beliefs about our own minds. If no adequate such inference is available, skepticism about the external world is apparently inevitable. EOF can sidestep this entire problem, however, by denying that any such inference is even necessary. If it is plausible to think that (some) beliefs about physical objects are basic, then it simply does not matter that we can't draw such beliefs as conclusions from beliefs about perceptual experiences.

It is thus easy to see why EOF of some sort or other has garnered so many adherents in recent years, perhaps even becoming the dominant view in current epistemology. EOF, or something very much like it, has been held by a number of recent authors with otherwise very different theoretical commitments, some calling themselves foundationalists, some direct realists, evidentialists, or even foundherentists, but all of whom agree that perceptual beliefs about physical objects are epistemologically basic. Such a view has been held by the likes of Robert Audi (1998), Bill Brewer (1999), Michael Huemer (2001), John Pollock (1986), James Pryor (2000), Anthony Quinton (1966), Steven Reynolds (1991), and Matthias Steup (2000).[3] Most externalist theories (e.g., Alston 1988; Goldman 1979; Plantinga 1993, 2001) also count as versions of EOF, as I explain in chapter 5. It is largely this rise to prominence of EOF that has debunked the much-rumored death of foundationalism and led to a renewed debate about the more traditional MSF. There has consequently been a "resurrection" (DePaul 2001) of foundationalism both old and new, of MSF and EOF.

Much recent discussion of MSF and EOF has taken place under the rubric of 'direct realism', a rather unfortunate term. There are three main reasons for framing the present discussion in terms of MSF and EOF, rather than direct and indirect realism. First, 'direct realism' is most often used to denote a combined set of metaphysical and epistemological commitments. Because I don't accept this whole package,

---

3. Some of these authors defend only the claim that there are epistemologically basic beliefs about physical objects without being full-blown foundationalists. The only defender of EOF that I am aware of prior to the last century is Thomas Reid ([1785] 1967, [1764] 1997).

it is important to separate the metaphysical and epistemological views. The very term strongly suggests the metaphysical view rather than the epistemological one. *Metaphysical direct realism* is a claim about the metaphysics of perception, rather than the epistemology of perceptual belief; it is a theory that is opposed to the idealism and representative realism discussed earlier. The epistemological implications of this metaphysical view are not straightforward, as anyone familiar with Hume's *no 'ought' from 'is'* dictum would expect, and as I argue in more detail shortly.

Second, even understood as an epistemological view about the basic status of perceptual beliefs, *epistemological* direct realism does not imply EOF, for it need not be committed to the rest of what distinguishes foundationalism from its rivals.[4] Epistemological direct realism, as I understand it, is simply the claim that some beliefs about external objects are basic. This does not require, as foundationalism does, that *all* justified beliefs ultimately owe their justification to a set of basic beliefs. It is hard to see why someone would deny this foundationalist claim while admitting that there are basic beliefs, indeed, so many of them. Strictly speaking, epistemological direct realism does not imply EOF, although I think—and I argue in chapter 2—that the plausible versions do. This is one reason why I focus on EOF rather than a more general epistemological direct realism.

Although epistemological direct realism does not imply EOF, EOF does imply epistemological direct realism. However, it must be stressed that EOF does not imply the view that is typically *called* 'direct realism.' Most epistemologists who embrace the name hold not only that there are basic beliefs about physical objects but also that these beliefs are based on and justified by nondoxastic experiential states, states of seeming or being appeared to.[5] This is a view that I dub 'experientialism' in chapter 2. It is a common enough version of epistemological direct realism that one might be tempted to equate the two, but there are other, important, versions of EOF that are not experientialist theories. In fact, the version of EOF that I prefer is one such.

This brings us to a final point regarding the term 'direct realism', which is that there is an important sense in which standard (i.e., experientialist) versions of direct realism are not—for my taste, at least—quite direct enough. The reliabilist foundationalism I eventually endorse has the justification of basic beliefs being more direct than standard direct realism does. Whereas standard, experientialist, epistemological direct realism holds that the basic beliefs are based on nondoxastic experiential states, the version of EOF that I endorse allows the basic beliefs to be justified without being based on anything at all.

2. Metaphysical and Epistemological Direct Realisms

I have mentioned that the epistemological implications of metaphysical direct realism are far from clear. In fact, I tend to think that the epistemological and metaphysical

4. I return to this in chapter 3. See also the preceding note.

5. A basic belief, again, is one whose justification does not depend on inferential or evidential connections to other *beliefs*, though its basicality is compatible with its justification depending on connections to other mental states, provided that these latter mental states are nondoxastic.

issues are more or less orthogonal. Epistemological direct realism, the view that perceptual beliefs about tables and rocks and the like are epistemologically basic, has little directly to do with the metaphysics of tables and rocks, or—more important for the present purposes—the metaphysics of perception. This is a good time to explain why a book with 'perception' in the title contains hardly a mention of sense-data.

Just as Descartes is the founding father of contemporary MSF, Thomas Reid ([1785] 1967, [1764] 1997) is the progenitor of EOF. Reid was the first major philosopher to respond to the problem of the external world, at least in its Cartesian formulation, by endorsing direct realism. However, he conflated the two types of direct realism, and it is essential to keep these separate. The epistemology I will be endorsing is in an important sense a Reidian epistemology, and I view his defense of epistemological direct realism as an insightful step forward. On the other hand, I want to strongly distance myself from his attack on the "ideal theory," for I see his defense of metaphysical direct realism as an embarrassing slide backward. The best and the worst of Reid's philosophy are tangled together right here, and it is unfortunate that Reid didn't seem to notice the difference between the two.

Cartesian-style skeptical arguments against the possibility of perceptual knowledge and justification begin with the claim that nothing is directly present to the mind but its own ideas, or that sensations are the immediate objects of perception, or some similar claim. This is the main point of Descartes's dream and demon hypotheses, as well as Hume's eye-pressing experiment.[6] My sensory experiences are distinct from tables and rocks and such, and my access to the latter is apparently mediated by my access to the former. In some sense that is difficult to articulate clearly, the central idea—call it the "primacy of experience thesis"—is that what is directly before the mind in perception is a perceptual experience. The skeptical problem results from the claim that tables and rocks and such are only indirectly present to the mind, and some conspicuously absent argument is needed to get from what is directly present to what is indirectly present. Here is one possible reconstruction of the skeptical argument:

1. The immediate objects of perception are sensations, rather than external objects.
2. We have no non-question-begging reason to think these sensations indicate or render probable the existence of real external objects.
3. To be justified in believing p on the basis of q, one must be justified in believing that q indicates or renders probable p.
4. Therefore, our perceptual beliefs about external objects are unjustified.

This is a fairly common even if problematic formulation of the argument. I have intentionally left a good deal of "straw" in the first premise for metaphysical direct realism to attack. If this premise, the primacy of experience thesis, is flawed, then the whole argument is undermined, and many direct realists have seized on the

6. In the *Treatise*, Hume invites the reader to press one eye and observe as the visual world doubles. Since the external world presumably did not double, the visual world and the external world are two different things.

unclarity of (1) in an attempt to avoid skepticism. As early as Reid and as recently as Michael Huemer (2001), authors have pointed out that, since we aren't properly said to perceive our experiences, these are not, contra (1), the objects of perception. These experiences are at best the *vehicles* of perception; it is tables and rocks that are the *objects* (Huemer 2001, p. 81).

This is an adequate objection to the letter of (1), but it completely misses the spirit. Representative realists (e.g., Locke [1690] 1975) often say things like (1), and some of them might even mean it, but (1) is a very poorly articulated statement of the primacy of experience thesis. The point is not that we actually perceive our experiences, in anything like the sense of 'perceive' in which we perceive physical objects; in fact, the central claim of representative realism is that our access to mental states is fundamentally different from our access to external objects. If the representative realist refers to sensory experiences as objects of perception, then 'objects of perception' is obviously being used as a term of art.

Perhaps (1) is a misleading way to formulate the primacy of experience thesis. An alternative formulation is this:

1'. Nothing is directly present to the mind in perception but sensory experiences.

It is statements like this that have led many to think that rejecting representative realism would provide a solution to the problem of the external world. Representative realism, again, claims that there are three things involved in normal (veridical) perception: (a) the mind, (b) a sensory experience or other representational state, and (c) the external object being represented, with (c) being present to the mind only insofar as (b) is in the mind. Just as the idealist hoped to avoid skepticism by paring this group down to two elements,[7] the naive, or direct, realist makes a similar move but does so by denying the intermediate, (b), rather than the external object.

Reid quite explicitly insisted that there are only two things involved in perception: the mind and the object:

> if by ideas are meant only the acts or operations of our minds in perceiving, remembering, or imagining objects, I am far from calling into question the existence of those acts....Nor do I dispute the existence of what the vulgar call the objects of perception....But philosophers maintain that, besides these there are immediate objects of perception in the mind itself: that, for instance, we do not see the sun immediately, but an idea; or, as Mr Hume calls it, an impression in our own minds. This idea is said to be the image, the resemblance, the representative of the sun, if there be a sun. ([1785] 1967, p. 298)

By denying this basic picture, Reid hopes to avoid the skepticism that he sees as being the inevitable result.

There are several ways one might go about denying the existence of mental intermediates. One is to endorse an extreme and probably incoherent kind of

---

7. However, as we have seen, it turns out on further examination that there are three elements after all, for objects, even if not external, are not (fully) directly present on a reasonably sophisticated idealist view either.

eliminativism: one that admits the existence of minds, (a), but denies the existence of sensory experiences or other representational states, (b). Reid is careful to point out that this is not his approach. It is less clear exactly what he is denying.

Sometimes it sounds as if Reid is denying that sensations are properly classified as *things*: in the language of his day, Reid is claiming that sensations are modes rather than substances. Anticipating more contemporary terms, he frequently insists that sensations are acts rather than objects. These are important and plausible claims, but their bearing on the problem of the external world is far from obvious. Descartes, whose *Meditations* serve as the defining source of both representative realism and the problem of the external world, was very clear about taking experiences as modes rather than substances. Hume does claim that ideas are substances, but he means it more as a reductio of the notion of substance than as a positive view about mental states. However, even supposing that (1') tacitly asserts that experiences are genuinely things, it is hard to see how dropping this supposition would make any difference. It is clear that the skeptical arguments can be formulated in a threatening manner without supposing that experiences are substances, since this is precisely what the *Meditations* does.

Nor is it at all apparent that it makes any difference whether experiences are given a sense-datum or an adverbialist treatment. It is perhaps easier to state the skeptical arguments in language that reifies experiences into sense-data than to state them in adverbialist language, but this is probably just because virtually anything is easier to state in sense-datum than adverbialist language. Still, I know that I'm being appeared to redly, but I also know that (it is possible that) in dreams I'm appeared to redly, even when there is nothing red nearby. So, following the basic Cartesian logic, to know that there is something red nearby right now, I would need some non-question-begging reason to think that my presently being appeared to redly really does indicate something red, and for this I would need some reason to think I'm not dreaming. The language of the argument may be slightly different than the standard formulations, but the spirit is the same. And there is good reason for this. Nothing in Descartes's theory of mind commits him to a sense-datum theory.

Whether experiences are modes or substances, sense-data or states of being appeared to, what matters is their status as intermediaries. Representative realism, as I construe it, is the metaphysical doctrine that external objects are perceived, or even thought about, only insofar as a (certain kind of) mental state representative of them is tokened. Representative realism is thus a species of representationalism more generally.[8] Berkeley was a representationalist in that he held that to think about something was to have (i.e., token) an idea of it, though he was certainly not a realist in any ordinary sense. Representationalism is neutral with respect to both the mode–substance debate and the sense-datum–adverbialism debate.[9] Reid also denied representationalism thus construed, and this is the part of Reid I am most concerned to disavow. While

8. "Representationalism" obviously means different things in different contexts; here I mean it as a view about cognition, not as a view about the nature of all mental phenomena, including, e.g., qualia.

9. Chisholm's original formulation of adverbialism (1957) was designed specifically to be ontologically neutral, a fortiori it was neutral with respect to the antirepresentationalist claim that thought and perception are unanalyzable, that, e.g., there's nothing internal to the states themselves that my belief that grass is green has in common with my belief that cows eat grass.

he now does have a genuine opponent, it is far from clear that he has a substantive view to offer in place of representationalism. If thinking about a horse is not a matter of tokening a mental representation of a horse, what is it? Representationalism is the only theory we have of what thinking and perceiving are, of what belief is, of why thought and inference exhibit productivity and systematicity and why they exhibit the particular systematicities they do.[10] Infighting among contemporary representationalists often concerns the existence of certain kinds of systematicity that the other group's preferred representational scheme cannot explain (Fodor and Pylyshyn 1988; Fodor and McLaughlin 1990; Cummins et al. 2001). Nonrepresentationalist theories (if 'theory' isn't too strong a word) cannot explain *any* of the systematicities. Though terms like 'systematicity' are fairly recent, the idea is quite old. A favorite argument of the British empiricists was that their view explained an alleged systematicity between past experience and conceptual capacity; it did so by positing a conceptual representational scheme with a combinatorial syntax and semantics and that derived its primitive semantic constituents from experiential representations.

Representationalism as here construed is the dominant view in contemporary philosophy of mind and in empirical cognitive science, and I think it is true. I won't argue this, however, for two reasons. The first is simply that it would take us too far afield. The second is that this metaphysical view is actually irrelevant to the epistemological problem at hand, the problem of the external world. If the primacy of experience thesis is read as a statement of representationalism, then the first premise is, as I say, fairly secure, but the resulting argument is invalid. Representative realism is the claim that experiences are metaphysical intermediaries, but the first premise of the skeptical argument must be the claim that experiences are epistemic intermediaries. The spatial metaphor of experiences being directly before the mind or directly present to it is innocuous if it is merely intended to convey the claim that thinking and perceiving involve the tokening of representations in virtue of which the thought or perception can be said to be *of* some particular object. Rather, the metaphor is intended to convey the claim that our perceptual beliefs depend *for their justification* on our perceptual experiences, or our beliefs about these experiences.

The primacy of experience thesis—the thesis that is relevant to the present epistemological concerns about skepticism and justified perceptual belief—is the thesis that experiences are *epistemically* prior to perceptual beliefs. This is not something that Descartes actually argues for. The purpose of the demon hypothesis, like that of Hume's eye-pressing experiment, is just to focus our attention on the inner experiential states instead of the external objects that we normally attend to. Having done this, it is simply assumed as self-evident that these experiential states are epistemically

---

10. A representational system is said to be productive if it has unbounded representational capacities. Thought is generally taken to be productive in the sense that we are capable of thinking indefinitely many different thoughts, and this is attributed to the productivity of the underlying representational system. Systematicity is a matter of certain cognitive capacities coming in clusters. Anyone who is capable of entertaining the thought that John loves Mary is capable of entertaining the thought that Mary loves John. The standard explanation for this is that thought involves a representational system that contains elements, 'John', 'Mary', 'loves', which can be rearranged.

prior to perceptual beliefs. The argument behind the problem of the external world needs to be written somewhat as follows.

1". Our perceptual beliefs about external objects are justified, if at all, by appeal to our having certain sensory experiences.
2. We have no non-question-begging reason to think these sensations indicate or render probable the existence of real external objects.
3. To be justified in believing p on the basis of q, one must be justified in believing that q indicates or renders probable p.
4. Therefore, our perceptual beliefs about external objects are unjustified.

If skepticism is false, then the present argument is unsound, but it is certainly an improvement over the earlier versions. Each of the three premises makes an epistemological claim; there is no attempt to derive an 'ought' from an 'is' here. Though each premise is controversial (each has been denied), each premise has some initial plausibility. And the argument, as thus formulated, makes no assumptions about the metaphysics of perception, so it cannot be deflected by endorsing a different metaphysics of perception. Whatever the metaphysics of perception, if perceptual belief depends epistemically on inferential support from our having such-and-such sensory experiences, the Cartesian problem will remain in need of a solution.

Reid's misguided attack on representationalism obscured his genuinely important contribution: the defense of EOF. Seeing where he went wrong, however, illustrates more distinctly where he went right. Once we see clearly that the notion of direct presence has to be an epistemological notion, we see that the crucial premise, the primacy of experience thesis, is a claim *for which no argument has been given.*

There are, of course, three different premises one might deny in responding to the present skeptical argument. Standard versions of MSF deny premise (2); the Cartesian claims that we have deductive reasons, the Lockean that we have abductive reasons. EOF, however, has two alternative options, and Reid himself is not clear which remaining premise he rejects.

Though I have been leading up to the rejection of (1"), most proponents of EOF actually reject (3) instead. I have left an intentional ambiguity in (1"). The claim could be either that our perceptual beliefs are based on beliefs about experiential states (a doxastic primacy of experience thesis) or that they are based directly on the experiential states themselves (a nondoxastic primacy of experience thesis). The typical defender of epistemological direct realism denies the former but accepts the latter. That is, she accepts *a* primacy of experience thesis, though perhaps not the traditional one. Thus, while the metaphysical direct realist attacks premise (1) or (1'), the epistemological direct realist typically actually *accepts* premise (1"), at least under one disambiguation. The fact that most proponents of epistemological direct realism accept the only premise to which metaphysical direct realism even speaks serves to reemphasize the important difference between these two views. On a standard direct realist epistemology (e.g., Pollock 1986; Audi 1998; Huemer 2001), my being appeared to redly is by itself sufficient for the prima facie justification of my belief that there's something red in front of me; I need not have any specific evidence for thinking that the nondoxastic state renders the belief probable.

There is another way out of the problem of the external world, and that is to reject (1″), the epistemological primacy of experience thesis, in both its doxastic and nondoxastic varieties. This is the route that I take, and it is the route that I see classic versions of reliabilism (e.g., Goldman 1979, 1986) as having taken. On this latter view, experience is irrelevant; it is process reliability that justifies our perceptual beliefs. One can accept premises (2) and (3) and still deny the skeptical conclusion (in chapter 7, I endorse something fairly close to, though not quite identical with, (3)).

Again, my strategy is to endorse an epistemological direct realism without taking on the difficult side project of defending a metaphysical direct realism. Partly because I am not sure how authors usually intend their talk about "direct presence" and the like, I'm not sure whether currently standard versions of metaphysical direct realism are at odds with representationalism in the philosophy of mind. If so, I will be assuming that metaphysical direct realism is false. I assume that our best science embodies our best guess as to how things are, and in particular, our successful cognitive scientific theories draw—to the best of our current knowledge—a fairly accurate picture of the nature of the mind. Our best cognitive science presupposes that cognition is a matter of standing in the appropriate relations to mental representations. And so will I.

3. Basic Beliefs

Although EOF is a promising and important theory, it forces us to examine more closely the notion of basic beliefs. The most traditional versions of MSF held that basic beliefs, being largely restricted to beliefs about one's present mental states and simple a priori truths, were infallible, incorrigible, and/or possessed of the highest possible degree of justification. These are strong claims even for MSF and certainly too strong to be endorsed by EOF. Perceptual beliefs about external objects can be mistaken, and thus can in principle be shown to be mistaken, so they are not incorrigible. It is also possible for an agent to persist in such beliefs even after they have been shown to be mistaken, in which case the beliefs are not justified at all, let alone possessed of the highest degree of justification.

These same considerations apply to MSF as well, since it seems that we are quite capable of having false, even unjustified, beliefs about our current mental states. (I may believe that I am appeared to redly simply because my psychic told me so.) But it is far more obvious in the case of EOF, and if we are not to foreclose the possibility of EOF *ab initio*, we will have to construe basic beliefs in terms of prima facie justification rather than justification full stop. To say that a belief is prima facie justified for S is to say that S is justified (i.e., ultima facie justified) in that belief, *provided* that there is no (epistemic) reason for S not to hold that belief. A prima facie justified belief has whatever positive epistemic support is necessary for justification, but it may fail to be justified if the agent also possesses contrary or undermining evidence. A basic belief, therefore, must be defined as one whose prima facie justification does not depend on evidential connections to other beliefs, though the ultima facie justification of the belief may very well depend on connections to other beliefs, at least in a negative way.[11] That is, basic beliefs

---

11. I will mean by this that the belief does not require evidential connections to other beliefs to have enough justification to meet whatever the threshold is for a belief to count as justified. One can endorse weaker claims on behalf of basic beliefs, though I don't feel that this one is in danger of being too strong.

can be defeasible. Nor is there any good reason to think that if a belief is basic, that belief cannot have its justification bolstered by additional, inferential evidence. Perhaps some enthusiasts have made such claims on behalf of basic beliefs, but I will not.

It is generally recognized that, because of defeasibility, it is possible for a belief to be basic but not (ultima facie) justified. However, it is frequently assumed that a basic belief must therefore be at least prima facie justified. This does not follow from the current definition of basic beliefs, and it is not something I will assume. A basic belief is one whose prima facie justification does not depend on evidential connections to other beliefs. To say that a belief is basic is to say merely that evidential support from other beliefs is not necessary for the justification of that belief; it is not to deny that something else is necessary. On the theory I will endorse, the factors that make a belief basic are quite different from and not sufficient for those that make a belief justified. I will argue that what makes a belief basic is the belief's having a certain psychological etiology and that what makes it justified is its being the result of a reliable process. The distinction between what makes a belief basic and what makes a (basic) belief justified will receive more attention later in this section; I mention it now only to avoid some possible misunderstandings.

External object foundationalism raises some even more pressing questions about the contents of the basic beliefs. EOF holds that some beliefs about external objects are basic. But which ones? Alternatively, which propositions are such that it is possible for an agent to have a justified basic belief with that content? Back when MSF was the only game in town, the answer to such questions looked easy: only beliefs about one's own current mental states (and perhaps all of these) are basic.[12] So, for example, my belief that I'm appeared to redly may be basic, though my belief that there's something red in front of me, according to MSF, would not be.

EOF makes this question of which beliefs are basic much harder to answer. Suppose that some beliefs about physical objects are basic. Then my belief that there's something red in front of me might be basic, as well as my belief (if I have such a belief) that there's a face with such-and-such properties in front of me. But what about my beliefs that Mark is here in front of me, or that my sister's second husband is here in front of me? Are any of these basic, or are they all inferential? When I look at a clock, which of the following beliefs are basic: that there's a white round thing in front of me with black markings and two black rectangular bars forming an obtuse angle, that there's a clock in front of me, that it's currently 3:55 (P.M.)?

A closely related problem involves the long-standing question of where we should (and whether we can) draw the line between perception and inference, or observation and theory.[13] The perception-inference distinction is typically framed in terms of such factive states as seeing F or seeing that p, but I want to focus on the nonfactive state of having the perceptual belief that p. One can have the false perceptual belief that there's a cat in the room, though one cannot falsely *see* that

12. So long as we restrict our attention to the beliefs involved in perception. The MSFist will typically also embrace basic beliefs about one's own current existence, a very hard-to-specify class of necessary truths, and perhaps some contingent a priori truths of an equally hard-to-specify nature.

13. The terminology of 'perception and inference' is more common in epistemology, 'theory and observation' in the philosophy of science. These aren't exactly the same issues, those in the philosophy of science traditionally being tied up with semantics in a way that those in epistemology are not.

there's a cat in the room. Taking the target to be perceptual belief rather than perception allows us to focus on the perceptuality, so to speak, rather than the factivity.

Looking around the room, I form a number of beliefs: my coffee cup is to the left of a pile of CDs; the light on the printer is on, and it is green; the dog is asleep (she is at least lying down with her eyes closed), and the carpet needs to be vacuumed. I smell a familiar odor and realize that I'm probably burning tonight's dinner. Which of these beliefs are perceptual beliefs, and which are inferential? From what beliefs are the inferential beliefs inferred? Descartes ([1641] 1985) claimed that when I look out a window and claim to see people on the street beneath me, all I genuinely *see* are coats and hats and *infer* from this that there are people inside them. Similarly, Berkeley ([1713] 1975) claimed that one does not actually *hear* the coach driving past but only hears a sound that leads one to infer the existence of the coach.[14] Reid ([1785] 1967, p. 184), on the other hand, claims that there is a sense of 'perception' (viz., acquired perception) according to which we really do perceive these sorts of things (in fact, Reid explicitly mentions Berkeley's coach example).

This general sort of debate has carried on into more recent philosophy. Churchland (1979, 1985) thinks that we (at least some of us) can taste the chemical composition of wine and see wavelength distributions. Brandom (1994) goes so far as to claim that a scientist can observe a mu meson moving through a cloud chamber. We do not (or do not merely) infer these things from what we perceive, but we actually perceive them. Presumably, these authors mean not only, for example, that we can perceive a meson moving but also that we can perceive *that* a meson is moving (the latter being opaque to substitution in a way that the former is not), and consequently that the scientist has the justified perceptual belief that a meson is moving, and so forth.[15] Other recent philosophers are somewhat less explicit but seem to have a far more restricted understanding of what we perceive, and they correspondingly assign more credit to inference. Consider, for example, the following discussion of Chisholm's:

> In reply to the question, "What is your justification for counting it as evident that it is Mr. *Smith* whom you see?" a reasonable man...would say...something like this: "(It is evident that:) Mr. Smith is a tall man with dark glasses; I see such a man; no one else satisfying that description would be in *this* room now...etc." (1982a, p. 81; italics and last ellipsis in original)

This is a challenging passage. Chisholm does not explicitly deny that the "reasonable man's" belief that he's seeing Smith (or that Smith is nearby) is a perceptual belief, but the description of the case certainly makes it sound as if the belief that Smith is nearby is not a perceptual belief. Chisholm does explicitly deny that beliefs about Smith are basic.

---

14. There are, to be sure, differences between the Cartesian and Berkeleyan claims, and not just in virtue of the fact that one is about seeing and the other is about hearing. Descartes is here just defending a traditionally narrow view of perception in the context of a commonsense metaphysics. Berkeley, however, thinks that the visible coach and the audible coach are actually different things, whose frequent conjunction must be inferred on the basis of experience. Similarly, the coach is a bundle of properties, of which the sound heard is only one.

15. Churchland, of course, would not himself put it this way, given his well-known eliminativism concerning the propositional attitudes, a view, however, that is independent of the one currently under discussion.

This raises an important question: what is the relation between perceptual beliefs and basic beliefs? The perception-inference distinction looks to be a mixed psychological-epistemic distinction: a perceptual belief is one that has a certain epistemic status and a certain psychological status. It is plausible to think, from the standpoint of EOF, that what is *epistemologically* distinctive about perceptual beliefs is that they are basic. For EOF, at least, there is a very close relation between the question of which beliefs are basic and the question of which beliefs are perceptual. MSF presumably won't see quite so tight a connection, since MSF may want to allow some beliefs about external objects to count as perceptual beliefs, while denying that any of these are basic. This points to another virtue of EOF over MSF: in giving an account of basicality, EOF will have partially solved the problem of which beliefs are perceptual beliefs; MSF will not have even begun. Similarly, it might be possible to get a handle on the problem of which beliefs are basic by first tackling the question of which beliefs are perceptual beliefs and generalizing from there.

Specifying which beliefs are basic will contribute to more than just our theories of perception. For example, not all a priori beliefs are basic; a complete epistemology needs to say which ones are and which ones aren't. The recent "reformed epistemology" movement (Alston 1991; Plantinga 1983, 2000) has raised the question of whether belief in God might be basic. Such questions are perhaps best answered by developing a general theory of basicality and seeing what implications it has for religious belief.

The problem of specifying which beliefs are basic is an important problem, one that needs to be solved for any kind of foundationalism that is to be taken very seriously. I have focused on this problem as it arises for EOF, in part because the problem is most vividly brought out in the context of EOF. In fact, however, the problem of which beliefs are basic arises for MSF as well. MSF claims that the basic beliefs involved in perception are first-person beliefs about one's own mental states. Let us say that an *appearance belief* is a belief about how one is appeared to, while a *perceptual belief* is a belief about external, physical objects. MSF thus claims that appearance beliefs are sometimes basic; perceptual beliefs never are. Even then, however, *which* appearance beliefs are basic? Is my belief that I'm appeared to my-sister's-second-husband-ly basic? Presumably not. However, we need some account of why not. Consider a more common and more difficult case. What should MSF say about the status of my belief that I'm appeared to table-ly? Is it basic, or does its justification depend on a more basic belief about being appeared to as if there is an object of a certain shape in front of me? And does this latter belief in turn depend on beliefs about patches of color having a certain arrangement in the visual field?

One might attempt to answer such questions by claiming that the basic beliefs are justified by the corresponding appearance states, and since it is impossible to be appeared to my-sister's-second-husband-ly, neither my belief that my sister's second husband is nearby nor my belief that I'm appeared to my-sister's-second-husband-ly can be basic. But even if this much is granted, it is far less clear whether I can be appeared to table-ly or whether I can be appeared to as if I am looking at so-and-so's face. Any claims one way or the other here are going to be in need of defense. Some appearance beliefs, like 'I'm appeared to my-sister's-second-husband-ly', are likely too "high level" to be basic, but is there any reason to think that only very low-level appearance beliefs, about arrays of color patches, shapes, and the like, are basic? Is 'I'm appeared to table-ly' already too high level?

What one says about the content of the basic beliefs will constrain and be constrained by what one says about how basic beliefs are justified. In fact, one reason EOF was so long in coming was that it was assumed that basic beliefs must be self-justifying. This concept is actually quite a bit more difficult than the familiarity of the term would suggest (as we will see in chapter 2), but it is natural to suppose at least that if belief B is self-justifying, then any belief token with the same content as B is (prima facie) justified. If so, then EOF cannot require basic beliefs to be self-justifying, for obviously it is possible to be completely unjustified in believing, say, that there is a rock in my hand. But if the basic beliefs are not self-justifying, what does justify them? It obviously can't be other beliefs, since this would contradict the definition of basicality. One popular answer is that what justifies a basic belief is a corresponding experiential state; another popular answer is that what justifies a basic belief is the reliability of the process that produced it. For EOF to be taken seriously, we will need some reason to think that one of these answers is plausible, and it would be good to know which one.

So we have at least two connected problems that must be faced by any theory committed to the existence of basic beliefs:

The Source Problem: Basic beliefs by definition don't receive their justification from evidential relations to other beliefs, so where do they get their justification? Reliability, experiential states, self-justification, etc.?

The Delineation Problem: Which beliefs are basic? The MSF-EOF distinction only marks off two very broad categories of responses to this question, and there are many more determinate choices that need to be made within these broad categories.

Thus, as mentioned before, the problem of what makes a belief basic is distinct from the problem of what makes a basic belief justified, though again, answers to these problems are mutually constraining.

I have been concentrating on the delineation problem because, of the problems raised in this section, it is the one that has received the least attention in the literature and will receive the most attention in what follows. We need an account of which beliefs are basic and which are nonbasic. In a sense, of course, we already have one in the definition of basic beliefs as those whose prima facie justification doesn't depend on inferential/evidential support from other beliefs. So a basic belief is one that can be justified even if it doesn't enjoy such evidential support. However, we need more than that. We need a theory that will tell us (at least in principle) which beliefs, specified nonepistemically, are basic and which are nonbasic. Although I will want the theory to do so without invoking any evaluative terms, even a committed nonnaturalist should require that we be in principle able to figure out, for any given belief, whether it is basic, without first knowing the epistemic status of *that belief*.

This is a question that most foundationalists haven't really tackled head-on. The usual approach is to offer a few sufficient conditions for a belief's being basic and leave it at that. I want to remedy that here. The theory I will eventually endorse is an externalist one in that it denies that an agent can tell on the basis of mere reflection whether a given belief is basic. It is externalist in another sense also, in that it is a kind of reliabilist EOF.

I will be adopting the aforementioned strategy of working out a theory of perceptual beliefs according to which such beliefs are basic and generalizing from there to get a full solution to the delineation problem. I endorse a position that I take to be so prima facie plausible as to sound nearly trivial: a perceptual belief is a belief that is the output of a perceptual system. If our perceptual systems deliver beliefs about tables as outputs, then these beliefs about tables count as both perceptual (rather than inferential) and basic. If these systems deliver beliefs about what time it is or who is nearby as outputs, then such beliefs are basic, perceptual beliefs. Such a theory generalizes to the view that whether a belief is basic is determined by the nature of the cognitive system that produced it. Very (*very*) roughly, the features of perceptual systems in virtue of which the beliefs they produce are basic include those properties that are characteristic of modular cognitive systems (Fodor 1983), so the basic beliefs are the ones that are produced by modular systems.[16]

Such an account can then be applied in principle to determine whether any given belief is basic, by looking at the nature of the system that produced it. This will make it possible to answer questions of the sort posed here. We can determine which of the beliefs that result from sensory processes count as epistemologically perceptual by determining which of them are outputs of the perceptual system itself. And we can (in principle) answer controversial questions about basic nonperceptual beliefs, such as belief in God.

As plausible as the theory of perceptual belief just sketched may be, it is at odds with a view that, though seldom explicitly articulated, seems to me to constitute a sort of orthodoxy. This is the view that perceptual beliefs are those that are accompanied by a corresponding sense experience. On this view, perception is essentially experiential; on my view it is not. The orthodox view is not merely an isolated claim about perceptual belief but is integrated into a—perhaps *the*—dominant view in epistemology, according to which the basic beliefs are justified by the corresponding experiential state.[17] I think that there are deep troubles for both this view of perception and its accompanying theory of the source of justification of the basic beliefs.

The theory of basicality I propose (my solution to the delineation problem) will be wedded to a more general reliabilist epistemology (an answer to the source problem). In fact, my theory of basicality is intended in no small measure to help solve certain recurring problems for existing versions of reliabilism. Again, however, such a view is incompatible with the experientialist orthodoxy; if being the reliably caused output of a certain kind of cognitive system is sufficient for prima facie justification, then having the appropriate experiential state is not necessary. Thus, to make room for the view I endorse, I will have to argue at length against the orthodox view.

Hence, I want to approach the delineation problem indirectly. I will start with the source problem and argue that only an externalist account of the source of justification of basic beliefs is plausible. This will narrow the field of possible answers to the delineation problem and make it easier to defend the one I prefer.

16. It is not merely the obviousness of the present proposal that makes it sound trivial. There is an appearance of circularity in the claim that perceptual beliefs are those that are the outputs of perceptual systems. To avoid circularity, we will need to be able to specify perceptual systems independently of their outputting perceptual beliefs. This is a difficult matter, one that I address in detail in chapter 4.

17. This claim is intended as an answer to the source problem, not the delineation problem. Absent an account of what the "corresponding" experiential states are—a significant problem on some popular theories of experience—and an account of what sorts of experiential states are possible, the delineation problem has barely been addressed.

2

Doxastic and Nondoxastic
Theories

The distinction between external object foundationalism and mental state foundationalism must be carefully distinguished from another important division within foundationalism. While the EOF-MSF distinction concerns the *content* of the basic beliefs, the distinction between doxastic and nondoxastic theories concerns the *source of justification* of beliefs. The standard taxonomy will be refined later, but according to it, a doxastic theory is one that claims that only beliefs can serve to justify beliefs, and a nondoxastic theory is simply one that denies this.

Though the question of the content of the basic beliefs is distinct from the question of the source of justification, there is a tendency in the literature to simply identify EOF with nondoxastic foundationalism and MSF with doxastic foundationalism. Thus Pollock and Cruz (1999, p. 29), for example, list Chisholm as a doxastic foundationalist, even though Chisholm never claims that only beliefs can justify beliefs. In fact, he clearly insists that the basic beliefs about self-presenting properties are justified, at least in part, by the facts that make them true (1966, p. 28; 1977, pp. 21–22; 1989, p. 19). What distinguishes Chisholm's view from Pollock and Cruz's own nondoxastic foundationalism is that Chisholm endorses a version of MSF, while they advocate EOF. Pollock and Cruz also cite the BonJour and Fumerton papers in DePaul (2001) as evincing a revival of doxastic foundationalism, even though BonJour and Fumerton both endorse nondoxastic versions of MSF there. (This is corrected in Pollock's (2001) contribution to that volume.) Steup's (2000) distinction between "restricted" and "unrestricted" foundationalism seems at first glance to map onto my distinction between MSF and EOF, respectively. However, Steup clearly thinks that a restricted foundationalist is ipso facto committed to denying that nondoxastic states can justify beliefs (2000, pp. 77–78). An MSFist is not so committed. Because so many of the beliefs it takes to be basic couldn't plausibly be self-justifying, EOF more or less requires nondoxasticism. MSF, however, can embrace either doxasticism or nondoxasticism. Many mental state foundationalists, in fact (e.g., Chisholm 1977, 1989; BonJour 2001, 2002; Fumerton 1995, 2001), endorse nondoxasticism.

Doxasticism and nondoxasticism are broad categories. Doxastic theories will include standard versions of coherentism, along with the version of foundationalism that holds the basic beliefs to be self-justifying. Among nondoxastic theorists are those who claim that the basic beliefs are justified by experiential states, as well as the more externalist theories, according to which the justification of basic beliefs depends only on nonintrospectible properties (e.g., reliability of the belief-forming process).[1] The theory I prefer is a nondoxastic theory of this externalist variety. That is, I think that there are basic beliefs that neither are self-justifying nor require corresponding experiential states for their justification. In fact, I doubt that experiential states per se can have any bearing on the justification of beliefs.

Before arguing for any of this, however, it is necessary to clarify the notions of doxasticism and nondoxasticism.

1. Evidential and Nonevidential Justifiers

The distinction between doxastic and nondoxastic theories concerns the sorts of things that can serve to justify beliefs. Discussions of doxasticism and nondoxasticism typically begin with a stipulative definition of a "J-factor" as anything that is relevant to the justificatory status of a belief. J-factors can be either positively relevant or negatively relevant, depending on whether they contribute to or detract from the justifiedness of a belief, though it is convenient to concentrate on justifiers, that is, positively relevant J-factors. Epistemologists have proposed a number of such positively relevant J-factors. Coherence, reliability, infallibility, clarity and distinctness—these are all controversial but well-known candidates. The fact that my belief is held on the basis of good evidence is something that can serve as a justifier; this is uncontroversial, even if not very informative. Some hold that nondoxastic experiential states can serve as justifiers, and clearly, known and/or justified beliefs can do so.

This class of putative J-factors makes up a diverse lot, however, and I want to distinguish two importantly different kinds. The sense in which justified beliefs confer justification is quite different from the sense in which reliability is said to do

1. I am following the bulk of the epistemological literature here in classifying coherentism as a species of doxasticism; most epistemologists think of it this way, following, perhaps, Davidson's famous formulation, "What distinguishes a coherence theory is simply the claim that nothing can count as a reason for holding a belief but another belief" (1986). I am going to follow the trend and treat coherentism as a doxastic view, despite the fact that it is mistaken. Nondoxastic coherentism is not only a logical possibility but a view that actually has adherents (e.g., Kvanvig 2003a; Gupta 2006) and is in many ways quite plausible. Nevertheless, there are too many *isms* floating around already, and I need to simplify matters. This simplification is a distortion, and I will try to remedy this somewhat by discussing nondoxastic coherentism early in chapter 3.

so. Justified beliefs justify other beliefs by serving as evidence for them; the former are *evidential justifiers* for the latter. Reliability, coherence, and the like are not taken to serve as *evidence* for beliefs; their purported role is one of being that in virtue of which a belief is justified, by being that on which justification supervenes, or to which justification reduces, or the like; their putative role is that of *nonevidential justifiers*. This distinction between evidential and nonevidential factors is well known; anyone who knows what evidentialism (e.g., Feldman and Conee 1985; Conee and Feldman 2004) is, is quite familiar with the distinction. Nonetheless, and as I illustrate later, this distinction is often forgotten when the topic is not explicitly evidentialism, and I want to say more to explicate the relation between the concept of evidence and the more general concept of J-factors.

Although it is controversial, I will assume that evidence is positively relevant to the justificatory status of a belief only if the belief is in some sense based on, that is, held on the basis of, that evidence. This notion of basing, though itself subject to certain controversies, is a familiar one.[2] I may believe that p and that p entails q, but when deliberating about whether to accept q, I fail to notice these reasons and instead accept q on the basis of my psychic's telling me that q. In such a case, my belief would be justifi*able* (since I possess good reasons for it) but not justifi*ed* (since my belief is not based on these reasons). This same distinction, or one very much like it, is sometimes formulated in terms of "propositional" versus "doxastic" justification (e.g., Kvanvig 2003b) or even in terms of "justification" versus "well-foundedness" (e.g., Feldman and Conee 1985).[3]

My concern at this point is not with the basing relation per se but with the notion of reasons operative in these discussions, which is that of an epistemological *ground*:

2. For discussions of the basing relation and the controversies surrounding it, compare Korcz (1997, 2000), Pollock (1986), and Kvanvig (2003b).

3. Thus, some of the controversy surrounding the assumption that opens this paragraph is more terminological than substantive. Evidentialism as Feldman and Conee see it (1985; Feldman 2003) is perhaps primarily a theory of what I am calling justifiability rather than justifiedness. (Others, such as Haack (1993), use 'evidentialism' differently.) Feldman and Conee use 'justification' to refer to a belief's fitting all the evidence S possesses and 'well-foundedness' for a belief's being based on appropriate evidence. What they call justified but not well-founded, I call justifiable but not justified. The dispute here is largely, perhaps entirely, terminological. I define evidential justifiers as justifying grounds, rather than, say, potential justifying grounds, because my concern is with justifiedness rather than justifiability. I believe that the major theses of this chapter could be translated into Feldman and Conee's language, though I won't pursue this.

There are, of course, some subtle differences among these distinctions, differences that sometimes matter. The justified-justifiable distinction, for example, normally applies equally to actual, occurrent beliefs, a justified belief being epistemically good and a justifiable (occurrent) belief being epistemically bad (though other beliefs may be worse). When this notion of justifiability is applied to beliefs that the agent might but doesn't hold, the distinction between beliefs and propositions collapses, and justifiability is equivalent to propositional justification. The *ex post–ex ante* distinction applies only to beliefs and not propositions, although *ex post* justified beliefs must be actual beliefs, while *ex ante* justified beliefs must be only potential. However, *ex ante* justification cannot be equated with propositional justification or justifiability. There is nothing epistemically wrong with *ex ante* justified beliefs. More important, a potential belief's being justifiable (being propositionally justified) does not imply that it is *ex ante* justified, that if the agent were to occurrently believe it, it would be justified; a belief's being *ex ante* justified is thus epistemically superior to its being merely justifiable. This could all be worked out in more detail, but this is plenty for my overall purposes.

that on which a belief is (at least partly) based. 'Reason' is notoriously ambiguous. To say that S has some reason for believing p could be to say (a) that there is a cause of S's believing that p, (b) that S is justified to some degree in believing that p, or (c) there is something on which S's belief that p is based. It is only this last sense that I am concerned with here; in this sense of 'reason', to say that S has a reason r for believing that p—better: that r is S's reason for believing that p—is to say that r is S's ground for believing that p, equivalently, that S believes that p on the basis of r, or that r is S's (putative) evidence for her belief that p. Having a ground or grounds for a belief does not imply that the belief is justified; for one thing, one's actual reasons are not always good reasons. However, when a ground does contribute to the justification of a belief, we can say that the ground evidentially justifies the belief, that the ground serves as an evidential justifier for that belief. An *evidential justifier* for a belief is any state that serves as part or all of the agent's justifying grounds, that is, evidence, that is, reasons, for that belief.

For something to be the ground of a belief, it must be the sort of thing that the believer can take into account. This is not a statement of internalism but merely an indication of how I'm using the term 'ground'. A ground must also in some sense explain the belief's being held, though there are typically a number of different kinds of explanations for the existence of a given belief, many of which do not invoke grounds. Compare the following:

(i) S believes that p because S believes that q and that q entails p.
(ii) S believes that p because S's desire that p causes S to form the belief that p.
(iii) S is being subjected to a strong magnetic field, which produces brain state #773291, which (in S at t) realizes the belief that p.
(iv) S is in brain state #773291, which (in S at t) realizes the belief that p.

The only item on the list that clearly offers one of S's grounds or reasons for believing that p is (i). S doesn't hold the belief that p *on the basis of* the magnetic field or being in brain state #773291. Nor, presumably, does S believe that p *on the basis of* wishful thinking—*as the result of* wishful thinking perhaps, but not on the basis of it. Still less does S believe that p on the basis of the reliability of cognitive processes that produce the belief—though continued belief in p may well be based on the (meta)*belief* that the processes that initially produced it were reliable.

There are a few classes of possible grounds whose status is controversial. Whether nondoxastic sensory/experiential states can serve as grounds is an important question and the main topic of chapter 3. Another controversial class of potential grounds would consist of certain nonmental, though still highly accessible, facts. One might claim, with some initial plausibility, that the fact that I exist is the sort of thing that could serve as a basis for my belief that I exist. Even among mental states, some claim that only conscious and occurrent mental states can serve as grounds (e.g., Feldman 1988), while others deny this (e.g., BonJour 1985). Finally, even if we were to admit self-justifying beliefs, it is unclear that this would commit us to anything more than the claim that some beliefs are justified whenever held. Perhaps a belief can literally be its own ground, though perhaps 'self-justification' is just a convenient shorthand for something else.

Sometimes when we ask what makes a belief justified, we are asking for the ground of the belief; that is, we are asking what, if anything, evidentially justifies the agent in holding the belief. This is especially true in nonphilosophical contexts and when speaking in the second person and about a particular belief token: for example, "What justifies you in believing that p?" At other times, however, we are not asking for the agent's evidence (or not merely for that) but are asking what it is in virtue of which the belief is justified. This is especially true in epistemological contexts. Here we are asking not for the evidential basis of justification but for the metaphysical basis of justification; we are not offering a challenge to provide evidence but are asking for a theory of justification. To specify fully what it is in virtue of which a given belief is justified, we will need to advert not only to evidential justifiers, but to nonevidential justifiers as well. In addition to the whole of one's evidence, there is the fact that that evidence is good evidence, and presumably some further, deeper fact in virtue of which this is true. Epistemic properties are probably not fundamental features of the world; they presumably supervene on, reduce to, or can somehow be cashed out in terms of something deeper—one hopes nonnormative, or at least nonepistemic, properties. Even if one holds that such epistemic facts are really fundamental, there is still a distinction to be drawn between S's total evidence for p and the fact that S's belief that p is supported by this evidence. Similarly, a part of what makes some belief justified is the ground on which it is based, and another part is the fact that it is based on that ground. Thus, there are often three significant J-factors for a justified belief: the evidence on which it is based, the fact that it is based on this evidence, and the fact that this evidence is good evidence.

There is, in this sense, more to justification than evidence. A *nonevidential justifier* is any positively relevant J-factor that is not an evidential justifier, that is, anything else that makes it the case that the belief is justified, or contributes toward making it the case that the belief is justified. Though nonevidential justifiers are by definition relevant to the justification of a belief, they are not themselves evidence, and their relevance to justification is constitutive rather than evidential.[4]

Consider by way of illustration B, my belief that someone exists, which I have inferred from my belief that I exist. What justifies B? Is it the belief that I exist (coupled perhaps with the knowledge that if I do, someone does), or the fact that B was deduced from a justified belief (namely, that I exist)? It is obvious that both are correct answers, though answers to different questions. The sense in which the belief that I exist justifies B is quite different from the sense in which its being the result of a deductive argument justifies it. Either could be said to *make* the target belief justified, but in very different senses of 'make'. My belief that I exist serves as evidence; it is what grounds, what evidentially justifies, the belief that someone exists, while the deductive relation is not (necessarily) *evidence* for anything but is one of the underlying properties in virtue of which the belief is justified; the relation nonevidentially justifies the belief.[5]

---

4. One might hold, as a matter of substantive doctrine, that a justified belief must be grounded in an at least tacit awareness of all the factors relevant to that belief's justification; though I will argue against such a view later, I am not denying it here but merely clarifying the conceptual distinction between evidential and nonevidential justifiers.

5. Though it may be uncontroversial that the deductive relation nonevidentially justifies the belief, epistemologists with different theoretical commitments will certainly disagree about why this is true. That is, we will disagree about what the deeper nonevidential justifiers are: does deductive inference justify because it is reliable? because it increases overall coherence? because it exemplifies intellectual virtue? and so on.

It is useful to look at major sorts of epistemological theory in terms of the evidential and nonevidential justifiers they posit. Reliabilism, for example, is primarily a theory of nonevidential justifiers; it specifies that in virtue of which beliefs are justified and lets the theory of evidential justifiers fall where it may. Process reliability per se does not figure into the agent's evidence and thus does not ground, or *evidentially* justify, belief (though, again, beliefs about reliability might do so). But if reliabilism is correct, reliability can still *nonevidentially* justify the belief, by being that on which the justification supervenes.

Foundationalism, on the other hand, is mainly concerned with evidential justifiers rather than nonevidential justifiers. It posits a class of basic beliefs, which are not evidentially justified by other beliefs, and claims that all other justified beliefs are ultimately evidentially justified by these. Foundationalism per se says little or nothing about what the nonevidential J-factors are (though, of course, some foundationalists have done so).

Coherentism combines a theory of nonevidential justifiers with a theory of evidential justifiers. The standard coherentist theory of evidential justifiers claims (a) that only beliefs can serve as evidential justifiers and (b) that no belief can either be evidentially justified by itself or be justified in the absence of any ground. Such a theory goes hand in hand with the standard coherentist account of the underlying nature of justification: that justification is a matter of coherence among a set of beliefs. Coherence is thus a nonevidential justifier; it is relevant to the justification of some belief, but it is not necessarily part of the justifying evidence for the belief.[6]

Evidentialism may seem to be the claim that there are no nonevidential justifiers—that nothing is relevant to justification but evidence. However, nothing about evidentialism precludes the claim that the adequacy of the evidence (i.e., the fact that the whole of the agent's evidence is good evidence) is a nonevidential justifier, even if the adequacy of a body of evidence vis-à-vis some belief is a necessary property of that body of evidence. On such a view, adequacy is nonetheless a property of the evidence, rather than a piece of the evidence.[7]

It will be convenient to proceed in terms of "evidential justification" and "nonevidential justification." However, such terminology might misleadingly suggest two different properties, rather than two different relations. There's just one property of being (epistemically) justified, but two relations things might stand in to justified

---

6. Epistemologists are often regrettably inexplicit about the distinction between evidential and nonevidential justifiers. It is hard to be sure, but some coherentists might propose coherence as a (the?) nonevidential justifier and abandon the notion of evidence altogether. This would yield a nonevidentialist view of the sort I discuss later. This reading would actually make sense of certain otherwise puzzling claims, like Lehrer's (1990b) insistence that justification is a matter of coherence with *all* the rest of one's beliefs, not just the justified ones. On the other hand, traditional versions of coherentism make quite an effort to argue for (a) and (b) and are left with little motivation once these are abandoned. Kvanvig (2003a) may endorse a nonevidentialist coherentism of the sort I've just sketched, though his is also nonstandard in being a nondoxastic theory.

7. Conee and Feldman (2005), for example, hold a doctrine of "strong supervenience," also known as "cognitive essentialism" (Pollock 1986), according to which evidential relations hold necessarily. This is presumably compatible with their mentalism: the view that only mental states can serve as evidence. Yet the fact that my evidence is good evidence is not itself a mental state. Thus, even on this strongly evidentialist and internalist view, there are things that are relevant to justification but do not serve as evidence; that is, there are nonevidential J-factors.

beliefs: the relation of nonevidentially justifying and the relation of evidentially justifying. If something stands in either of these relations to a belief, then that belief has the property of justification; that is, the belief is justified.

It may help to keep in mind that the relation of evidential justification is at least in certain instances a causal relation. Grounds sometimes cause the beliefs they justify to be tokened, thereby causing those beliefs to be justified. Nonevidential justification, on the other hand, is constitutive, rather than causal. The belief's being justified *just is* (or reduces to, or supervenes on, etc.), its being the result of a reliable process. The relations here are far too intimate—and necessary—to be causal.

Although I won't pursue the possibility in much detail, the concept of nonevidential justification is equally compatible with a metaphysical nonnaturalism in epistemology. Even if epistemic properties do not reduce to or supervene on anything nonepistemic, there is a distinction between my evidence for some belief and the (now supposedly brute) fact that this is adequate evidence. Suppose my belief that q is evidentially justified by my belief that p. Part of what makes my belief that q justified is the fact that p is a good reason for q. If epistemic properties are nonnatural, then this fact has no deeper metaphysical underpinning, but this has no bearing on the claim that this fact makes my belief justified, in the sense of nonevidentially justifying the belief.

The goal up to this point has merely been to elucidate the distinction between evidential and nonevidential justification. I do not presuppose that there in fact are any nonevidential justifiers. A very strong kind of internalism might insist that nothing can be relevant to justification unless it is taken into account by the cognizer, that not even the adequacy of the evidence contributes to justification unless this adequacy is itself part of the cognizer's evidence. I think this view is mistaken, and I argue against it later, but I have been careful to be neutral up to this point, discussing candidate nonevidential justifiers and theories about nonevidential justifiers.

The distinction between evidential and nonevidential justification is quite familiar, and I have perhaps belabored the obvious for too long. Perhaps everyone at least tacitly recognizes the distinction between evidence and nonevidence. The import of this distinction, however, has often gone unnoticed, both in arguments for and against doxasticism.

2. The Supervenience Argument

To illustrate the distinction further and to set the stage for the argument to follow, consider a well-known argument, which infers the possibility of nondoxastic justification from the claim that epistemic properties supervene on nonepistemic properties. I call it the supervenience argument (SA):[8]

1. Epistemic properties supervene on nonepistemic properties (perhaps, e.g., reliability, incorrigibility, coherence).
2. So beliefs ultimately receive their justification from something that does not itself have justification.

8. Versions of this argument have been espoused by Sosa (1980), van Cleve (1985), and Steup (1996, 2000).

3. Therefore, there is something that makes beliefs justified but is not itself a justified belief.
4. Unjustified (or nonjustified) beliefs cannot confer justification on other beliefs.
5. Therefore, there is something that makes beliefs justified but is not itself a belief.
6. Therefore, not all justification is doxastic, so doxastic theories are false.

The most sophisticated formulation of SA is due to van Cleve (1985), who invokes an important distinction between two kinds of epistemic principles: transmission principles and generation principles. The former tell how justified beliefs give rise to justified beliefs, and the latter tell how something that is not itself a justified belief gives rise to justified beliefs. The point of the supervenience thesis (that epistemic properties supervene on nonepistemic properties) is that it guarantees the existence of true generation principles. And if there are true generation principles, then it is possible—indeed, perhaps necessary—for something nondoxastic to confer justification on beliefs.

A closely related argument is sometimes offered as an ad hominem against coherentists, the chief proponents of doxasticism: coherentists claim that justification supervenes on coherence. But this is the claim that coherence justifies beliefs, and coherence isn't a belief, so coherentism is committed to nondoxastic justification after all (Sosa 1980; Steup 1996).

The problem with all of this, however, is that such phrases as 'confers justification', 'makes beliefs justified', 'gives rise to justified beliefs', and the like are ambiguous between evidentially justifying and nonevidentially justifying. Suppose that supervenience does imply that something nondoxastic justifies beliefs; it does not follow from this that nondoxastic things can *evidentially* justify beliefs. A Cartesian foundationalist, for example, could endorse a doxastic theory of grounds by claiming that only beliefs can evidentially justify beliefs. This would be perfectly compatible with the Cartesian claim that a belief is justified iff it is clear and distinct, even though, patently, neither clarity nor distinctness is itself a belief. If the Cartesian foundationalist were to say that nothing can justify a belief except a belief, we should read this as an infelicitous way of claiming that only beliefs can *evidentially* justify beliefs, not as a repudiation of the epistemic role of clarity and distinctness. This is presumably what coherentists are doing when they claim that only beliefs can justify beliefs. They are not denying that coherence nonevidentially justifies beliefs; they are insisting that evidential relations obtain only among beliefs and thus that only beliefs can evidentially justify, can serve as justifying *grounds* for beliefs.[9]

Doxasticism is best viewed as a theory about evidential justification rather than justification more generally. For one thing, there are few if any prima facie constraints on what sorts of things can serve as nonevidential justifiers: reliability, coherence, clarity and distinctness, even perhaps the right sort of unjustified or nonjustified beliefs about epistemic principles. The correct theory of nonevidential justifiers will be the one that gets the cases right; if doxasticism were the unrestricted claim that

9. This sort of point generalizes to all so-called doxastic theories, but I will restrict my attention to coherentism here to simplify matters.

only beliefs can be relevant to the justification of beliefs, there would be very little reason to take doxasticism seriously. Additionally, it is not obvious that anyone has ever endorsed such a view. Most extant theories of nonevidential justification have posited something nondoxastic as that in virtue of which beliefs are justified. Witness coherentism and Cartesian foundationalism, which are paradigm instances of "doxastic theories" as the term is generally used.

So if doxasticism is to be taken seriously, it must be read as a thesis about evidential justifiers. But this is where SA falls flat. The fifth step of SA claims that there is something that is not itself a belief but that makes beliefs justified. To refute doxasticism, however, what is required is the stronger claim that this nondoxastic thing *evidentially* justifies beliefs, and this is not something the supervenience premise supports. Supervenience may imply that there are nondoxastic justifiers, but it does not begin to imply that there are nondoxastic *evidential* justifiers.[10] What SA needs to refute doxasticism is a thesis about evidential justifiers; what it offers instead is a thesis about nonevidential justifiers.

A detailed theory about nonevidential justification might have implications concerning evidential justification, but the supervenience thesis claims only that justification supervenes on *something or other* that is nonepistemic. This generic claim, however, though plausible for its generality, is compatible with any theory whatsoever about grounds. The fact that there are true generation principles indicates that there must be justifiers that don't themselves have justification, but that doesn't yet tell us whether there must be—or can be—justifying *grounds* that don't themselves have justification.

3. Doxasticism and Nondoxasticism

It is possible to sharpen the notions of doxasticism and nondoxasticism in light of the previous discussion. Doxasticism is sometimes characterized as the view that any two doxastically identical agents are ipso facto epistemically identical (e.g., Pollock 1986, p. 19). Such a theory would be rather implausible. First, it founders on the possibility that two agents share all the same beliefs, where these beliefs are differently based. In such a case, the two agents might very well differ epistemically.[11] Furthermore, I could have exactly the same beliefs as you do, and perhaps even the same basing relations, even though my beliefs are the result of a perverse stubbornness (which I don't acknowledge, of course, and which is nowhere reflected in my belief set), while yours are the result of an honest effort to seek the truth. Any reasonable theory ought to admit that there is an epistemic difference between us.

A weaker form of doxasticism claims only that an agent's *evidence* is limited entirely to that agent's beliefs. Two doxastically identical agents will, on this view, be evidentially identical, but perhaps not epistemically identical, for the reasons just glossed. I will understand doxasticism to be this weaker, more plausible, view. Even

---

10. It is unclear that supervenience implies even this much. Premise 4 of SA is only obviously true if we read 'confer justification on' as 'evidentially justify'.

11. Not all doxastic theories claim that the basing relation is a causal one, of course, but as long as there is more to the matter of which beliefs are based on which beliefs than is captured by the sum of an agent's beliefs at a time, this objection will stand.

this notion of doxasticism needs clarification, however. The rallying cry of doxastic theories is that nothing can justify a belief but a belief. Viewing doxasticism as a thesis about evidential justification, however, requires us to go beyond the traditional slogans. Doxasticism must be more than the claim that only beliefs can evidentially justify beliefs, since this is something reliabilists can accept, and reliabilism is a paradigmatically nondoxastic theory. Instead, doxasticism must be viewed as a conjunction of two claims:

The Belief Principle: only beliefs can evidentially justify beliefs

and

The Grounds Principle: all justified beliefs have grounds, that is, evidential justifiers.

Although the Belief Principle is the only one mentioned in standard formulations of doxasticism, the discussion up to this point reveals the Grounds Principle to be far more than just the trivial claim that all justified beliefs have justifiers. All justified beliefs do have justifiers, of course, but the Grounds Principle makes the stronger claim that all justified beliefs have evidential justifiers. Doxasticism claims not only that no nonbeliefs evidentially justify beliefs but also that every justified belief has a belief that (evidentially) justifies it.

Doxasticism thus understood may have fewer proponents than is generally thought. Standard versions of coherentism are clearly doxastic theories in this sense, but it is not obvious that many foundationalists, even of the more conservative variety, really accept doxasticism. For a foundationalist to accept the Belief Principle and the Grounds Principle both would require a very literal reading of the claim that the basic beliefs are self-justifying. A doxastic foundationalist cannot intend talk about self-justification as metaphorical shorthand for the property of being justified whenever held, or the like. If every justified belief has a doxastic ground, then a basic belief must really be its own ground; self-justification so literally construed presents a situation that van Cleve (1985) likens to improving one's financial situation by lending oneself money. It is not obvious that such a view is even intelligible. A nondoxastic foundationalist, however, can still talk in terms of self-justification, but what will be meant is merely that the belief is justified whenever held or something similar.

A nondoxastic theory is simply one that is not a doxastic theory, and there are at least two important kinds: one that endorses a more liberal conception of grounds than doxasticism does and one that rejects the need for grounds altogether. An *experientialist nondoxasticism* ("experientialism" for short) agrees with doxasticism in accepting the Grounds Principle but rejects the Belief Principle in allowing nondoxastic experiential states to serve as justifying grounds. If there is a standard view in contemporary epistemology, it is probably this.[12] Such a view is not restricted to fully internalist theories; Alston's (1988) "Internalist Externalism" is a kind of

---

12. This is also probably the classic doctrine of the given, though it is hard to be sure that those authors intended the experiential states to play a specifically evidential role.

experientialism on my taxonomy, since he explicitly endorses the Grounds Principle while allowing nondoxastic experiential states to serve as grounds.[13]

Other versions of reliabilism, however, make no such requirement of grounds. A *nonevidentialist nondoxasticism* ("nonevidentialism") is one that denies the Grounds Principle, thereby allowing beliefs to be justified without being evidentially justified. Primary examples are externalist theories of the sort Goldman (e.g., 1979, 1986) has defended: so long as the relevant processes are suitably reliable, the belief will be (prima facie) justified, whether or not it is based on a ground; thus grounds are not necessary for justification. A nonevidentialist theory need not be a reliabilist theory, but as far as I can see, the only attractive versions of nonevidentialism are externalist theories. Thus nonevidentialist theories carry with them a commitment regarding the internalist-externalist debate in a way that the broadly evidentialist theories of doxasticism and experientialism do not.[14]

Since nonevidentialism is gotten merely by denying the Grounds Principle, a nonevidentialist can accept the Belief Principle without compromising her view. So long as one denies that every justified belief has a ground, one can insist that only beliefs can evidentially justify beliefs. Later, in fact, I will defend the Belief Principle as part of an argument *for* nonevidentialism and thus, indirectly, for reliabilism.

4. Doxastic Theories

Doxastic theories have been in decline in recent years, and there is good reason for this. Though I cannot give this important issue the attention it deserves, it is worthwhile to rehearse the familiar arguments that I take to militate against doxasticism. The following is intended less as a knockdown refutation of doxasticism than as an explanation of why I will be assuming nondoxasticism in ensuing chapters.

The main objection to doxastic theories is the famous isolation objection. It is typically offered as an argument against coherentism, though, as Pollock (1986) notes, it is really an argument against doxastic theories more generally. Consider an ordinary agent with ordinarily justified beliefs, but an agent who lives in an extraordinary world, perhaps of the sort common in fairy tales. So this agent has justified beliefs—including perceptual beliefs—about trolls, dragons, damsels in distress, and the like. But an agent in the actual world—which is conspicuously lacking in dragons and the like—could be doxastically identical to the agent just described, could share all of the first agent's basing relations, could believe out of the same motivations, and so forth. This second agent would, according to doxasticism, be justified in most

13. Is *any* view that endorses the Grounds Principle and denies the Belief Principle an experientialist view? No, one might hold, as mentioned previously, that internal but nonmental facts can serve as grounds (or, I suppose, that mental states other than experiences and beliefs could). I don't think such a view is very plausible, largely for reasons that will emerge later. Consequently, I will ignore such a view and treat experientialism as equivalent to the view one gets by endorsing the Grounds Principle and rejecting the Belief Principle.

14. Although doxasticism is usually taken to imply internalism, one could conceivably maintain that what determines whether a given belief counts as evidence for some other belief is some factor external to the agent. Such a view would parallel Alston's externalist yet evidentialist view.

of her beliefs, since the first agent was. Since the second agent clearly would not be justified in her beliefs, doxasticism is false.

The isolation objection is often expressed in terms of causal contact with reality or truth-conduciveness. Such formulations are unlikely to move internalists much and detract from what I think is the real point of the objection, which is little more than epistemic arbitrariness. Isolation is just a more general case of vicious circularity, and circularity is just arbitrariness multiplied.

Suppose I take some random proposition, say,

p: I've been abducted by aliens,

and I decide to believe it. Obviously, the belief is epistemically arbitrary and thus completely unjustified. I have no reason to believe it but am simply *making things up*. If I'm even moderately clever, however, I can concoct an argument for this belief: I claim that the abduction would explain why

q: I have a computer chip implanted in my brain.

This might actually be a reasonable move if I had some independent reason to believe that q, but suppose that my only reason for believing this is that I also believe (justifiedly or not) that

r: Aliens typically implant chips in the brains of their abductees.

Then r, together with p, does provide an argument of sorts for q, but not a justifying argument, for the whole business is obviously (viciously) circular. My belief that p is just as epistemically arbitrary as it was initially. What was wrong with it before is still wrong. The "argument" I've produced is not a matter of justification, but confabulation.

I lay out the example, as is common, by allowing that the agent in question is deliberately making things up. Though this makes the issues more vivid, it is inessential to the argument. The beliefs in question need not result from my voluntarily adopting them; the beliefs are just as unjustified if they result from my having a fever, or paranoid delusions (or, given appropriately specified background details, if they actually result from the chip the aliens have implanted in my brain). Victims of paranoid delusions are—not to put too fine a point on it—*crazy*, and 'crazy' here is just as much an epistemic as a clinical term.

Coherentism is sometimes characterized as the view that *large enough* circles do confer justification, though such a view is understandably not usually taken very seriously. More confabulation ought to make my epistemic situation worse, not better. Just as stringing together affirmations of the consequent doesn't make the inference any better, there's no reason to think that large circular arguments should be any better than small ones.[15] Nor, for the same sorts of reasons, should the *shape* of

---

15. That is, except in the relatively uninteresting sense that the circularity might be harder to detect in larger arguments; agents thus might have an additional defeater for beliefs based on smaller circular arguments—that is, that the argument for the belief is circular, hence bad—that is lacking in the case of larger arguments. Surely, however, this is not what coherentists have ever had in mind.

the confabulation matter. A complicated confabulation will have the shape of a web or a network, rather than a circle, as the mythical "linear conception of justification" would have it, but it remains a confabulation.

The problem with circular arguments does not obviously have to do with a lack of causal connection to the external world or with a failure of truth-conduciveness.[16] In fact, it is surprisingly difficult to say just what is wrong with circular arguments without parroting platitudes from our youth, such as 'two wrongs don't make a right'. Tired as the cliché may be, it seems to be on the right track. The reason circularity does not confer justification is just that unjustified beliefs can't serve as justifying evidence for beliefs, and if a given belief is in need of justification, then it can't serve as a premise for its own justification. If the only "justification" I have for a certain proposition is a circular argument, then I have *no independent* justification for the proposition, so unless the proposition in question is self-justifying, it is not justified at all. One could insist that webs and networks of interconnected beliefs are ipso facto not circular, and in a strictly geometric sense this is right, but this wouldn't change the epistemic situation at all. Instead of a single belief for which the agent has no independent justification (and thus no justification), it is a whole belief set. Again this makes the agent's epistemic situation worse, rather than better. It is not as if circularity detracts from the justification of the target beliefs; it's rather that circularity fails to add anything other than more unjustified beliefs where there had previously been only one.

Much of this comes fairly close to begging the question against coherentism. The coherentist claims that circular arguments can justify beliefs, and I reply by denying that circular arguments can justify beliefs. Such a response, however, is sometimes the only appropriate one. When a thesis is as thoroughly and fundamentally implausible as the kind of coherentism under consideration, the best way to argue against it is simply to point out the obvious truth of its denial. The claim that adding more fabrication to an initially arbitrary belief somehow justifies it simply strains credulity.

Unless...unless there is some reason to think that the very existence of a large enough and coherent enough set rendered it virtually certain to be true (or mostly or nearly so) (Davidson 1986). This is perhaps the best reason for taking doxastic coherentism seriously.[17] Consider, by way of analogy, a cryptogram where the letters of some passage of text are systematically replaced by numbers or different letters. To solve the puzzle, one must try substituting various combinations of letters for the symbols given. The fact that a given combination produces a sensible (coherent)

---

16. Lehrer's (1990b) response to the isolation objection is his "transformation argument": if the agent really is isolated from reality, then her belief depends on a false proposition (viz., that she is not isolated), and this prevents the belief from constituting knowledge. This only addresses the isolation objection to a coherentist theory of *knowledge*, where what is at issue here is the isolation objection to a coherentist theory of *justification*. In addition, it considers only a version of the objection according to which isolation is a causal issue.

17. The other main reasons are the apparent lack of alternative options and something like the Quine/Duhem thesis, that our beliefs face the tribunal of sensory evidence as a corporate body. The Quine/Duhem thesis, however, does not offer an argument for doxasticism. In fact, the very notion of a "tribunal of sensory evidence" suggests that experiences play an essential role. As far as the lack of other options, a major point of this book will be that there are pretty good alternatives.

result is very good evidence for thinking that the solution arrived at is the correct one, simply because it would be vanishingly improbable to get a solution that is coherent but wrong. Similarly, one might think, for beliefs.

Such an analogy is of only very limited use, however, for the cryptogram is constrained by external factors (like the symbols given in the puzzle and the rules for solving it), the analogues of which are barred by doxasticism from playing any role in the epistemological account. Coherence is supposed to be an internal property of the belief system. But it is exactly the feature of being subject to external constraints that makes cryptograms (more or less uniquely) soluble. The inference from the coherence of a belief set to its probable overall truth is plausible only if either there are enough external (i.e., nondoxastic) constraints or the standards for coherence are so incredibly high that only very few belief sets could count as coherent. The latter option is incompatible with the fact that many people have different belief sets (for one thing, they include incompatible *de se* beliefs),[18] which are nevertheless justified. And the former option is incompatible with doxasticism, the only constraints available to which are internal.[19]

BonJour's (1985) response was to add the "observation requirement," stating that in addition to coherence, a justified belief set must contain a large number of laws attributing a high degree of reliability to a wide range of cognitively spontaneous beliefs (p. 141). A cognitively spontaneous belief is a belief that is involuntary, "coercive," and not the result of any introspectible train of reasoning (p. 117). Because the observation requirement is an internal constraint (though it seems initially to bridge the gap between internal and external constraints), it is insufficient. Supposing that Napoleon was justified in most of his beliefs, my adopting *all* of his beliefs will include my satisfying the observation requirement as well, for I will have all of his metabeliefs about what cognitively spontaneous beliefs he (/I) has (/have). Any coherentist who is now willing to bite the bullet and claim that I'm justified in believing that I'm a French army general would have fared just as well without the observation requirement.

Additionally, the observation requirement imposes no constraints on which cognitively spontaneous beliefs the agent takes seriously.[20] What if my belief set contains laws attributing a high degree of reliability to cognitively spontaneous beliefs about monsters, dragons, and alien abductions? Perhaps I think that wishful thinking is reliable (at least in my own case) or that my television or my dog is communicating telepathically with me and is thus a reliable source of cognitively spontaneous beliefs. I might in addition lack beliefs about the reliability of ordinary perceptual beliefs since they so frequently conflict with my preferred cognitively spontaneous

18. I am assuming here a scheme for belief individuation that counts two tokens as being of the same type if they have the same character, in Kaplan's (1989) sense; that is, if I think (of myself that) I'm Napoleon and Napoleon thinks (of himself that) he's Napoleon, we share this belief. If one refuses to allow such an individuation scheme, the same points could be made by appeal to analogous and equally coherent sets.

19. Although the cryptogram analogy argues for a certain role to be played by coherence, it is not the role that coherentists need it to play. This should not be surprising, since the first (to my knowledge, anyway) epistemologist to appeal to this sort of case was Descartes ([1644] 1985, Principle CCV).

20. With the exception of introspective beliefs about what other cognitively spontaneous beliefs one has (BonJour 1985, p. 141).

beliefs. The cognitively spontaneous beliefs I do endorse might cohere fairly well with the rest of what I believe, but surely these beliefs aren't justified.

More important, the observation requirement fails to address the real problem, which involves particular beliefs. Even if the observation requirement entailed that *some* of the beliefs in a coherent set were suitably connected to reality, it doesn't entail that all are. Those that aren't would count as justified even though they shouldn't. My current belief that it's raining coheres reasonably well with the rest of my beliefs, and I take seriously a wide range of cognitively spontaneous beliefs, but this doesn't imply that my belief that it's raining—which I just pulled out of the air—is at all justified.

This is exacerbated by the fact that I may be sitting and looking out a window, having a visual experience as of a sunny, perfectly rainless day. For whatever reason, my brain has not produced a cognitively spontaneous belief that it's not raining, so there is nothing in my belief system that can serve as a defeater for my belief that it's raining. Thus, a doxastic theory has to count the belief as undefeated, and if coherence (in a system that satisfies the observation requirement) is sufficient for prima facie justification, then the belief has to be classified as justified, which it very clearly is not. This point about the negative role of experiential states as defeaters is clearly a problem with doxastic theories more generally; if only beliefs can evidentially justify a belief, then there is no obvious reason to deny that only beliefs can evidentially *unjustify* beliefs.

Again, the isolation objection is an objection to doxasticism in general, not just coherentism. The central point is that something outside the system of beliefs is required to justify beliefs. Pollock and Cruz (1999) have an argument against doxastic theories that assimilates the insights of the isolation objection but without understanding isolation as a causal or verific notion. Although their argument does not quite succeed, I think that a modified version of it does.

Pollock and Cruz (1999, pp. 84–86) argue as follows (translating into my own terminology):

1. Assume doxasticism, that is, every justified belief has a justifying ground, and only beliefs can serve as grounds.
2. The *rest* of one's beliefs cannot evidentially justify a given perceptual belief, since they generally do not determine what perceptual beliefs one should adopt.
3. Therefore, justified perceptual beliefs must evidentially justify themselves; that is, they must be prima facie self-justifying.
4. But perceptual beliefs are ordinary physical-object beliefs and as such can be held for bad reasons (or no reason at all). And when they are, they are not prima facie justified, which shows that they were not prima facie self-justifying.

Because (4) conflicts with (3), which followed from (1), (1) must be false.

As formulated, the argument is open to several responses. The MSFist will deny either (2) or (4), depending on whether perceptual beliefs are construed as beliefs about appearances or external objects. The coherentist will object at a number of points.

To avoid some of the terminological worries, I will retain the stipulated usages from chapter 1 and use 'perceptual belief' to refer to beliefs about external objects, in contrast to first-person beliefs about how one is appeared to, which I have been calling 'appearance beliefs'. It is also helpful to have at hand a notion of a 'pure perceptual belief'. Let us say that S's belief that p at t is a *pure perceptual belief* iff S's belief that p at t is a perceptual belief, and S has no independent evidence for p at t.[21] It may very well be that many of our perceptual beliefs are not pure. We spend a great deal of time in familiar environments, where prior beliefs do give us some information about what to expect. However, the existence of *justified* pure perceptual beliefs is uncontroversial, and it is really this notion that epistemologists typically have in mind in discussing perceptual belief. Henceforth, all talk about perceptual belief should be understood as talk about pure perceptual belief unless marked otherwise. I will occasionally use 'pure' as a reminder.

Given this terminology, it is clear that the proponent of MSF will deny (2). Some of our other beliefs do determine whether we should hold a given perceptual belief or not, namely, our *appearance* beliefs. My belief that there seems to be a book in front of me does serve as evidence for my perceptual belief that there's a book in front of me. Pollock and Cruz dismiss this possibility, on the grounds that we rarely explicitly formulate such appearance beliefs. This rejoinder, however, only succeeds on the controversial assumption that nonoccurrent beliefs can't serve as evidential justifiers.

There is a better response, which is to notice that on a doxastic foundationalism, these beliefs would have to be prima facie self-justifying, and even appearance beliefs can be held for bad reasons or no reason at all. If I really like being appeared to redly, I may, as the result of wishful thinking, come to believe that I'm appeared to redly. I may believe that I seem to smell frankincense because my dial-up psychic told me I do. Pollock and Cruz's argument is insufficiently general. *Any* belief can be held for bad reasons or none at all (compare Goldman 1979), in which case it is not even prima facie justified. There is simply no proposition such that, necessarily, if S believes it, then S is prima facie justified in believing it. The problem here is just the problem of isolation, of epistemic arbitrariness, all over again. It is not only beliefs about aliens and dragons that can be adopted arbitrarily but also beliefs about one's own mental states.

Coherentists will also have to deny premise (2) of Pollock and Cruz's argument, but such a move is even less plausible once appearance beliefs are seen not to help. For, barring appearance beliefs, (2) is just the claim that there are justified pure perceptual beliefs, and this is surely true. I have no idea what to expect behind door number 2, but once it opens, I am perfectly justified in believing that it's a (new?) car.

Perception often justifies our beliefs not just in the nonexpected but in the unexpected. Even if I know perfectly well that it is extremely unlikely to snow on Easter in Tucson (and that it's Easter in Tucson), my belief that it's snowing may be justified. The only beliefs that might justify such perceptual beliefs are appearance beliefs, but the isolation objection applies to these as well; there must be something outside

21. I won't bother defining independence, but the idea is intuitive enough. Importantly, being appeared to as if p and believing that one is appeared to as if p are not to be understood as independent here.

the system of beliefs that accounts for the justification of perceptual beliefs. The question to be addressed next is whether this outside something is an experiential state, as the experientialist maintains, or whether it is, as the nonevidentialist thinks, something more external than that. With doxasticism out of the picture and the playing field thus limited to experientialism and nonevidentialist nondoxasticism, any argument against the former becomes an argument for the latter.

The argument against doxasticism makes it possible to seek assistance from an unlikely source: Sellars. Though the famous Sellarsian dilemma has served for many years as one of the main arguments against experientialism, it will strike many readers as wildly ill advised to align myself with Sellars. First of all, the Sellarsian dilemma is usually offered as an argument for coherentism,[22] and I am trying to defend reliabilism. Second, the argument is, as a matter of sociological fact, notoriously unconvincing, as is witnessed by the proliferation of experientialist theories. Even the Sellarsian dilemma's most vigorous proponent, BonJour (1999, 2002), has abandoned it.

However, the distinction between evidential and nonevidential justification yields a version of the Sellarsian dilemma (or something like it) that is at once stronger and weaker than the standard version. It is stronger in that it really does provide a good argument against experientialism but weaker in that it leaves nonevidentialism completely untouched. The basic idea is this: the dilemma shows that experiential states cannot serve as evidential justifiers for beliefs, thus establishing the truth of the Belief Principle and consequently the falsehood of experientialism (which by definition denies the Belief Principle). Coherentism or doxasticism more generally only follows if the Grounds Principle is also assumed. Since doxasticism is false, and since the Belief Principle is true, the Grounds Principle must also be false. Therefore, a nonevidentialist nondoxasticism must be true.

---

22. James Pryor (2004) calls the Sellarsian dilemma "the Master Argument for Coherentism."

3

Experientialist Theories

Experientialist nondoxasticism (or simply 'experientialism') I have defined as the view that endorses the Grounds Principle while rejecting the Belief Principle, by allowing nondoxastic experiential states to serve as grounds for beliefs; every justified belief has a ground, but some nondoxastic states can serve as justifying grounds. Since the experiential states are nondoxastic, the target beliefs may satisfy the definition of basic beliefs: though they are evidentially justified, they aren't evidentially justified *by other beliefs*. This makes experiential states prime candidates for solving the famous regress problem by serving as justifiers and regress terminators at the same time. They can terminate the regress because they aren't themselves beliefs, so the question of their being justified doesn't arise; yet they can provide reasons for beliefs in much the way that (justified) beliefs can. Consequently, experientialism has been enthusiastically embraced by many foundationalists, MSFists and EOFists alike.[1] In the argument to follow, I will take the standard proponent of experientialism to be a foundationalist of one of these two sorts. I should say a few words up front, therefore, about the *nonstandard* varieties of experientialism.

Experientialism, as I have defined it, endorses the Grounds Principle but denies the Belief Principle. The experientialist is thus committed to the claim that some justified beliefs are ultimately based on experiential states. I think it would be natural

1. Proponents of experientialism include Alston (1988, 2002), Audi (1998), BonJour (1999, 2001, 2002), Brewer (1999), Chisholm (1966, 1977, 1989), Feldman and Conee (1985), Fumerton (1985, 2001), Haack (1993), Huemer (2001), Pollock (1986), Pollock and Cruz (1999), Pryor (2000), Quinton (1966), Reynolds (1991), and Steup (1996, 2000).

to take this a step further and claim that all justified beliefs are, but the experientialist per se is free to incorporate elements of both doxastic foundationalism and coherentism. An experientialist can hold that some beliefs are literally self-justifying, though as we saw in the previous chapter, such a claim is stronger than it usually sounds. An experientialist can even deny foundationalism, claiming that there are some beliefs whose justification depends entirely on coherence and not ultimately on basic beliefs, even though there are some basic beliefs, and these are grounded in experiential states. Allowing experiences to serve as terminal justifiers, however, certainly undercuts the standard motivation for this coherentist element. If experiential states can confer (prima facie) justification on beliefs, there will surely be enough basic beliefs to make foundationalism plausible and thus little reason to take on all the burdens of coherentism or some other nonfoundationalist alternative.

The extra burden, of course, is the isolation objection again. As seen in the last chapter, the isolation objection works just as well for proper subsets of the belief set as it does for the whole thing. It is interesting in this connection that Pryor (2000) thinks that it is foundationalism that takes on the extra burden; he claims that perceptual beliefs get their justification from experiential states but explicitly backs away from claiming that all beliefs do. However, allowing experiences to justify some beliefs only solves the isolation problem for those beliefs. The isolation objection does not demand merely to know how *all* justification could be purely doxastic, but how *any* could be. The only way to really solve this problem is to insist not only that some justification is nondoxastic but also that all justification ultimately is.

Another way to allow experiential states an epistemic role without thereby embracing foundationalism is to claim that they have a merely negative epistemic role, rather than a positive one. Experiential states can play a nonfoundationalist role if they serve only as defeaters for belief but not as positive grounds.[2] However, if these states are intended to serve as evidential rather than nonevidential defeaters (a view any evidentialist will have to accept), it is very hard to see how one might deny that they can also serve as positive evidential justifiers. And if they can, it is hard to see why one might continue to court problems about isolation in favor of just adopting foundationalism.

Another kind of nondoxastic coherentism, of the sort defended by Gupta (2006), denies that the evidence for perceptual beliefs is either purely doxastic (as traditional coherentism claims) or purely nondoxastic (as EOF claims); instead, nondoxastic experiences serve as evidence for perceptual beliefs, but only in conjunction with ancillary beliefs about the evidential relation between the experience and the perceptual belief. These ancillary beliefs must themselves be justified, and though a regress threatens, the standard coherentist responses will be made. This may be the most plausible type of experientialism, but I won't discuss it much, in part because it is not

---

2. Kvanvig *sounds like* he endorses a coherentism that is nondoxastic in at least this sense: "It is open to coherentists to deny that appearances [i.e., nondoxastic experiences] impart, or tend to impart (even in the absence of defeaters), any degree of positive epistemic status for related beliefs. The coherentist can maintain, instead, that appearances are necessary (in the usual situations) for those beliefs to have some degree of positive epistemic status, but in no way sufficient in themselves for any degree of positive epistemic status" (2003a, sec. 2.1). This may also have been what he and Riggs (1992) had in mind. Alternatively, they may be endorsing something like Gupta's view, which I discuss shortly.

the most common; most experientialists endorse a foundationalist theory concerning the role of experiences.

My guess is that there are two main reasons that experientialists have tended to avoid nondoxastic coherentism. The first is that, while nondoxastic coherentism might avoid the isolation objection in a way that standard doxastic coherence theories never could, it is still a kind of coherentism, and the standard coherentist responses to the regress argument simply aren't very satisfactory. In particular, there is something troubling about the notion of a belief literally conferring justification on itself, even if through the intervention of other beliefs. The second reason is that any coherentist theory requires far too much cognitive sophistication on the part of the believer, who must now have a host of beliefs about perceptual beliefs, experiential states, and the like. The coherentist requirement would deny justified perceptual beliefs to animals and small children, it fails to do justice to the phenomenology of perceptual belief, and it might spawn a new, infinite, regress of the sort Lewis Carroll (1895) discussed.

I find these two reasons fairly compelling, although, with the exception of Carroll's regress (which I mention later, in section 2.4, and discuss in more detail in chapter 7), I don't have anything new to say on these already familiar topics. In any case, I want to streamline an already complicated discussion and more directly address the larger audience by assuming that all experientialists are foundationalists, at least as far as perception is concerned. It is important to flag this simplifying assumption for what it is, because, although most of my arguments against experientialism apply to any kind of experientialism, one only applies to the foundationalist versions. Nondoxastic coherentism will be immune to this particular argument.

Thus, to make the exposition manageable, I will treat all experientialists as foundationalists of one sort or the other. I will also continue to treat coherentism as a form of doxasticism, despite the caveats entered here and in the previous chapter. These simplifications should introduce little further distortion, since most experientialists do endorse a foundationalist view, at least about perception, which is the almost exclusive focus of the present discussion.

Experientialism is probably the dominant view in epistemology, and I will have to do some work to show that it should be abandoned in favor of nonevidentialist nondoxasticism. However, there are too many variants on the basic experientialist approach for me to address them all. Instead, I want to offer a general argument designed to show that experiential states cannot play the evidential role required of them by any experientialist theory of perception. I will take an EOF version of experientialism as representative, in order to avoid having to run each argument two or more times, though I will occasionally make explicit reference to MSF where appropriate. It is, however, the putative justifier that I am worried about; the justificandum beliefs will be discussed only for the sake of examples.

The diversity among experientialist theories is not exhausted by the MSF-EOF divide (even restricting our attention to foundationalist versions). The term 'experiential state' is notoriously equivocal, and although authors are frequently regrettably unclear about what they are taking experiential states to be, there is likely to be a diversity of opinion here. I will thus pursue a familiar strategy in arguing that experiences cannot play the role experientialism requires of them. The general argument is roughly as follows. The nondoxastic experiences that are alleged to justify the basic beliefs are either sensations or percepts (about which much more in the next section). Sensations cannot justify the basic beliefs, in part because they cannot stand in the appropriate evidential relations to beliefs. Neither can percepts justify the basic beliefs, unless the percepts are construed as themselves beliefs, in which case they are not nondoxastic, and the beliefs they justify are not basic after all.

All of this sounds highly reminiscent of the famous Sellarsian dilemma. As it happens, I think the Sellarsian dilemma does contain some important insights, though I want to distance myself from the package deal. The standard formulation, due to BonJour (1978, 1985) has amassed few converts, and understandably so.[3] It is worth rehearsing briefly to explain just how much of this I am not committing to. BonJour presents the dilemma as follows:

> The givenist is caught in a fundamental dilemma: if his intuitions or immediate apprehensions are construed as cognitive, then they will be both capable of giving justification and in need of it themselves; if they are non-cognitive, then they do not need justification but are also apparently incapable of providing it. This, at bottom, is why epistemological givenness is a myth. (1978, p. 269)

It is little surprise that there are still experientialists, for there is much not to like about this argument. The dilemma is supposed to present us with two unacceptable alternatives, but neither alternative (at least as presented in this summary form) seems so obviously unacceptable. Why deny that noncognitive apprehensions can justify beliefs? And why think that cognitive apprehensions would have to be themselves justified to do so? Other versions of the argument substitute 'propositional' or 'conceptual' for BonJour's 'cognitive,' frequently proceeding in terms of the experiential states themselves, rather than apprehensions of them, but none of these variations seems to help much.

Though I will argue that neither sensations nor percepts can play the role experientialism requires, this may not be for particularly Sellarsian or BonJourian reasons. I won't claim, for instance, that being propositional or conceptual or cognitive makes a mental state somehow "in need of justification"; nor does my argument here even really take the form of a dilemma. The main features that the present argument shares with the Sellarsian dilemma are the claims (a) that the term 'experience' is importantly ambiguous and (b) that however the ambiguity is resolved, experiences cannot serve as justifying grounds for basic beliefs. This provides an argument for the Belief Principle of the previous chapter, which, of course, was a crucial element in the Sellarsian/BonJourian argument for coherentism. But the move from the Belief Principle to coherentism is legitimate only if the truth of the Grounds Principle is assumed and if literal self-justification is dismissed. However, if the Grounds Principle is not a mere platitude but a substantive, controversial thesis, as I have argued, then we can use the conjunction of the Belief Principle and the failure of doxasticism to argue against the Grounds Principle and thus in favor of nonevidentialist nondoxasticism.

---

3. I follow established convention in referring to the ensuing argument as "the Sellarsian dilemma"; I do not thereby intend to make any exegetical claims about what the historical Wilfrid Sellars himself meant by any of the famously obscure arguments in "Empiricism and the Philosophy of Mind" or elsewhere.

It is important to reiterate exactly what the target is. Because terms like 'the doctrine of the given' and 'givenism' have such a long and murky history, I won't assume that all those who have called themselves givenists have intended experientialism as I define it. The doctrine of the given claims that experiential states (or apprehensions of them, acquaintance with them, etc.) can justify beliefs; experientialism imposes the stronger requirement that the experiential states not only justify, but evidentially justify, the basic beliefs. One could claim that having the corresponding experiential state is a necessary condition for justification (for a certain class of beliefs), even though the experience serves as a nonevidential justifier. Such a strange form of givenism might seem to be deserving of the title 'experientialism', but I am reserving this term for a view that maintains the Grounds Principle. The main motivation for experientialism is the intuitive plausibility of the Grounds Principle, but it is not obvious what the motivation might be for this "bare givenism": the view that experiential states serve as nonevidential rather than evidential justifiers. (I return to this view later, in section 5.)

I take the friends of the given to be, at least in the standard case, experientialists. Experiential states are invoked to stop the evidential regress and avoid the isolation objection by serving as (nondoxastic) grounds without themselves being in need of justification. They guarantee a sort of contact with reality (since they are part of the extradoxastic reality) but an evidential, and not (or not merely) causal, contact. Thus Pollock and Cruz (1999) and Brewer (1999) talk about experiential states serving as *reasons* for beliefs; Feldman and Conee (1985) and Haack (1993) are quite explicit about such states being part of one's *evidence*; and Alston's (1988) motivation for the internalist component of his view invokes the practice of giving reasons—his appeal to experiential states is as *grounds*, and not just items in the epistemic supervenience base.[4]

On the other hand, it is less clear what the rationale might be for bare givenism, especially if the claim is not merely that experiential states *can* enter into the epistemic supervenience base, but that having a corresponding experiential state is actually necessary for the justification of the relevant class of beliefs, despite the fact that this experiential state is not serving as a ground. If experiences are grounds, then the requirement that all justified perceptual beliefs be accompanied by a corresponding experience is a straightforward consequence of the Grounds Principle (conjoined with the rejection of self-justification). If experiences merely serve a nonevidential role in justification, however, it is hard to see why we should think them necessary. Thus I will concentrate here on experientialism, only returning to nonexperientialist versions of givenism afterward, though they are not really my target.

My goal in attacking experientialism is to pave the way for a nonevidentialist nondoxasticism that allows beliefs, including perceptual beliefs, to be justified even in the absence of the corresponding experiential states. Experientialism is a threat to this project (though bare givenism is not), because if the Grounds Principle is true, then the experiential states are not only sufficient for the (prima facie) justification of pure perceptual beliefs but necessary as well (assuming, again, that the relevant beliefs involved in perception are not literally self-justifying). A pure perceptual

4. It is not entirely clear that his (2002) response to the Sellarsian dilemma is compatible with this older theory, and I'm not sure whether this is an oversight or a change of view. I return to this issue later, in section 5.

belief is one for which the agent has no independent evidence. If such a belief has a ground, it would have to be a nondoxastic ground.[5]

1. Sensation and Perception

Experientialism is the view that experiences evidentially justify beliefs, but what is meant here by 'experience'? When I open my eyes and look across the room, there is not just one state I am in, my "visual experience". Though my experience may appear to be a single seamless unity, it is actually composed of parts. Which of these components of experience are held to be responsible for evidentially justifying beliefs, and what features of these states equip them to do so?

I want to invoke a well-known distinction here, which, although in fact a somewhat outdated oversimplification of perceptual experience, allows us to pick out two ends of a spectrum and will help to bring some order to the discussion of nondoxastic experience. Most introductory psychology textbooks draw a well-known distinction between sensation and perception. This distinction, or the terminology at least, is originally due to Reid ([1785] 1967). As I will use the terms, *sensation* is the raw, direct experiential consequence of the stimulation of the sense organs, while *perception* involves processing of information.[6] The sensation is what a Lockean *tabula rasa* would experience, while the perception is the result of the mind's unconscious and involuntary attempt to make sense of the world.[7] Perception transforms James's "blooming buzzing confusion" of sensation into meaningful experience.

Standard formulations of the distinction are usually quite vague and never aimed at elucidating the current issues. Perhaps the best way to clarify these matters is by example. When I look over toward the corner of the room, where the walls meet each other and the ceiling, I see a 'Y' shaped confluence of lines, forming three roughly 120° angles. That is, if I situate myself in just the right location, I can make it so that the three angles look equal, and each one looks to be 120°. Or so it would seem reasonable to claim. Yet at the very same time that these 120° angles are apparent, the corner looks like three surfaces, extended in three dimensions, meeting each other at right angles, where each of the surfaces is bounded by a 90° angle. So what does it look like, three 120° angles meeting in a plane or three 90° angles meeting in three

---

5. This argument proceeds on the assumption of EOF, though it is easily modified to encompass MSF. According to MSF, the perceptual belief is based on a corresponding appearance belief. If the belief in question is a *pure* perceptual belief, however, then this appearance belief must be such that none of the agent's other beliefs is relevant to *its* justification, so this appearance belief must be grounded in something nondoxastic. Either way, the Grounds Principle implicates nondoxastic grounds for pure perceptual beliefs.

6. These terms, though quite common, are not very well or canonically defined; different authors frequently draw the distinction in slightly different ways. Thus, I don't mind if my formulation of the distinction is somewhat stipulative, though it will surely be recognized as *a* standard formulation.

7. Thanks to Jeff Stripling (in conversation) for this way of depicting sensation. None of this makes any particular assumptions about why we (adults) are not *tabulae rasae*; however, it is no surprise that this distinction has been pressed into service by empiricists, from Locke to Helmholtz to Russell, whether they used Reid's terminology or not. The sensation-perception distinction provides a nice way to characterize empiricism: sensation is ontogenetically (and epistemically) prior to perception; sensation is innate, but perception is learned.

dimensions? Well, both, but in different senses of 'look'. There is a sense in which the corner looks like three 120° angles meeting in a plane: if I move, I can get one of the angles to approach 180° while the other two approach 90°. This sense of 'look' describes the sensation. There is another sense, however, in which no matter where I stand, the corner itself looks like it isn't changing at all but is remaining a rigid confluence of 90° angles in three dimensions. This sense of 'look' describes the percept (or the perception; more on this distinction shortly).

As another example, consider the famous Necker cube (figure 3.1):

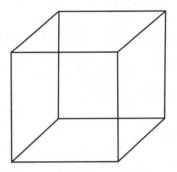

FIGURE 3.1

What is interesting about this figure is that it alternates between looking like a three-dimensional cube viewed from above and to the right, and looking like a three-dimensional cube viewed from below and to the left. That is, there is a clear enough sense in which the figure looks three dimensional. But 'looks' here describes the content of the *percept*, not the *sensation*. When the cube shifts from facing down and to the left to facing up and to the right, this is a shift from one percept to another competing and incompatible percept. The drawing only produces a single sensation, however.[8] There is no conflict in the raw, unprocessed information; the conflict only arises as the result of the visual system's attempt to interpret the sensory information. In the sense of 'looks' that describes the sensation, the drawing looks like exactly what it is: a series of lines joining each other at certain angles. There is no *cube* here, only squares and lines. Only some of the angles in the sensation are right angles; others are 45° or 135°. Even this description, however, may be a bit misleading. The sensation does not represent the lines and angles *as being* lines and angles, and certainly not as being 135° angles. That is the kind of interpretation or categorization that occurs higher up; the sensation is raw, qualitative, uninterpreted.

Consider one more famous example. A lump of coal in bright light reflects the same amount of light as a snowball in dim light; the sensation produced by the former is qualitatively similar to the sensation produced by the latter. The respective percepts, however, are formed by the visual system's taking into account the ambient

8. Note that by 'sensation' here I mean the *visual* sensation, and the term is being used in the technical sense introduced previously. I don't deny that there's an introspectible, experienced difference when the cube shifts, just that this is a difference in the visual sensation.

lighting conditions, and thus the two percepts are quite different. The snowball *looks* white and the coal *looks* black; that is, one percept is of a black thing, the other of a white thing. So the coal and the snowball look the same, yet they look different; that is, they produce similar sensations but different perceptions.

Not only are there many-to-one mappings from percepts to sensations but also, perhaps even more common, there are many-to-one mappings from sensations to percepts: the various perceptual constancies. The visual sensation produced by the coal changes when the coal is brought indoors, but the coal does not appear to change color. That is, the percept does not change. A receding object produces a changing sensation as the retinal image gets smaller. The percept, however, is not of a change in size but rather of a rigid body in motion. A shadow crossing a smooth surface produces a variegated sensation but a perception of a uniformly colored object under different lighting conditions.

Attending to sensations is actually relatively difficult, and it is often easier to attend to the percept than to the sensation. This may be why it took so long for artists to come up with the rules of perspective. Untrained artists frequently make the mistake of trying to reproduce the percepts rather than sensations. Predictable mistakes ensue—railroad tracks are drawn using parallel rather than converging lines, and objects are given coloring-book outlines. A bit metaphorically, they are reproducing the scene the way it looks to the mind, not the way it looks to the eye, so when it's fed back to an eye, everything looks wrong. This is why aspiring artists must be "trained to see" (actually, to introspect), and it is also one reason that the introspectionist school in psychology employed trained introspectors. Naive observers were susceptible to what Titchener (1926) called the "stimulus error": attributing to the sensation properties believed to belong to the object.

Another indication of the relative difficulty in attending to sensations is that almost no one notices that the geometry of sensation is different from the geometry of perception. We *perceive* the world to be Euclidean, but the geometry of sensation is closer to Riemannian than Euclidean geometry:[9] parallel lines converge, and lines that are perceived to be straight can intersect twice. The mathematical proof of this is more convincing than the introspective one, which is further evidence of the difficulty in attending to sensations.[10]

It is easy to quibble about the correct way of describing the phenomena in question. Does the object that is partly in shadow *look* uniformly colored, or does it merely look *to be* uniformly colored? Does 'color' have the same meaning in both of these occurrences? Is it really plausible to claim that *the corner* looks like it's changing when I move my head around the room, or is it better to say that it looks like my relation to the corner is changing? Such worries don't cast serious doubt on the sensation-perception distinction; they presuppose the distinction or something significantly like it and concern themselves with the proper language with which to frame it. Something changes as I move my head around the room, the sensation; something remains the same, the percept.

9. It is actually a spherical geometry, which is something like a finite version of Riemannian geometry, and is compatible with Euclid's parallel postulate. See van Cleve (2002) and Yaffee (2002).

10. Reid's proof of this occurs in section IX of Chapter 6 of his *Inquiry* ([1764] 1997).

There is a concern in this neighborhood, however, that is much more than merely verbal. There are two importantly different ways in which the sensation-perception distinction has been understood. The primary contrast here is sometimes drawn between two different kinds of mental states, sensations and percepts, where both are taken to be nondoxastic. Alternatively, the contrast may be between two phenomena, sensation and perception, where the latter is taken to be a kind of belief, perhaps even a species of knowledge. On the former view, perception is a matter of nondoxastic experience; on the latter, it is a matter of belief. This is a crucial difference, for if anything is clear about the experientialist's understanding of experiences, it is that they must be nondoxastic states in order to play the distinctive role attributed to them in responding to the regress argument.

Though the view of percepts as nondoxastic states is the contemporarily more common view, Reid's original distinction is between the nondoxastic sensation and perception construed as a doxastic state: "This conception and belief which nature produces by means of the senses, we call perception. The feeling which goes along with the perception, we call sensation." Others, including Gibson (1966), Russell ([1912] 1997), and Titchener (1926), have followed Reid in holding that the sorts of states that are being classified here as percepts are in fact beliefs, rather than non-doxastic states.[11] When I describe the table under a shadow as uniformly colored, I am reporting my belief about the table, not how the table visually appears to me. When I describe that same table as looking rectangular rather than, say, trapezoidal, I am describing what I think the shape of the table to be, not how the table actually nondoxastically appears, according to this view.

There is a standard response to this doxastic view of perception, and that is that things can look a certain way to me, even though I don't believe them to be that way, where—crucially—their looking that way is not a matter of the sensation they produce. An object moving away from the observer casts a shrinking image on the retina. Titchener and Russell would say that the sensation is of shrinking rather than of motion; on the basis of this sensation, however, we believe that the object in question is moving away. This, they claim, is the only sense in which the object looks like it is moving. Yet, the standard response goes, clearly I can have this perception of motion without actually believing that anything is moving. The object producing the shrinking sensation might be a patch of color on a movie screen, which I know perfectly well isn't going anywhere. Still, it *looks* like there is a horse riding away (and not shrinking). For similar reasons, the shift of the Necker cube must be a matter of nondoxastic experience, because I know perfectly well that the stimulus is two-dimensional and unchanging. I might have suspended belief in physical objects altogether, but still the corner looks like three right angles meeting at 90°. Perception—and not just sensation—is notoriously belief independent. This is not to say that expectations can't affect perception, or that there are never top-down effects on perception. It is merely to say that something can look, perceptually, to be a way that the subject does not believe things to be.

11. Gibson cites this passage in Reid and explicitly adopts the latter's terminology; Russell and Titchener eschew Reid's terminology but are quite clear about holding the view described here. This is especially true of Titchener; for Russell on this issue, see Kelly (1999).

For these sorts of reasons, contemporary psychologists and philosophers usually distinguish percepts from perceptual beliefs. The belief can go away without the percept doing so. Having the percept probably includes having a number of dispositions of various strengths to believe—this is likely part of the functional role definitive of something's being a percept—but these dispositions are defeasible, and having the percept does not include having the perceptual belief per se.[12] Not on the standard view, at least. We will have reason to reexamine this standard view later, but it can be assumed for now. Because experientialism requires experiences to be nondoxastic states, percepts are only of particular interest to experientialism if they are nondoxastic.

One important moral to be drawn already is that what seems on casual introspection to be a single unitary experiential state is actually quite a bit more complicated. If we fail to recognize this, it is partly because we don't pay much attention to many of these 'experiences' and partly because we are very bad at imagining what anything else would be like. Guessing at what sensationless perception might be like is almost as hard as guessing at what perceptionless sensation might be like. Talk about *the* experiential state associated with such-and-such distal phenomena does serious violence to the actual complexity of the psychology of experience. Furthermore, the very existence of a genuine debate over whether the table's "looking" to be uniformly colored is a matter of belief or some nondoxastic state indicates that introspection is not to be unreservedly trusted on such matters. It is possible for careful thinkers (and professional introspectors!) to be wrong about whether a given state is doxastic or nondoxastic.

The sensation-perception distinction is not entirely unproblematic, but my motives for invoking it can be served even if, as I am fully convinced is actually the case, the distinction only hints at a more complicated reality. The sensation-perception distinction provides a convenient and familiar taxonomy for distinguishing some kinds of experiential states from others. For these purposes, it matters little if the distinction as offered is somewhat stipulative, even dogmatic.

The standard account of the sensation-perception distinction suggests that sensations, even though they are sensations *of* something, do not have full-blown intentionality in the way that percepts do. Perception involves the categorizing of distal stimuli and thus subsumption under one or more concepts. Sensations, though rich in qualia, either lack content altogether or at least lack conceptual and propositional content (though, of course, we must invoke concepts in *describing* them and propositional contents in forming *beliefs* about them). I think that this suggestion is essentially correct, and although the complexity of the relevant issues precludes my giving a thorough argument for it here, I will adopt it as a working assumption. I will thus stipulate that sensations, for the present purposes, are those low-level mental states

---

12. Audi (1988) uses the term 'disposition to believe' to pick out a particular kind of what is often simply called a dispositional belief: a wildly dispositional one that has never been explicitly entertained but would be assented to on reflection, for instance, that dogs don't grow on trees. I don't just mean (wildly) dispositional beliefs here. Since the dispositions at issue here are defeasible, one can have what I am calling the disposition to believe that *p* without having the dispositional belief that *p*. This is presumably what happens when I discover, for example, that the Müller-Lyer illusion is an illusion. I have a (now defeated, or overridden) disposition to believe that one line is longer than the other, though I lack the belief—occurrent or dispositional—that that line is longer. I would not assent to the claim that the one line is longer, even though I have a (defeated) disposition to believe that it is; that is, were it not for that defeater, I would so assent.

that have qualia associated with them (and thus perhaps a kind of qualitative content) but lack conceptual and propositional content, while percepts are those higher-level states that involve the subsumption of distal stimuli under concepts and hence have a conceptual—and I will assume propositional—content.

I introduce this stipulation as a temporary, simplifying assumption. I don't intend this to be either a dissolution of a very real debate in the philosophy of mind/ language/epistemology concerning the propositional/conceptual content of experience or a dismissal of representationalist theories of sensation in the metaphysics of mind. I intend it rather to be a way of sidestepping these issues. However, I think that the assumption is actually compatible with many of the positions taken in these literatures. The Peacocke-McDowell debate (e.g., McDowell 1994; Peacocke 1983), though perhaps rooted in epistemology, actually has little to do with the present concerns, which are largely Sellarsian. Sellarsian worries are not about whether a certain state has some content *in addition to* conceptual/propositional content, whether its content goes beyond that of conceptual representations, or whether this content can be fully expressed conceptually. Having conceptual content-*plus* clearly would not preclude a state's playing an evidential role. The question is whether some component of experience (viz., the sensation) *lacks* conceptual/propositional content, for this really might prohibit that state from serving as evidence. By asking whether a state lacks conceptual content, I mean to ask not whether we have concepts (including demonstrative concepts) that adequately characterize the sensation, but whether we have any concept C such that a given sensation is a representation that represents something as being C. If sensations are not representational, then it follows trivially that they lack conceptual content in this sense.

Even if sensations are representational, they may very well have nonconceptual content (e.g., Tye 1995). Communicative exigencies often lead to formulations of the contents of sensations using English words, which presumably have roughly the content of some of our concepts. This should not be taken to indicate that the representational content of sensations is adequately characterized either by English words or by ordinary concepts.

As mentioned already, the very distinction between sensations and percepts, like the claim that the former have merely nonconceptual content while the latter have conceptual content, is a simplification. Historically, Descartes's intentionally broad conception of ideas was exploded by Hume's distinction between impressions and ideas, which, in turn, was exploded by Reid's sensation-perception distinction. The sensation-perception distinction itself is probably still too crude. Recent work on perception suggests several layers of representations, not just two.

Marr (1982), for example, famously posits a raw primal sketch, a full primal sketch, a 2½-D sketch, and more, all prior to final percept formation. More important, we have, according to Marr, conscious access to certain features of these representations (p. 73). Visual experience certainly includes several different representations, with various kinds of potentially incompatible content. Information from V1 projects to at least thirty-one other anatomically and functionally distinct visual areas (Felleman and Van Essen 1991). Each of these presumably produces its own representations, and we don't yet know how many of these are consciously accessible. There seems to be plenty of room here for both propositional and nonpropositional content in the representations that make up experience.

Distinguishing these functionally distinct elements of experience is introspectively impossible—a situation that is again exacerbated by our difficulty in separating the components even in the imagination: we have a very hard time telling even what the elements *might be*. It is hard to guess, for example, what visual experience must be like for prosopagnosics (do faces look the same to them as to us but just not ring any bells, or do they actually look different? if the latter, how?) or visual object agnosics or patients with movement blindness, Capgras syndrome, and so on In a somewhat similar vein, one is likely to think that it is impossible to experience something's moving but not going anywhere. Any of the motion aftereffects (e.g., the waterfall illusion) disproves this rather quickly. It seems intuitively impossible to experience color and visual texture without shape or to see stripes without having any idea whether they are vertical or horizontal. Yet Goodale and Milner's (2004) now famous patient DF exhibits both of these dissociations.[13]

The important point for the moment, however, is that there is not just one monolithic way or state of being appeared to and merely different ways of describing or conceptualizing it. The dominant tradition in epistemology is a phenomenological one, which takes the deliverances of introspection at roughly face value and tends to think of experience as a single state that can be differently characterized: comparatively, noncomparatively, and so forth (Alston 2002; Chisholm 1957). There is also a phenomenological tradition in psychology, which sees experience as composed of two importantly different states: the sensation and the percept. A third tradition is the cognitive scientific one, which approaches the issues in terms of the theoretical posit of mental representations. In this nonphenomenological tradition, introspection delivers not the basic ontology of the theory but merely a set of data that the theory needs to explain. On this view, the sensation-perception distinction is somewhat artificial, given that the reality is so much more complex. Experience, on this view, is a matter of the introspectible features of a host of different representational states. Though my sympathies lie with the cognitive scientific approach, I will retain the sensation-perception distinction, as it is familiar even if somewhat outdated, and it will be useful in splitting experientialist theories into two broad categories. I will use 'experience' and 'being appeared to' and the like when I want to remain neutral about which type of experiential state is under discussion, but we need to know which aspect or element of "experience" is doing the epistemological work, the high-level percept or the low-level sensation. I will come back to the multilevel approach in due time.

---

13. Subjects with agnosias are not blind, but they have visual recognition deficits. Visual object agnosia patients can see objects—they can sometimes reach for and even describe the objects—but they cannot identify them: they see the cup but can't tell it's a cup until they laboriously figure it out or use another sense modality. Prosopagnosia is a visual agnosia that is more or less specific to faces. Movement blindness is just what the name describes; patients report seeing a series of stills, like a strobe-lit room but without the dark gaps. A patient with Capgras syndrome is convinced that familiar objects (especially people) are imposters. He will insist, for example, that this person looks exactly like Mom but that he knows she is an imposter. The delusion does not occur if Mom is presented via a different sense modality (e.g., the telephone). The waterfall illusion can be experienced by keeping a fixed gaze on some point through which the water is passing, for a half a minute or so. Subjects who do this and then look at the surrounding, unmoving area experience a sense of motion, even though nothing actually seems to be going anywhere.

2. Sensations as Grounds

Crude as it is, the sensation-perception distinction allows us to distinguish two importantly different types of experientialism: sensation experientialism (SE) views sensations as the evidential justifiers of perceptual beliefs, while percept experientialism (PE) makes percepts the evidential justifiers of perceptual beliefs. Experientialists tend not to say which of these theses they are defending. Pollock and Cruz (1999) explicitly and intentionally frame their discussion in terms of percepts, and obviously a number of authors have held that the experiential states they are concerned with have propositional content, though they are generally less overt about these being percepts rather than sensations. I think, however, that most experientialists actually have sensations in mind, for some of the same sorts of reasons that motivate experientialism in the first place.

Though it is difficult to imagine what perception might be like without sensations, the fact that most of the qualia distinctive to perceptual experience reside in the sensation gives us some inkling of what it may be like to have a percept without a corresponding sensation: it would presumably be, from the agent's perspective, a lot like a hunch.[14] Without the relevant sensations, I might just find myself with inexplicable dispositions to believe various things about my environs. Obviously, however, not all hunches are prima facie justified; in fact, no *mere* hunches are. I may be strongly disposed to believe that it's going to snow a lot this winter or that nominalism is true, but neither disposition suffices to even prima facie justify the corresponding belief. A plausible suggestion, especially for the internalist, is that what distinguishes the good hunches (e.g., 'there's a cup in front of me' while visually presented with a cup) from the bad hunches (e.g., 'it's going to snow a lot this winter') is that the former but not the latter are accompanied by—indeed, epistemically based on—a corresponding sensation.

Such considerations motivate a version of experientialism according to which perceptual or appearance beliefs are evidentially justified by the corresponding sensation, namely, SE. As prima facie plausible as SE is, however, I think it is mistaken. Because it is the best motivated version of experientialism, a great deal of the present case against experientialism will consist of an attack on SE. Sensations cannot serve as justifying grounds of beliefs and thus, on pain of (an unmotivated) skepticism, cannot be *required* for justified perceptual beliefs.

There is a facile sort of argument from the nonpropositional content of sensations to the claim that sensations cannot serve as evidential justifiers, one which I want to disavow. It starts with the stipulation that an inference is a move from one or more propositions (premises) to another (conclusion), in accordance with rules of deductive or inductive logic. It follows quickly that a sensation cannot be a premise, and if only premises can evidentially justify, sensations cannot evidentially justify.

Obviously, the experientialist, to the extent that she sees evidential relations as inferential, is operating under a relaxed sense of 'inferential' and a correspondingly relaxed sense of 'premise'. Such relaxed usage must be allowed, partly to avoid

---

14. I don't deny that percepts have qualia associated with them. Some authors find it obvious that beliefs lack qualia (e.g., Clark 1993); I myself am not so sure that there is not something it is like to believe that it's raining (nor am I sure that there *is*). If beliefs have qualia, percepts surely do as well, but the qualitative character had by percepts is likely to be more like that had by beliefs than like that had by sensations.

trivializing the debate but partly because the operative concept of inference is scientifically invaluable. There is a sense in which physical object beliefs must be inferable from low-level visual representations; otherwise, the only psychological story we've ever had about vision (or just about any other psychological phenomenon, for that matter) would have to be rewritten, from scratch. Nearly all psychological explanations invoke inference in the sense of well-behaved symbol manipulation;[15] the famous slogan, due to Helmholtz (1962), insists that perception, in particular, is unconscious inference.

Although there is no serious question about the inferability of physical object beliefs from lower level states, two important questions remain: (1) is this an inference that is available to the agent? and (2) does this inference take sensations as premises?

To avoid a certain tempting misunderstanding, it is important to emphasize that I am concerned with the *justifying* role of sensations in perceptual belief, not any *constitutive* role they might have. It is initially plausible—though I think incorrect—to claim that sensations are necessary for justified perceptual beliefs, because without the sensation, the belief in question wouldn't be a *perceptual* belief. Part of the argument against this claim follows immediately, though the rest has to wait until chapter 4. In what follows, I must ask the reader to assume that it's at least an epistemic possibility that one could have perceptual beliefs without sensations; this will make it easier to focus on the *epistemic* relation between sensations and perceptual beliefs.

2.1. Sensationless Perception

One immediate problem for SE derives from the central role of qualia in sensations. Sensations, I assume, are individuated by their qualitative character, so if two agents have different qualia, then they have different sensations, and if an agent has no qualia, that agent has no sensations. Inverted and absent qualia arguments can thus be brought to bear on the plausibility of sense experientialism. The assumption just made, however, is dispensable, for we can simply develop analogues of the classical inverted and absent qualia arguments.

Suppose my color sensations are inverted with respect to yours: grass looks to me the way that ripe tomatoes look to you (i.e., grass produces in me the same sensations that ripe tomatoes produce in you), and so on. Even in such cases, you and I might agree about what color grass is: green. This is possible because our belief contents are fixed at least partially externally. Just as my belief is that H_2O is wet, while my twin's belief is that XYZ is wet (Putnam 1975), you and I can share the belief that grass is green, even though we have different sensations. Similarly, it does not seem as if the sensation inversion ought to make any difference regarding the epistemic status of the beliefs in question; both of our beliefs are justified. But then consider what is going on: I'm having a red sensation (better: a red* sensation, where 'red*'

---

15. I mean all this sufficiently generally to count connectionist representations as symbols and connectionist processing as inferential, since it involves the manipulation of symbols, subsentential though they be. A logic can be devised for any symbol system, even nonpropositional ones. Sun Joo Shin (1994), for example, has a logic for Venn diagrams that is provably sound and complete. It allows for transformations—inferences!—from pictures/diagrams to other pictures/diagrams.

characterizes the intrinsic character of the state) while holding the justified belief that there's something green in front of me. Meanwhile, you are having a green* sensation while holding the justified belief that there's something green in front of you. In addition, while your green* sensation accompanies your justified belief that there is something green nearby, my green* sensation accompanies my justified belief that there is something red nearby.

So the same sensation (the green* sensation) can accompany either of two very different but nonetheless justified beliefs (that there is something green nearby or that there is something red nearby), and two agents can have very different sensations while being justified in holding the same belief. Clearly, however, if any old sensation is compatible with the justification of the belief that there's something green nearby, then the sensations aren't doing any real epistemological work vis-à-vis that belief. A fortiori, they are not grounding that belief. Similarly, if the sensation is compatible with the justification of any old belief, then again the sensation is epistemically irrelevant.

Again, this argument assumes EOF, but it is clear how a modified version would work for MSF. A more serious assumption is a thesis I will call "*evidence essentialism*," which holds that evidential relations hold essentially: if e is evidence for h, then necessarily, e is evidence for h.[16] A few authors (Alston 1988; Plantinga 1993) have explicitly denied evidence essentialism, and I discuss this possibility in more detail in section 2.4. However, I think that evidence essentialism is the standard default view about evidential relations, often taken to be a trivial consequence of our ordinary concept of evidence, and this makes it at least dialectically appropriate to assume it here (I will continue to assume it until section 2.4). So more precisely, the argument is this: the conjunction of evidence essentialism and the claim that inverted sensations are compatible with sameness of justified belief entail that sensations are not the justifying grounds for these beliefs.

A related problem arises for cases of absent qualia, or absent sensations. A variant on the standard zombie theme in the philosophy of mind provides another argument against SE. There are two senses of the term 'zombie' in play in philosophy. In some circles, a zombie is an exact physical duplicate of some actual normal person, where, unlike its normal counterpart, the zombie lacks conscious experiences entirely. There is nothing that it's like to be a zombie, yet the zombie is physically, functionally, and otherwise psychologically identical to its counterpart.[17] Zombies thus construed are metaphysically and even conceptually possible only if certain plausible supervenience claims about conscious experience are in fact false. There is a less common but weaker and less controversial sense of 'zombie', according to which a zombie is merely as psychologically similar to one of us as possible,

---

16. I mentioned in an earlier footnote that Pollock (1986) calls this view "cognitive essentialism"; Conee and Feldman (2005) call it "strong supervenience." I introduce the new terminology quite reluctantly and only because the existing terms are so opaque.

17. Zombies are generally held to be quite a lot like us, despite their lacking qualia; Chalmers (1996) insists that they are psychologically *exactly identical* to us, though phenomenologically very different. Zombies presumably act, in any interesting sense of the term, and do so for reasons; they are presumably moral agents, and I presume epistemic agents as well. Because they are psychologically like us, zombies will believe—though falsely, of course—that they have sensations and other conscious experiences.

consistent with its lacking conscious experiences. Zombies in this latter sense may have to be physically different from us, and if conscious experiences have psychological consequences, they will have to be somewhat different psychologically as well. A zombie in this sense (and this is the sense in which I will be using the term 'zombie') is certainly possible, and they would still be capable of having beliefs, desires, hopes, some perceptual states, and the like, and much of its psychology would be like ours.[18] Intuitively, some of this creature's beliefs might count as perceptual beliefs (because, e.g., they are the result of visual processing that starts with retinal irradiation and produces 3-D information about distal objects), and intuitively, some of these perceptual beliefs would be justified. Certainly the creature could have empirical beliefs of some sort, and surely some of these could be justified. But if having sensations is necessary for having justified perceptual beliefs, then having sensations would be necessary for having justified empirical beliefs of any sort.

Even if any creature lacking sensations is therefore strikingly unlike us, it must be possible for some, perhaps radically different, kind of creature to have beliefs without sensations, perhaps even to have perceptual beliefs without sensations. Intuitively, some such creature could have some justified empirical beliefs. Block's (1995b) hypothetical super-blindsighter, who has visual beliefs just like a normal subject but lacks visual experiences, intuitively has justified visual beliefs. It is hard to see how the fact that we sometimes have sensations would make it so that we have to have a sensation on every occasion of justified perceptual belief, while those who lack sensations altogether do fine—epistemically—without them.

We needn't go so far into the realm of science fiction, however, to find such examples. The actual world provides us with many instances of what Gibson (1966) calls "sensationless perception." One such example (in fact, one of Gibson's own) concerns the obstacle sense, or facial vision, of the blind. Blind people (and sighted people while blindfolded, too, though less reliably) can detect obstacles—walls, chairs, and the like—without having any (conscious) sensation. In fact, they tend to think that they are picking up information somehow through the skin of the face (hence "facial vision"), when in truth the information is coming in through the ears as a subtle form of echolocation (1966, p. 2). Because the subjects don't have introspective access to any relevant sensation, this looks to be a case of sensationless perception. Though *philosophical* zombies may be things of fiction, such "minor zombies" actually exist.

We might want to know more details before delivering any firm verdicts here, but there is nothing about the case as so far described that rules out the intuitive claim that these subjects have justified perceptual beliefs on the basis of their obstacle sense. One might insist that the beliefs are justified inferentially if at all, that the agent is only justified in believing that there's a large object to the left if the agent is justified in thinking her facial vision reliable. I don't find this line of response very convincing, nor, I expect, do others with EOF-friendly intuitions. If, per EOF, meta-beliefs about reliability are unnecessary for the prima facie justification of visual beliefs, then they are quite plausibly not necessary for the prima facie justification of

---

18. Whether or not beliefs have qualia (see note 14), it is generally agreed that qualia are not essential to the individuation of beliefs and desires; that is, it is possible to have the latter without having the former, and which belief state one is in has no necessary connection to the qualitative character of that belief. Nor, presumably, are sensations essential to the individuation of beliefs.

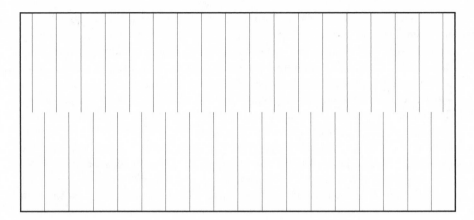

FIGURE 3.2

obstacle sense beliefs. Nonetheless, it is probably best to turn to examples that are even closer to home.

We all *perceive* a horizontal discontinuity in the center of Figure 3.2. We do not, strictly speaking, *sense* any such discontinuity; the perception is of a discontinuity, though the sensation is not. It takes a good deal of processing to extract the discontinuity from the retinal image, and the visual representations that include the discontinuity are higher level representations than sensations. To take another classic example, many of our perceptions are of partially occluded objects. The object itself isn't given in sensation; it is constructed in perception. I'll have a sensation of a partially occluded building and a concomitant perception of a (whole) building. It seems to me that I actually *perceive* (and don't merely believe that there are) whole disks being occluded by the square in Figure 3.3.

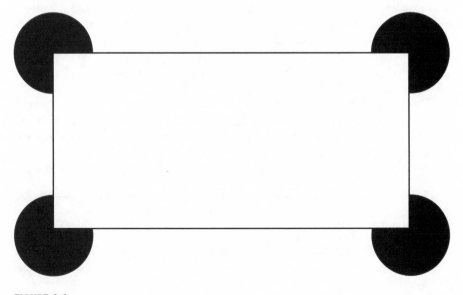

FIGURE 3.3

My perception here is not of four Pac-man shapes butting up against a square but of four solid disks being occluded by a square. These sorts of instances are extremely common; it is doubtful that any ordinary perception would be possible were it not for such phenomena. Though it may be an exaggeration on Gibson's part to classify these more mundane cases as instances of sensationless perception, the crucial fact is that all these cases do involve *perception without a sensation of what is perceived*. The kinds of cases under consideration here fall along a spectrum. Zombies have no sensations at all, yet they have justified perceptual beliefs. The facial vision subjects do have sensations, presumably—at least of ambient odors, temperature, and the like—yet they have justified beliefs about objects they do not sense. Finally, all of us have justified perceptual beliefs in ordinary circumstances, of objects we do not sense. We are in this respect similar to the blind with their facial vision, who are in turn similar to the zombies. There is thus something to the claim that sensationless perception is real and in fact quite common.

2.2. The Sensation-Perception Gap and Collateral Information

Even if it is an exaggeration to describe the ordinary cases as sensationless perception, the preceding section draws our attention to a very important point: if sensations do justify perceptual beliefs, they must do so by way of a nontrivial inference. It is not merely a matter of my being appeared to Φ-ly and inferring that Φ is exemplified nearby; it is more a matter of my being appeared to Γ-ly and inferring that Φ is exemplified nearby.[19] There is, in short, a sensation-perception gap. The motivating problem of perceptual psychology is that there is information explicit in the percept that has to be constructed, partly on the basis of what is only implicit in the sensation.[20] Sensations don't represent subjective contours or, typically, whole objects; percepts do. Similarly, the overarching function of perception is to enable the recovery of information that is only implicit in the sensation, or derivable from the sensation with the aid of collateral information. If sensations play the role of premises in inferences having perceptual beliefs as their conclusions—and this is basically what SE claims, with 'premise' and 'inference' understood in the relaxed way described previously—then these inferences are highly enthymematic. The collateral information I am speaking of plays the role of missing premises.

To see the essential role of this collateral information, consider the famous sort of display shown in figure 3.4. Four of the five objects inside the rectangle look (perceptually) to be convex, while the other looks to be concave. But there is nothing in the sensation alone that determines that. Turn the page upside down, and most of the objects will appear concave. This, according to the standard story in perceptual psychology,

---

19. The same argument applies to MSF, though here there is some flexibility about where to locate the nontriviality. Either my being appeared to Γ-ly (prima facie) justifies my belief that I'm appeared to Γ-ly, which in turn justifies my belief that Φ is exemplified nearby, or my being appeared to Γ-ly (prima facie) justifies my belief that I'm appeared to Φ-ly, which in turn justifies my belief that Φ is exemplified nearby. Either way, one of the "inferences" is nontrivial.

20. "Information" is being used here in the way psychologists use it and does not imply either accuracy or belief.

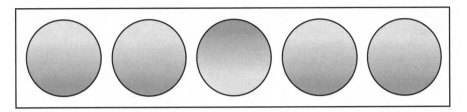

FIGURE 3.4

is because the visual system "assumes" that objects are uniformly shaded and lit from above. This assumption, however, is independent of and collateral to the sensation itself. Organisms that evolved and matured in a world in which things were generally lit from below might have the same sensations as we do, but different percepts and beliefs, seeing the upright array as mostly concave and the inverted one as mostly convex. Again, convexity and concavity are constructed in perception rather than given in sensation.

This raises the question of the epistemic role of this collateral information, such as the assumption that objects are generally lit from above. If a single sensation is compatible with the perception of concavity as well as convexity, then it is hard to see how the sensation might justify—evidentially justify, that is—the perceptual belief that there is something convex out there unless the possessor of the perceptual belief also (justifiedly) believes that things are generally lit from above. If a piece of evidence is equally compatible (both logically and probabilistically) with p and $\sim p$, then it cannot, by itself, evidentially justify either one. So the sensory state cannot (evidentially) justify the convexity belief by itself, but only in conjunction with additional evidence about the light source location. Thus, the agent cannot be justified in this perceptual belief unless she—and not merely her visual system—has a belief about the light source and actually believes that things are lit from above.[21]

The first consequence of this is that SE is incompatible with EOF. The sensation could evidentially justify the belief about convexity only if the latter also depended evidentially on a collateral belief about the light sources. In such a case, the convexity belief would be nonbasic. Since, however, this sort of case is ubiquitous, it would follow that few or none of our perceptual beliefs are basic, which is exactly what EOF wants to deny.

The role of sensations currently under consideration ought to be unappealing to MSF as well. The standard sorts of worries arise: there is no obvious way for an agent to have justified beliefs about the location of light sources *prior* to having justified perceptual—indeed, visual—beliefs, so it seems wrong to insist that perceptual beliefs depend evidentially on justified beliefs about light sources. Threats of circularity and skepticism loom. The collateral information involved in perception is often highly

---

21. Two qualifications: (1) I am still working under the assumption that evidence essentialism (p. 51) is true; more on this in section 2.4. (2) The agent might be ignorant of the light source but still have some other belief that links the shading sensation with convexity, such as 'when things look lighter on the top, they are generally actually convex'. The belief about the light source is only intended as an example of the sort of collateral belief that would be needed, and the argument to follow should stand regardless of the exact content of this belief.

contingent information of the sort that can only be obtained by reliance on the very perceptual system that requires that information.

In addition, the sorts of assumptions made by the perceptual systems are often not going to be the contents of any of the agent's beliefs, and if not, then these assumptions cannot be part of the agent's evidence. The point is not merely that we do not consciously and occurrently form such beliefs (Pollock 1986) but that we don't even dispositionally believe much of the collateral information on which our perceptual systems depend. In any case, we don't have to in order to have justified perceptual beliefs. Some of the cues involved in depth perception, like texture gradients and aerial perspective, are far from obvious, and few people without training in perceptual psychology or the visual arts are aware of them. Things just "look far away" without the agent being able to specify what the cues are, what looking that way consists in.

Even when the cues that the perceptual systems use are consciously accessible cues, agents typically do not recognize, even implicitly, their status as cues. Many subjects who encounter the display of figure 3.4 for the first time are surprised to see the convexities and concavities reverse upon inversion. This suggests that they do not know that it is the circle's being lighter on the top that makes it appear convex or being lighter on the bottom that makes it appear concave. Discovering perceptual cues is a difficult, experimental, endeavor and not simply a matter of drawing out what we, as opposed to our visual systems, already know.

Berkeley ([1709] 1975) famously but misguidedly denied Descartes's ([1637b] 1985) rationalist theory about the role of eye convergence in depth perception, on the grounds that children and peasants lack the required trigonometry to determine the distance from the eyes to the point of angular convergence. Berkeley's argument in effect requires that in order for me to perceive depth from eye convergence, I must utilize information about angular convergence, trigonometry, and eye distance as premises in an inferential justification. While this is bad psychology, it is not such bad epistemology.[22] It is bad psychology because as long as my visual system is doing the trigonometry, *I* don't have to. It is good epistemology because if my awareness of eye convergence is serving as my evidence about distances, then I do have to be doing the trigonometry, at least in a rough-and-ready way. Berkeley is right in thinking that the information about angular convergence of the eyes is not sufficient for an ordinary agent's being inferentially justified in beliefs about the distance of the object on which the eyes have converged. For those of us who are not trigonometry geniuses, those beliefs about depth or distance that result from eye convergence will have to be basic if they are to be justified at all. Though the brain uses information about eye convergence to determine depth, it does not follow that this sensation has any evidential

22. It might also be bad Descartes exegesis. Descartes seems to offer two accounts of eye convergence in the *Optics*, only one of which is really rationalistic. The other account suggests that the impressions made on the pineal gland by the animal spirits will differ with differences in eye convergence, and these different impressions will convey different ideas of depth. On this account, the idea that pops into the mind is already one of depth, without the mind having to *infer* depth from information about eye convergence. For Descartes, the relation between the impression on the pineal gland and the resulting idea is always an arbitrary one, God having assured that the right ideas would accompany the right physical impressions. In essence, the trigonometry problem could be handled by the hydraulics (i.e., the nerves, the animal spirits/cerebrospinal fluid, and the ventricles), rather than by the mind.

role to play in the agent's justification for believing that an object is a certain distance away, even when the agent has a discriminable sensation of converging eyes.

Certain neuropsychological phenomena make a similar point. Subjects with associative agnosia are virtually incapable of visual identification, although evidence suggests that they have normal, intact sensations (Farah 1990), perhaps even normal percepts.[23] These patients are able to describe what they are looking at, draw pictures of it, copy drawings, and the like, even though they are unable to identify, or recognize, what they are seeing or copying. The fact that these patients can accurately draw objects they cannot identify suggests that the low-level information is getting in, and that the patients have the normal introspective access to it, despite their inability to form normal perceptual beliefs. This strongly suggests that the sensation is evidentially inadequate for the justification of the perceptual belief, for one can have the sensation without having the slightest evidence for the corresponding perceptual beliefs. To press this a little more, let us again make evidence essentialism an explicit constraint. Now the proponent of SE would have to either embrace sensation experientialism while denying that these sensations are adequate evidence for *our* perceptual beliefs, or insist that an associative agnosic is indeed justified when she bases a perceptual belief on the appropriate sensation, even though, given her brain damage, *this belief is just a lucky guess.* The standard view among experientialists, I think, is that one simply couldn't have the relevant sensory experience and not have a reason for believing that there's cup in front of one (provided of course that the agent has the requisite concepts). Associative agnosia seems to empirically refute this view.[24]

All these examples serve to illustrate the nontriviality of the construction of perceptual beliefs out of the sensations that SE takes to be their grounds. The lesson is that perceptual systems have a kind of intelligence that normal people lack (Hoffman 1998); our perceptual systems are much smarter than we are when it comes to deriving external world information from sensations. The ordinary person is simply not knowledgeable enough about geometry, trigonometry, optics, electromagnetism, and the like—let alone inferentially quick enough—to form inferentially justified perceptual beliefs on the basis of sensations. It is likely that none of us could calculate such information without the benefit of the special-purpose hardware; we certainly couldn't do so in real time.

23. Associative agnosia is usually contrasted with apperceptive agnosia. Patients with the latter condition clearly have visual sensations, though they can't even copy simply line drawings (although they can often draw well from memory). The traditional interpretation of these two agnosias is that apperceptive agnosia involves spared sensations with impaired percepts, while associative agnosia involves intact sensations and even "a normal percept that has somehow been stripped of its meaning" (Teuber 1968, p. 293). I could press the present case against SE using apperceptive agnosia and return to associative agnosia in my discussion of PE, but since one might object that apperceptive agnosics don't really have fully intact sensations, it is better to make the stronger case here and appeal to associative agnosia, where the evidence very strongly indicates intact sensations. The reader will kindly recall the resulting argument in section 3, when the topic turns to PE, though I won't rehearse it again there.

24. There is a large literature surrounding associative agnosia, and like anything in psychology—especially where brain damage is concerned—it is complicated. Farah (1990), for example, questions whether the associative agnosic's visual experience is genuinely normal, given the "slavish" nature of their copying of line drawings. All I really need for the present purposes, however, is the claim that associative agnosia, as I've understood it here, is metaphysically possible. The actual neuropsychological results should at least break us free of intuitive resistance to this claim.

The fact that one of my perceptual modules bases its outputs on certain assumptions, for example, about the location of the light source or about the rigidity of objects, does not mean that my belief is based on these assumptions, for these may be assumptions I do not share. I may not believe that things are lit from above or I may fail to appreciate its relevance to how things look, yet things continue to look a certain way precisely because my visual system makes and utilizes such assumptions. It is not obvious just how to make this precise, but it is intuitively clear that the larger organism need not *believe* everything that its subpersonal modules "assume." And again, it is not merely that the agent need not consciously or occurrently believe it; the agent need not believe it in any sense, even a wildly dispositional sense.

A related reason for denying that perceptual cues have evidential status for the subject is the fact that subjects can explicitly doubt the relevant assumptions or doubt that the cues are reliable indicators without thereby losing prima facie justification. Not only are the agent's perceptual beliefs more or less the same but also the epistemic status of these beliefs is unchanged. Suppose that, like most people, I fail to realize that the nearby object looks convex to me because the upper parts are reflecting more light my way than the rest. In such a case, I could come to doubt that the nearby objects are lit from above, but I would retain my perceptual belief that the object in front of me is convex. Supposing that everything else is normal, there is no reason to suppose this belief is unjustified.

Not only does my suspending belief about whether nearby objects are lit from above not undermine the justification of my beliefs about nearby convexities but also my having positive evidence to the contrary need not constitute defeaters for my perceptual beliefs. In particular, my justified but false belief that nearby things are lit from below is not, absent any justified beliefs about how this affects perception, a defeater for my belief that this object in front of me is convex. (Of course, were I to come to believe that the nearby objects are lit from below *and* that in such circumstances thing that look convex generally are not convex, then this would serve as a defeater for my perceptual belief that the object is convex, but this is importantly different from the case at hand.) Such failure of defeat shows that the collateral information was evidentially unnecessary. But this collateral information was necessary to connect the sensation with the perceptual belief. The evidential status of the sensation depended on that of the collateral information, so if the collateral information is evidentially inert, the sensation is, too.

Helmholtz was certainly right in claiming that perception involves a kind of inference; that is, the causal processes that make percepts and perceptual beliefs possible are inferential processes. It does not follow from this, however, that perceptual beliefs are *epistemically* inferential. Gilbert Harman (1973) once argued that it does, which suggests that the very inferences that are causally responsible for perceptual beliefs might evidentially justify them as well. Although such a view is not usually endorsed by defenders of SE, closing the sensation-perception gap seems to require this claim or something much like it. Additional premises besides the sensation are needed for the justification of the perceptual belief, and the only plausible candidates are roughly those that the relevant modules are already using.

I have been arguing against this view on the grounds that the agent need neither actually believe these additional premises nor appreciate their perceptual significance to be justified in her perceptual beliefs. An additional problem for such a view is that if the collateral assumptions are serving as evidential justifiers and not just causal mediators, they would have to be themselves justified to confer justification on the perceptual beliefs. However, there are good reasons for denying that the premises actually used by the perceptual modules are likely to be justified. As Fodor (1983, 1987) has convincingly argued, the operation of the perceptual modules is the result of *not* taking seriously certain epistemological strictures.[25] In particular, their modularity entails that they violate the total evidence requirement by being insensitive to the rest of the agent's beliefs, no matter how relevant. I can believe whatever I want about the light source; my perceptual beliefs are going to be determined by my visual system's dogmatic assumption, so to speak, that things are lit from above. Perception works partly *because* the modules get to make a host of useful but in some sense unwarranted assumptions about how the world is. The overall reliability of perception might require that the assumptions made by the perceptual modules will hold most of the time, but this doesn't show that these assumptions are epistemically justified.

I have just scratched the surface here, concentrating mostly on vision, though the sensation-perception distinction is certainly not limited to vision. Auditory localization of sound sources utilizes very subtle (mostly unconscious) cues about phase, amplitude, and timbre difference between the two ears. Such information, along with collateral information about the speed of sound, the acoustical properties of the head and ears, and a host of complicated mathematics, allows a percept to be constructed that represents the location of the sound source. Again the sensation is not nearly sufficient to justify the perceptual belief, given the information actually available to the perceiving subject.

2.3. Problems Concerning Basing

In the previous two sections, we saw a number of intuitively justified beliefs whose justification cannot be accounted for by their being based on the corresponding sensation. Here I want to temporarily set aside such problems and ask whether perceptual beliefs usually or ever *are* based on the corresponding sensations. That is, though I have argued that sensations are not justifying grounds, the question I now want to ask is whether they are even grounds. There are two reasons to worry that they may not be.

First of all, as discussed earlier, we tend to have better access to our percepts than to our sensations. With a good deal of care, one can learn to attend to the sensation itself, but this is unusual. It is plausible that our everyday access to our sensations—when we aren't paying special attention—is mediated by perceptual beliefs, rather than the other way around. Why do I think I am having an elliptical sensation right now? Because I'm looking at my coffee cup, and I know that tops of cylinders produce elliptical sensations when viewed obliquely. At the very least, this is a coherent story, and there is no obviously good reason to deny it. Such a story is even more plausible in cases like face recognition. Often the only way to conceptualize the sensation is at least partly in terms of the percept or the object that the percept represents. It is not at all clear that we have the sort of independent access to the sensation that would be required for it to justify the perceptual belief. We tend to assume that sensations are causally or in some other sense prior to perceptual beliefs, but this does not imply that the perceptual beliefs are

---

25. Although he now (2003) seems to endorse roughly the view just attributed to Harman.

epistemically dependent on the sensations. If my beliefs about my sensations are based on introspection of my perceptual beliefs about external objects, then it is odd (even if not straightforwardly contradictory) to claim that these perceptual beliefs are based on the sensations.

This brings us to the second point. Although it is quite natural to assume that sensations are causally implicated in the fixation of perceptual belief, this assumption is a bit of folk psychology that very well may not turn out to receive serious support from cognitive science. This is a potentially important issue for anyone who holds a causal theory of basing, as many do (e.g., Alston 1988; Pollock and Cruz 1999).[26] For all we can determine *on the basis of common sense and introspection*, visual sensations may play no causal role in the generation of perceptual beliefs.

The mechanisms responsible for visual sensations may be completely distinct from those responsible for perceptual identification. It is by now well known that visual processing separates quite early on into a dorsal pathway, which extends from early visual areas in the occipital lobe into the posterior parietal lobe and which is involved in visually guided motor responses, and a ventral pathway, which extends into the inferotemporal lobe and which is responsible for perceptual identification. Perceptual beliefs of the sort 'that's a dog' are outputs of the ventral pathway. The relative independence of the two pathways is evidenced by the fact that some brain-damaged patients are able to "see" well enough to visually guide motor responses (including adjusting size, type, and orientation of grip aperture) without being able to visually identify objects; other subjects exhibit the reverse deficits (Goodale and Milner 2004). When we think of the qualitative aspects of sensation, we think of color and viewpoint-dependent shape information, neither of which has any indispensable role in normal visual object identification, according to influential theories of vision like those of Marr (1982) and Biederman (1995). Perhaps visual sensations occur in the dorsal stream, thus contributing little or nothing to our perceptual identification of objects. Perhaps they occur in offshoot substreams of the ventral stream, only the main stream being causally relevant to perceptual identification. Perhaps these sensations occur in the main ventral stream, but as more or less epiphenomenal consequences of the representations that really are causally relevant to downstream perceptual identification.[27] Most likely, there simply is no one such thing as the visual sensation; rather there is low-level information about color, about texture, about viewpoint-dependent shape, and so on. We don't yet know which, if any, of

26. Though they are not explicit about this, both Fumerton (2001) and BonJour (2001) seem to concede that evidential justification or something like it—perhaps well-formedness in the sense of Feldman and Conee (1985)—requires a causal connection between the ground and the belief it justifies.

27. Consider, for example, the enhancement processes responsible for phenomena like the Mach band effect (Ratliff 1965) or the Hermann grid illusion (Spillmann 1994). Although these processes are certainly causally relevant to perception, it is an open question whether—and in what capacity—the illusory sensations themselves are. The Mach band contrast enhancement usually goes unnoticed, and its contribution to vision is one of increasing perceptual salience and facilitating boundary detection. This is obviously useful and contributes to the reliability of vision, but the enhancement could occur without the phenomenology, that is, without the sensation (indeed, it usually does). The perception and the sensation are surely causally linked, but SE requires that they be part of a single chain, and there is no reason yet to think they aren't simply joint effects of a common cause.

EXPERIENTIALIST THEORIES   61

these are causally implicated in perceptual identification, and we are not going to find out by introspecting.

Throughout this discussion, I have been appealing to unconscious inference and attributing this idea to Helmholtz. The view that I want to back, however, is more of a *neo*-Helmholtzian view than a straightforward Helmholtzian view. Helmholtz assumed that perception was a matter of unconscious inference from *sensations*; contemporary vision science from Marr onward assumes it is a matter of unconscious inference from *retinal stimulations*.[28] The standard contemporary view is neutral as to where in the causal nexus the various sensations fit.

The point here is merely this: the causal relations between sensations and perceptual beliefs cannot be discovered by mere introspection. We tend to assume that sensations are causally implicated in perceptual belief, but this assumption is a tenet of folk psychology that might turn out to be false. Which, if any, sensations are causally involved in which, if any, perceptual beliefs is an open empirical question. If sensations and perceptual beliefs are correlated only because they have a common cause, then sensations do not contribute to the formation of the perceptual beliefs. If only causes can serve as grounds, then the claim that sensations serve as grounds for belief is subject to empirical refutation. Correlatively, the claim that a corresponding sensation is necessary for the justification of a perceptual belief, conjoined with a causal theory of basing and certain empirically possible findings about the relationship between sensations and perceptual beliefs, will imply that few or none of our perceptual beliefs are justified. Surely we are not so certain that sensations are epistemically necessary that we should be willing to court such skepticism.

Note that even on some weaker theories of basing than the causal theory, these results still obtain. The fundamental idea of a belief being based on ground *g* is that the belief is held in some sense *because* of *g*. It seems that virtually any way of making this more precise would subject the resulting version of SE to the threat of empirical refutation. Suppose, for instance, that *S*'s belief *b* is based on ground *g* only if the counterfactual 'if *g* hadn't been in *S*'s possession, *S* wouldn't have believed *b*' is true.[29] Such a counterfactual relationship between sensations and perceptual beliefs might hold. But it also might not.

Empirical refutability per se is not a problem for an epistemological theory; my own theory is empirically refutable, and this might even be a virtue of an epistemological theory. The point I want to make is that SE requires a certain psychological connection—most likely a causal one—between sensations and perceptual beliefs, and there is little or no scientific reason to think that such a connection exists. SE is premised on an empirical assumption about the causal or counterfactual relation between sensation and perception. The proponent of SE simply helps herself to this assumption, presumably on the grounds that it is a truism. Unfortunately, there are no truisms about psychological processes.

28. Not necessarily *just* retinal stimulation; nothing in this view precludes vision's also getting information from "efference copies" of motor signals to the oculomotor muscles, from inputs from vestibular-proprioceptive systems, or whatever.

29. Counterfactual dependence is notoriously weaker than casual dependence. Such a theory might be more attractive than a causal theory of basing to coherentists and others who hold that nonoccurrent beliefs can serve as justifying grounds.

2.4. SE and the Content of Sensations

A final problem with SE concerns the very possibility of sensations as evidential justifiers. On the face of it, sensations lack the kind of content necessary to serve as evidential justifiers for beliefs. Perhaps sensations lack content altogether, but they at least lack propositional/conceptual content; the mental representations that involve categorizations of distal stimuli are percepts, not sensations. Consequently, sensations are not capable of standing in evidential relations to perceptual or appearance beliefs, any more than my foot or a rock is. This is a familiar, Sellarsian, point, but one worthy of elaboration.

The distinction between nonevidential and evidential justifiers is crucial here. As conceded in chapter 2, there are few or no prima facie constraints on what can count as a nonevidential justifier, thus nothing about the nature of experiences that precludes them from serving as justifiers. Experientialism, however, involves the stronger claim that experiential states are not merely justifiers, but *evidential* justifiers. There is no obvious reason to deny that items lacking conceptual/propositional content can serve as justifiers; such a denial seems like little more than a bit of Sellarsian dogma.[30] Perhaps, however, there are good reasons for denying that items lacking conceptual/propositional content can serve as *evidential* justifiers.

It is a commonplace that not everything is evidence for everything. That my dog barks is evidence neither for Cartesian foundationalism nor for the claim that the universe is billions of years old. My beliefs that p and that p entails q are evidence for my belief that q. What is it that makes certain things evidence (for some things) and other things not? There must be some kind of nonarbitrary relationship between the evidence and that which it evidentially justifies, but it is hard to say just what this relationship consists in.

Note that the concern here is with the epistemologist's understanding of evidence, and epistemologists typically use the term 'evidence' in a restrictive way; this is because an epistemologist is concerned with some agent's evidence for some belief. Common usage and legal usage, having different sets of concerns, are far more liberal with their terminology. Murder weapons are tagged and labeled as "physical evidence"; a broken window is taken to be evidence of a break-in. The sagittal crest of *Australopithecus robustus* is cited as evidence of its vegetarian diet.

Surely it is legitimate to use 'evidence' in this broad way, but this is just as surely not the epistemologist's sense of the term. The broken window itself does not *ground* my belief that someone broke in. My *belief* that the window is broken certainly might ground the belief that someone broke in, but the window itself is simply not evidence in the epistemological sense—the current sense—of the term. If *A. robustus*'s sagittal crest *itself*—and not my cognizance of it and/or of its significance—were really my evidence, my ground, for my belief that *A. robustus* had a vegetarian diet, this belief might be basic (since the sagittal crest is obviously not a belief). But clearly such a belief could not be basic for me. The existence of sagittal crests or broken windows might be important phenomena that indicate, to those in the know, certain other important phenomena. But they are not evidential justifiers, grounds of belief.

---

30. This way of putting the point is due to James Montmarquet, in correspondence.

Not, at least, according to the standard epistemological usage of the terms. Though I say a bit more immediately following in defense of the epistemologist's sense of 'evidence', I will return to this issue later, in section 6.

So the issue here is the evidential relation, in the epistemologist's sense of 'evidence'. To my knowledge, there are only four plausible candidates that purport to characterize that relation. Restricting our attention to evidence for beliefs (rather than propositions, claims, or what have you), there are four likely relations that might hold between the evidence e and the belief h it evidentially justifies:

(i) a broadly semantic relationship, that is, one that holds merely in virtue of the contents of e and h: p is evidence for $p \lor q$ 'All observed emeralds have been green' is evidence for 'All emeralds are green'

(ii) a believed connection: the holder of h (justifiedly?) believes that e is evidence for h, or that e implies h, or that e renders h sufficiently probable, or some variant on these

(iii) e and h are related by virtue of the cognitive system or faculty that produces h: perhaps the faculty that is designed to produce h is designed to do so on the basis of e (Plantinga 1993)

(iv) a reliability connection: e is a reliable indicator of h, or the conditional probability of $h \mid e$ is suitably high (Alston 1988)

I will discuss these in reverse order.

Notice first that (iii) and (iv) offer externalist theories of evidence in the sense that they deny that whether e is evidence for h (for S) is something that S can determine on the basis of mere reflection or introspection. One who endorsed such an externalist theory of evidence could agree with evidentialism in holding that the justificatory status of a belief is determined by that belief's fit with the agent's evidence, while denying what Conee and Feldman (2005) call "mentalism," the claim that any two mentally identical individuals are therefore epistemically identical. Two mentally identical agents might nonetheless differ with respect to their evidence, because the very same mental state that serves as evidence for p for the one agent might not bear the appropriate external relation to that belief for the other agent.

Similarly, these theories of evidence conflict with evidence essentialism: the view that evidential relations hold necessarily. At least one important motivation behind evidence essentialism is an assumption it shares with internalist theories of evidence: that whether one has evidence for some belief is something that ought to be fairly directly knowable, without having to investigate contingent facts about the external world. Perhaps this is simply part of what it means to say that something is evidence; nonessentialist theories might not be coherently intelligible as actually offering theories of *evidence*, a possibility to which I return later.

Traditional internalists are thus not likely to be attracted to (iii) or (iv), but not all experientialists are internalists. Why couldn't a hybrid internalist-externalist view like Alston's endorse one of these? Could the presence of a reliable connection (even if the agent does not believe there is one) suffice for evidential justification? As important as Alston's (1988) internalist externalism is, some problems with it are well known. The mere presence of a reliable indicator relation between a ground and some belief does not make that ground justifying evidence for that belief. My concern for the moment is not with the evidence essentialist's contention that there is something incoherent about the notion of contingent evidential relations (though I have some sympathies for this view). Rather, it is simply that Alston's theory doesn't get the cases right.

On Alston's (1988) view, an experiential state prima facie justifies a perceptual belief iff the experience is internally accessible in the right sort of way and is a reliable indicator of the truth of the perceptual belief. There are hosts of counterexamples to such a view. Suppose that the visual experience I have when I look at the moon causes me to believe that the moon is 2,187 miles in diameter. Because the moon is in fact 2,187 miles in diameter, the probability of the belief conditional on the ground is high (in fact, 1), so we have here a state that serves as a reliable indicator. Clearly, however, the belief that the moon is 2,187 miles in diameter is not even prima facie justified. Further counterexamples can be gotten by exploiting the fact that, on Alston's view, there need be no intuitive relation at all between the experience and the belief. A twinge in my left knee might reliably cause me to believe that bats are more closely related to primates than to rodents. Since that belief is true, we have a reliable connection again, but clearly the twinge experience does not justify that belief. Even more clearly, it does not *evidentially* justify the belief.[31]

It may be objected here that the reliable connection is gotten too cheaply in the previous two examples, since the target beliefs are true regardless of the occurrence of the experiential states. The conditional probability of $h \mid e$ is high, but only because h is true. A modified Alstonian view would require that evidential justifiers be not merely reliable indicators, but probability raisers: an adequate ground is one such that the conditional probability of the belief given that ground is sufficiently high, and higher than the unconditional probability of the belief. Even then, counterexamples are easy to come by. Suppose a mad neurosurgeon rearranges some of my neural connections while I sleep, in such a way that excessive pressure on my right big toe now reliably causes a sensation of warmth on my left cheek, but for some reason, I'm prone to infer from this that there's pressure on my right big toe. Suppose that the cheek sensation only occurs when there is pressure on the toe. Supposing that I have no idea that this odd connection holds, the intuitive verdict is that the belief is not prima facie justified. And even if our intuitions are so externalist that we are inclined to grant that the belief is justified, it's the reliability of the connection between the physical event and the belief that is doing the epistemological work, not the connection between the sensation and the belief. The sensation is not *evidence*—not for me at least—for the belief about the state of the toe.[32] And it presumably cannot become evidence for me until I am aware of the connection, and this would lead us to (ii), which I discuss shortly.

---

31. Tom Senor has helped me to see the importance of cases where the experiential state bears no intuitive relation to the belief it purports to justify, although I think that the import of such examples is especially clear if we restrict our attention to evidential justification rather than justification in general.

32. I do not mean to discount the importance of reliability; the theory I will eventually endorse is a version of reliabilism. Reliability, however, is a nonevidential justifier and has few direct implications for evidential justification. As we will see in chapter 5, this indicates that reliabilists typically lack a theory of evidential justification, and this is one of the major problems with reliabilism.

Perhaps (iii) offers an improvement over (iv) in claiming that it is the nature of the belief-producing mechanisms that determines what is evidence for what. Plantinga's (1993) discussion of perceptual warrant suggests that what makes a given experiential state serve as evidence for a given perceptual belief is that the perceptual faculty is designed to produce the belief in response to that experiential state.[33] Counterexamples of the sort just offered in response to Alston's view can be developed here as well. To take a quick example, suppose that the neurosurgical rewiring just discussed constitutes—unbeknownst to me, of course—my acquisition of a new (reliable, truth-aimed) faculty, which is designed to produce the toe beliefs from the cheek sensations. Intuitively, this belief would still not be justified.[34]

In addition, the sort of view on offer is only nominally a kind of experientialism, perhaps not one worthy of even the name, for once again, the experience is doing no real epistemological work. Here it is the faculty that is doing all the epistemic work, rather than the experiential state. Suppose that our visual faculties were in fact designed to produce perceptual beliefs on the basis of visual sensations and that the faculties are well designed and meet all of Plantinga's other conditions (reliability, etc.) for producing justified beliefs. Sensations might serve as grounds on such a view, though not, I think, in a way that would satisfy experientialists. Our visual faculties could easily have been designed to produce perceptual beliefs even without the corresponding sensations while still satisfying the other conditions for producing justified beliefs. If this counterfactual design plan had been our actual design plan, the beliefs would have been justified even in the absence of the sensations. This mere possibility should modify our sense of the epistemic contribution of the sensation, even given what we're supposing the actual design plan to have been. It seems to be the theory of nonevidential justifiers that is running the show here, not the theory of evidential justifiers, for the relevant belief could have been justified in the absence of any evidence whatsoever, had the design plan been slightly different. Thus, it is far from clear that (iii) offers a theory of evidence that would be acceptable to an experientialist. The epistemic role of experiences is not typically taken to be a mere quirk of our evolutionary history.

This argument proceeds in terms of Plantinga's own theory of nonevidential justification, but this is only for the sake of having a concrete example. In chapter 4, I will offer a different account of the justification of perceptual beliefs, according to which it is in large part the nature of the faculty that produces the beliefs (though not the *function* of the faculty) in virtue of which those beliefs are justified. Clearly, though, the nature of the generating faculty serves as a nonevidential, rather than an evidential, justifier. And even if the theory required that justified perceptual beliefs always be accompanied or preceded by sensations (on my theory, it will not), this would not clearly entail that the sensations are therefore *evidential* justifiers, any more than process reliability would be an evidential justifier merely because the theory required that justified perceptual beliefs be reliably produced. Even if we were to claim that sensations are necessary for the justification of perceptual beliefs, we

33. I say this is *suggested* by Plantinga's discussion; he speaks neither of evidence nor of justification, his topic being warrant.

34. I discuss these problems in more detail in chapter 5, section 3.4.

would need to say something more to give substance to the claim that their role is that of evidential justifiers and not merely as nonevidential justifiers.

All this can be taken a step further, for there seems to be something deeply incoherent about proposals like (iii) and (iv), at least within the context of experientialism. Experientialism, recall, is a broadly evidentialist view, in that it requires that every justified belief have an evidential justifier. My own nonevidentialist externalism makes no such requirements and thus views the possession of evidence as just one possible way of achieving justification. But what could possibly be the rationale for requiring that an agent have some evidence for every justified belief, while allowing that the status of that evidence *as* evidence (i.e., good evidence) is utterly beyond her ken? What could the resulting conception of evidence even amount to? If, as the experientialist insists, mere process reliability is insufficient for (prima facie) justification, why should the agent's possession of some ground—the relevance of which to the belief in question is absolutely unrecognized by her—make any difference? If this is what is meant by 'evidence', who needs it?

This brings us to the internalist proposals (i) and (ii). Perhaps what makes an experiential state evidence for a belief is some believed connection between the two. This, at least, seems to be a sufficient condition for something's being evidence, for it seems that pretty much anything can serve as evidence for pretty much anything else, provided that the agent justifiably believes that the former reliably indicates the latter. Recall, however, that the point of experientialism was to provide an account of the evidential justification of basic beliefs. Experiential states were to serve as regress terminators. On the straightforward reading of (ii), it couldn't possibly be of any assistance to the experientialist. True as it may be that anything can serve as evidence for a belief when the agent believes there is the appropriate connection, (ii) introduces another belief into the mix, which must be justified to play the role in question, and the regress is on again.[35]

There is an alternative reading of (ii), which may be of use to the experientialist. The claim might be that the agent's beliefs (or something like beliefs) serve as nonevidential rather than evidential justifiers. Perhaps my belief that e is evidence for h, or the fact that I would, on reflection, believe that e is evidence for h, or the fact that my procedural knowledge for how to reason allows me to infer h from e, is what makes e evidence for me for h. Such a background "belief" about e's evidential status might not actually be a premise in my argument for h but could nonetheless be what makes my argument from e to h a good one.[36]

This is a coherent proposal—the mere fact that the J-factors in question are beliefs does not force them to play a specifically evidential role—but it is not a very

---

35. Here is the argument, mentioned earlier, that can be avoided by endorsing a certain kind of nondoxastic coherentism.

36. Either reading of (ii) makes for an internalist theory of evidence, assuming that the background "beliefs" of the alternative reading are indeed introspectively accessible. Only the straightforward reading, however, offers a version of evidence essentialism. In a sense, of course, it is contingent whether p is evidence for me for q because it is contingent whether I believe that p indicates that q is likely to be true. But clearly, in such a case, p is only part of my evidence, and it plausibly is necessary that my whole evidence— p conjoined with the belief that p indicates q—is evidence for q. The alternative reading of (ii), by leaving these background beliefs out of the agent's evidence, really does make evidential relations contingent.

compelling one. The main problem with such a view is that, intuitively, certain *unjus-tified* higher order beliefs about the evidential status of *e* should have no bearing on the evidential status of *e*, and because these beliefs are held to play a merely nonevi-dential role, there is no principled ground for denying that unjustified higher order beliefs can have this effect. To take a concrete example, suppose a source I know to be unreliable tells me that wide black stripes on a certain kind of caterpillar indicate that a mild winter is coming, and I accept and internalize this, working it into my procedural knowledge of how to reason. My consequently inferring that this winter is going to be mild from the wide stripe on this caterpillar seems intuitively to be unjustified.

This leaves us with (i), that to serve as evidence for a basic belief, something must bear an appropriate semantic relation to the belief; what evidentially justifies which beliefs is determined solely by the contents of the evidence and the justifican-dum beliefs. This is the only plausible way left for the experientialist to make sense of the nonarbitrariness required of the connection between basic beliefs and their evidential justifiers. However, the experientialist would owe us an account of which semantic relations will do the job.

A standard view is that logical or probabilistic relations are necessary but not sufficient for something's being evidence for something else. Not every entailment relation is an evidential relation for a given agent, and the natural response is that only those that the agent recognizes as (i.e., justifiedly believes to be) evidential are such.[37] This brings us back to (ii), however, and such a move is blocked for the experientialist foundationalist, who requires some belief-independent relations to be evidential rela-tions. This is an important problem, one I try to say something about in chapter 7.

An additional problem arises for SE, since sensations do not seem to bear the relevant semantic relations to beliefs. Sensations might, like rocks and peanut shells, lack content altogether and thus simply not bear any semantic relations to anything. If so, they don't bear evidential relations to anything either. If sensations do have contents, however, they have nonpropositional and nonconceptual contents and thus cannot stand in logical or probabilistic relations to beliefs. Consequently, it is dif-ficult to see how they can stand in *evidential* relations to beliefs, unless logical or probabilistic relations are not in fact necessary for evidential relations.

The experientialist is likely to simply dig in and claim that there is more to evidence than entailment and probabilification. Perhaps, but we would like to know what. Certainly the experientialist will be at no loss in generating ad hoc principles: being appeared to greenly is evidence for the belief that there's something green nearby; having a pain is not evidence for the belief that there's a chair nearby, and so forth. The problem is that this is the beginning of an open-ended and indefinitely

---

37. Lewis Carroll's (1895) regress threatens, but one way to avoid it is by denying the Grounds Principle. If this principle is false, then one can have the justified belief that *p* is evidence for *q* without having any evidence for the proposition that $p \supset q$ (or that *p* is evidence for *q*). This, of course, is no con-solation to the experientialist, who endorses the Grounds Principle.

Fumerton's (1985, 2001) Principle of Inferential Justification is a similar claim, but he only claims that the believed connection is necessary in cases of inferential justification. Though all inferential justi-fication is evidential justification, the experientialist denies that all evidential justification is inferential in Fumerton's sense (since the latter involves beliefs).

large list, with no guiding principles specifying what gets put on and what gets left off the list. It is tempting to simply cite the following principle:

> If S is appeared to Φly, then S is prima facie justified in believing that there is something Φ nearby.

This, however, is no use to sensation experientialism, since the contents of sensations, by definition, are nonconceptual. No one ever has the *sensation* of being appeared to Φly, if 'Φ' has a conceptual content, and if it doesn't, then it's not involved in belief.

The closest principle that SE can consistently maintain is something more like this:

> If S is appeared to Φly, then S is prima facie justified in believing that there is something Γ nearby.

But clearly we are now in need of some principled account of which values of Φ get matched up with which values of Γ, and it is doubtful that the sensation experientialist can provide this. As Reid noticed, we are so accustomed to a covariation between a particular sensation and a particular belief that we tend to think that the connection between them is nonarbitrary, that, for example, the sensation of solidity "fits" with the belief in solidity in some way that is not just a contingent matter of our cognitive wiring. But if sensations lack conceptual content, the relation will be at least *semantically* arbitrary.

SE, like experientialism more generally, is committed to the existence of belief-independent evidential relations: e's serving as evidence for h, independent of the agent's beliefs about e and h. This leads to the view that e is evidence for h iff the right semantic relation obtains between the two, but the experientialist is in no position to tell us what that relation is. The only plausible contenders are incompatible with important facts about the contents of sensations. While it is perhaps mere Sellarsian dogma to insist that only items with conceptual/propositional content can serve as justifiers (full stop), there is nothing dogmatic about the claim that only these can serve as *evidential* justifiers. In fact, what seems dogmatic is the stubborn insistence that some unspecified—and perhaps unspecifiable—class of items, which just so happens to include SE's favored sensations, can serve as evidence for beliefs, despite the apparently unbridgeable semantic gap between them.

3. Percepts as Grounds

Some of the problems facing SE could be avoided by construing experiences, in the relevant sense, as higher level states than mere sensations. In particular, by taking the relevant states to be percepts with conceptual and propositional content, the defender of percept experientialism (PE) might hope to both close the sensation-perception gap and find a state that can stand in the right semantic relation to a basic belief. Perhaps this is the way to defend the view that experiences can serve as belief-independent evidence for perceptual beliefs.

3.1. In Search of the Percept

PE is a difficult view to argue against, partly because it is so difficult to know just what percepts are supposed to be. As the present discussion illustrates, this is a problem with experientialism generally. One who claims that experiential states are justificatory grounds for beliefs owes us an account of which experiential states or which aspects of experience are supposed to do this work. Though introspection suggests that experience is indivisible, monolithic, and unproblematic, in fact experience is a patchwork whose seams go unnoticed largely because of our inability to imagine the component pieces individually. The phenomenological approach to experience has us believing in one unified whole, called 'experience', or perhaps two: a sensation and a percept. The cognitive scientific approach tells us that there is in fact a host of representations tokened by the perceptual system in the process of normal perceptual belief production, some of which (or some features of some of which) are consciously available. It is far from clear which of these representations count(s) as "the" percept.

Perhaps this wealth of representational states will come as good news to the defender of PE, for surely one of them is bound to have the right kind of content to ensure belief-independent evidential relations while remaining nondoxastic. Recall, however, the prima facie objection to PE that motivated the examination of SE: without sensations, having a percept would be introspectively little different from having a hunch, a strong inclination to believe. What motivates experientialism is a commitment to some kind of internalism; there must be something available from the agent's perspective, which counts for that agent as evidence for thinking that this hunch is something more, something that may, perhaps must, be taken seriously. The problem is that the higher up on the hierarchy one begins the justificatory process, the less there is to distinguish mere hunches from genuine perception. But the lower one goes, the wider the sensation-perception gap becomes and the less plausible it is to think the nondoxastic state in question can bear any belief-independent evidential relation to beliefs.

At the low end of the hierarchy, the states are introspectively vivid and qualitatively rich, thus apt for serving the subjective role experientialism requires. But the evidential import of these states is far from clear; it takes either a genius or a special-purpose perceptual system to decipher them. As we ascend the hierarchy, the colors drain away from the states. Informationally rich but qualitatively impoverished, the higher level states close the percept-belief gap but leave nothing subjective for the agent to go on. At the extreme high end, the percept has the same content as the belief (plus perhaps some more determinate, maybe even nonconceptual content of its own). There would be no semantic gap between a percept thus construed and the belief, and this is the best-case scenario for belief-independent evidential relations. But such a state does little to appease the internalist worries that motivated experientialism in the first place.

This general concern can be formulated in the current cognitive scientific idiom. Early perceptual representations, to the extent that they are introspectibly accessible at all, only represent very low-level features: intensity differences and discontinuities in the visual field and the like. Somewhat higher level representations represent whole surfaces and their orientations; higher level yet are representations of object boundaries. None of these stages represents objects as the kind of objects they are: we have representations of boundaries and surfaces, not of cups and saucers. The highest level perceptual representations do involve object categorization and represent an object as a book or a desk, or the like. But there is nothing particularly *experiential* about this highest level representation. The states that most deserve to be counted as experiential states are the lower level states, to which the arguments of section 2 apply.

Moderation and ecumenicalism immediately suggest themselves. Moderation would urge that PE choose some state between the two extremes, one that has high-level content yet also has qualitative character. Reasonable though this may sound, it is not actually an improvement over SE. The proponent of this view will still have to respond to the arguments of section 2 and explain how the qualitative component contributes evidentially to the belief in question, and insofar as this state is a mid-level state, the sensation-perception gap (or its analogue) has opened up again. The ecumenical approach would be to argue that a whole range of states be brought to bear; even if any individual representation is incapable of playing the role experientialism requires, perhaps the congeries of states that is experience can serve as belief-independent evidence. However, it is hard to see how the whole experience can serve as evidence if none of its component states can.[38] Sensations cannot serve as evidence for perceptual beliefs or high-level appearance beliefs without additional beliefs. So adding them into the mix of experience doesn't help in any obvious way.

Experiences have two kinds of properties: semantic properties and qualitative properties. Both kinds of properties are important, for experiences are supposed to function as ground-level evidence, presumably in virtue of their semantic properties, while at the same time offering something to appease internalist scruples, presumably in virtue of their qualitative properties. The sensory component of experience is subject to the arguments presented against SE, leaving only the higher level states and their semantic properties. But a percept with only semantic properties won't do the work that PE wants it to.

3.2. Percepts and Beliefs

The trick for PE is to find a level of representation that is not yet doxastic but has the sort of content necessary to avoid some of the aforementioned problems for SE. A percept must have a content that suits it for serving as belief-independent evidence for beliefs. Furthermore, to avoid the kinds of problems posed by the sensation-perception gap, it seems that the percept will have to have, or contain, the same content as the belief it justifies. Anything less will raise the question of whether it is really sufficient to provide the agent with evidence for the perceptual belief.

But then it is far from clear that what is being called a percept is not a belief after all, in fact, the very belief whose justification is in question. The standard argument for distinguishing percepts from beliefs (section 1) is actually quite unconvincing upon closer scrutiny. Recall that the argument was that the percept can remain while the belief goes away—the one line continues to look longer than the other even though I believe they are the same. So the line's being longer is the content of

---

38. An indiscriminate generalization of this claim would be clearly fallacious. Obviously it is possible that p is not by itself evidence for q, though the conjunction of it and '$p \supset q$' is. In the present case, however, the other experiential states are not proposed to be serving the role of additional premises, and certainly not conditional premises.

the percept; their being the same is the content of the belief. Since they have different contents, the percept is distinct from the belief. But the case where my belief conflicts with my percept cannot be fundamentally different from the case where my belief agrees with the percept; thus the percept and the belief must be distinct even in cases where the two have the same content.

So goes the standard argument. But whether this conclusion follows depends on substantive cognitive scientific theses. Suppose that among the outputs of the visual system is the representation R: a sentence in Mentalese with the content that the upper line (say, of the Müller-Lyer illusion) is longer. The rest of the organism is wired so as to—defeasibly—rely on such outputs of the visual system in inference and practical deliberation and so forth, in short, to treat it in such a way that it has the functional role appropriate to beliefs. In normal conditions such as these R *just is* the belief that the upper line is longer. Once we've measured or become familiar with the illusion, other information from outside the visual system inhibits R from taking on the role appropriate to belief. In these conditions, that very same representation, R, is not a belief. The standard argument for the percept-belief distinction assumes that being a belief is an essential property of a mental state, that something cannot be a belief at one time and not at another: once a belief, always a belief. The story just sketched suggests otherwise. In very crude terms, the idea is that "accepted" percepts may actually be beliefs even though "rejected" percepts are not.

The standard view in the philosophy of mind (e.g., Field 1978; Fodor 1978) holds that (occurrently) believing that p is a matter of standing in a certain functional relation to a representation, R, which has the content that p. As it is sometimes put, this is a matter of tokening R in one's "belief box" (Schiffer 1987), that is, tokening an R representation in such a way that R is poised to have the causal role definitive of belief: R is used as a premise for inference, for practical syllogisms, and the like. When R has this causal role, it is a belief; when it doesn't, it is a mere percept. But when R has both this role and the role appropriate to percepts (e.g., it causes the subject to make claims of the form 'it looks as if p'), there is no obvious sense in which the percept is something distinct from the belief. We mustn't let the box metaphor mislead us into thinking a representation token can occupy only one box at a time.

Whether different functional roles require separate representations depends on the cognitive architecture. In a von Neumann machine, a "belief box" may be a separate register where representations are rewritten and stored, contingent on the functional role assigned to them. In such a case, R's appearing in the visual output register might typically cause the system to make a copy, R', in the belief register. In this architecture, a belief box would really be a functionally, perhaps even physically, separate part of the system. Here R is not the belief; R' is, and we have a very clear delineation between the percept, R, and the belief, R'. Talk about boxes, however, certainly has to be read far more metaphorically in other architectures. If the architecture is instead a production system, for example, then for R to "be in the belief box" is nothing more than for R to have a certain functional role, and this will depend not on where R is stored but on what other representations are vying with R for control. It is far more plausible to think that we have decentralized control architectures: that we are production systems, blackboard systems, connectionist networks, or some such, than to think that we have centralized control architectures like a von Neumann machine. In these decentralized control architectures, the percept-belief distinction, of the kind observed in the von Neumann machine considered here, generally does not obtain.[39]

The standard argument for distinguishing percepts from beliefs only seems compelling if we assume that being a belief or not is an intrinsic or essential property of a mental state. But the dominant philosophical theory about the nature of belief gives us no good reason to believe this. Because functional roles can come and go, the property of being a belief is not an essential property of a state. In accordance with this view, I am suggesting that a representation may be tokened and for a time have a certain causal role that makes that representation a belief token; later that representation may trade that causal role for a different one, whereupon it ceases to be a belief and becomes a mere percept. Because the "boxes" in human cognitive architecture are almost certainly not physically distinct locations, the very same representation token can be in the belief box and in the percept box at the same time, even though these are different "boxes." If I come to believe that vision is unreliable, this representation might "move out of" the belief box while remaining in the percept box; that is, it ceases to be a belief and becomes a mere percept.

Thus, the fact that what I believe and what percept I'm having are not *necessarily* the same does not show that individual percepts are not beliefs, in cases where the two agree. The kinds *belief* and *percept* are distinct; being a belief is a different thing from being a percept. What matters, however, is whether the token percept is distinct from the token perceptual belief it is alleged to justify. If not, then the picture proposed by PE is a nonstarter. PE, like experientialism more generally, holds that perceptual beliefs are based on things other than themselves, in particular, nondoxastic percepts. If these percepts are in fact doxastic after all—worse, if they are in fact the very beliefs whose justification is at issue—then this view collapses. I have argued that the percept and the belief may very well be token identical, and if so, the percept is obviously not going to be able to play the role PE requires.[40]

The present argument is intended to suggest, not to establish, that percepts and beliefs are not as distinct as PE requires them to be. This is a large and complicated issue, and one that I take up again in chapter 4.

3.3. The Zombies Return

If PE is really to embrace a form of experientialist nondoxasticism, percepts must be understood as some nondoxastic state. I have been arguing that an analogue of the

39. A bit roughly, a von Neumann machine is a serial computer with a CPU and several input/output devices; all of our Macintoshes and PCs have this general architecture. Though classical computationalism is sometimes parodied as the view that we are von Neumann machines, virtually no one, including classical computationalists, believes either that we are serial machines or that we have central processing units. Production systems, blackboard systems, and the like all have control (the issue of what to do next) determined not by some central processing authority (they don't have a CPU) but dynamically by the individual components: the conditional statements that constitute a production system, the individual nodes of a connectionist network, and so forth. This is a large part of what makes parallel computation possible in these architectures. For a good overview of such architectural differences, see Harnish (2002).

40. I have only argued that the belief and percept may be numerically identical in cases where the percept and belief agree; I grant that they are distinct otherwise. Clearly, however, it is only cases of agreement that are of any importance to PE, for justified perceptual beliefs on this view are cases where the percept that *p* justifies the belief that *p*.

sensation-perception gap causes trouble for this view; if the percept is to remain non-doxastic, it should have a different content from that of the belief it purports to justify, but then a nontrivial inference will be in order, and there is little reason to think that percepts thus construed can serve as belief-independent evidence. Similarly, analogues of the inverted and absent sensation arguments from section 2.1 plague PE. If the percept is numerically distinct from the belief, then the two can come apart, and the same belief can occur either in the presence of some other percept or without any percept at all. My argument will focus on the latter.

Just as sensationless perception posed a problem for SE, perceptless perception would pose a problem for PE.[41] Perceptless perception may be less common than sensationless perception, but it is not nonexistent. Return to the facial vision of the blind. Not only does the subject lack any introspectible sensation but also there seems to no introspectible experiential state at all[42] and thus nothing that would count as a percept in the sense required by PE. Still, these beliefs might be justified, even in the absence of any related beliefs.

Do zombies ipso facto lack percepts? Let us use the term in an even more proprietary sense than before, so that my zombie counterpart is a creature that is doxastically identical to me and otherwise as psychologically and physically similar to me as possible, consistent with his lacking experiences altogether. Such a creature has beliefs, and let us assume perceptual beliefs. Intuitively, some of the zombie's empirical beliefs would be justified, despite the fact that none is based on an experiential state. There seems to be no good reason to insist that zombies couldn't have knowledge or justified beliefs that result from the operation of their perceptual processes; otherwise, they could not have any empirical knowledge whatsoever. But if these beliefs are justified despite the zombies' lacking experiential states of any sort, then this is as much a problem for PE as it was for SE.

It would actually be quite odd for an internalist to deny that zombies are justified, for some of the reasons internalists think their view is superior to externalism. One important argument against externalist theories is that it treats inhabitants of a demon world (who are deceived by a demon in just the way Descartes supposed he might be) as unjustified. But since the demon worlders can't possibly tell that they're living in a demon world, they should be no different epistemically than us. It seems plausible that the same could be said about zombies. Since they're doxastically identical to us, they think they do have experiential states. Intuitively, it seems that zombies have no more way of telling they're zombies than demon worlders have of telling they're demon worlders. I am not claiming that the demon world

---

41. The term 'perception' is ambiguous between having a percept, having a perceptual belief, and perceiving. I mean it here in the second sense, of having a perceptual belief. Obviously, if 'perception' is intended in this first sense, there could be no such thing as perceptless perception. Recall, too, that the present question is an epistemological question and is not concerned with whether something could count as a perceptual belief without there being a corresponding experiential state.

42. How do I know there is no introspectible experience? Facial vision is actually quite common; everyone has the ability to some extent, though it can be more highly developed (and trusted) in the blind. I have done a fair job of navigating a hallway with my eyes closed, apparently on the basis of this facial vision, and I at least discerned no associated experiential state. It doesn't seem to be a necessary truth that to further develop the skill one would have to have more vivid, discernible experiences.

objection is a good one; if it is, however, there seems to be no nontheoretically moti-vated reason to deny that zombies are justified.[43]

The possibility of justified zombies aims us in a direction I want to take further in the next section. Experientialism is a moderate, middle-of-the-road view, avoid-ing the extremes of externalism and doxastic internalism. If zombies have justified empirical beliefs without experiences, then this must be either because some kind of doxasticism is true or because some kind of externalism is true. Given the implausi-bility of doxasticism, if I can convince the reader of this disjunction, I will feel that my argument for externalism has been made.

4. The Belief Principle

I want now to expound a general argument that I believe shows that no kind of experientialism can be true. Whether it is high-level or low-level experiential states that are at issue, neither can evidentially justify beliefs; only (justified) beliefs can do that. Suppose that the broadly Sellarsian worries from earlier have been satisfactorily addressed, and experiential states can stand in (broadly) logical relations to percep-tual beliefs; either they have propositional content, or it is possible for nonproposi-tional items to bear logical/probabilistic/evidential relations to beliefs after all. This is still a long way from supposing that experiences can actually serve as evidence for beliefs. My desire that p, my fear that q, and my wondering whether r can stand in logical relations to my belief that p or q or r. But it is quite clear that none of these states can serve as evidence for this belief. Neither can the proposition that p by itself or *your* belief (of which I have no idea) that q. Standing in logical relations to beliefs may be necessary, but it is not nearly sufficient, for evidentially justifying those beliefs.[44] To be an evidential justifier, a ground must stand in an evidential rela-tion to the justificandum belief, but it also must stand in a justifying relation. Thus far I have been concerned mainly with the former relation; now I am turning my attention to the latter.

It is worth asking on this score what it is that makes justified beliefs capable of evidentially justifying beliefs, for it is one thing to insist that they can do so and another to explain how this is possible. The answer, I suspect, has something to do with the fact that, if p entails q, then anything that makes p probable also makes q probable. Moving to the agent's perspective, if I know that p entails q, then—*ceteris*

43. Certainly there are differences between zombies and demon worlders to which certain theories might appeal; for one thing, the latter have experiential states while the former do not. The question, however, is whether there is any *intuitive* difference between the zombie case and the demon world case. Just as the experientialist can draw a motivated, though not intuitively motivated, difference between us and zombies, the reliabilist can draw a motivated, though not intuitively motivated, difference between us and the demon worlders: our perceptual processes are actually reliable.

44. This point has also been arrived at—independently, I think—by Aaron Champene (2003). It is brought out vividly, though inadvertently, by Steup (2000), who argues that experiential states, though propo-sitional, are not thereby in need of or susceptible to epistemic justification, just as other nondoxastic propo-sitional attitudes, like desiring, are not in need of or susceptible to epistemic justification. This analogy does him more harm than good, since it is obvious that desires cannot serve to evidentially justify beliefs.

paribus and within limits—anything that justifies me in believing that p should justify me in believing that q, since my knowing that p entails q results in my rightly treating any evidence for p as ipso facto evidence for q. Similarly with nonevidential justifiers: whatever nonevidentially justifies my belief that p will—*ceteris paribus* again—at least partially justify my belief that q, if I know that the former implies the latter. Since it is in some sense or other the agent's perspective that matters, we should expect that S's being justified in believing that p implies q should have much the same effect. The same will hold, though to a lesser degree and within tighter limits, when p does not entail, but merely renders probable, q.

On the view just sketched, it is not that one belief literally transmits justification to another belief as if justification were some kind of caloric-like fluid—that would be taking the transmission metaphor too seriously. On the present view, the inferred belief derives its justification not from the premise beliefs themselves, but from whatever justified them.[45] If we suppose that this is the only way for something to evidentially justify beliefs, we can use this supposition to explain why unjustified beliefs cannot evidentially justify other beliefs.[46] It is because what justifies a conclusion belief is whatever justified the premise belief, which, in the case of an unjustified premise belief, is nothing. Analogous reasoning explains why desires, fears, bare conceptions, and the like cannot evidentially justify beliefs. It is not so much because they are not *beliefs* but because they are not *justified*. Of course, since only beliefs can be epistemically justified, it follows that only beliefs can evidentially justify beliefs, and this just is the Belief Principle from chapter 2. Now, however, we have this principle as the conclusion of an argument, not a mere dogmatic postulate. We are not *assuming* that something can evidentially justify a belief only if it is itself a belief; we are inferring this from the fact that something can evidentially justify a belief only if it is justified. Unfortunately for the experientialist, this reasoning, which explains why unjustified beliefs cannot serve as justifying evidence, also implies that nondoxastic experiences cannot evidentially justify beliefs—whether these experiences have propositional content or not.

Some of BonJour's formulations of the Sellarsian dilemma (e.g., 1985) suggest that if a state is propositional, then it is somehow ipso facto in need of justification, and that is why propositional states must be justified in order to justify beliefs. But the present point is merely that only things that are justified can evidentially justify beliefs. This reveals the standard claims that nondoxastic states are not in need of justification, because they aren't propositional (e.g, Alston 2002) or because they aren't susceptible to justification (e.g., Steup 2000), as non sequiturs. Perhaps they do not "need" justification for their own sake—whatever that might mean—but they do need it if they are to evidentially justify beliefs.

The caloric view, dismissed before as too literal minded, has the same result. Here evidential justification is a matter of justification transmission—this is an

---

45. The justifiers of the premise beliefs may not suffice for the justification of the inferred belief, of course; other necessary conditions might well hold. For instance, the agent may need to believe or be justified in believing that the premises support the conclusion.

46. It is obvious, I take it, that unjustified beliefs cannot evidentially justify beliefs. It is not obvious that unjustified beliefs cannot *nonevidentially* justify beliefs.

important difference between evidential and nonevidential justification—and one cannot transmit what one does not already possess. This is why unjustified beliefs can't evidentially justify beliefs, but again, the theory implies that experiential states, not having any justification to transmit, cannot evidentially justify beliefs.

The caloric view and the view I have proposed both offer explanations of (i) how justified beliefs evidentially justify other beliefs and (ii) why it is that unjustified beliefs cannot (evidentially) justify beliefs. Nothing here depends much on which, if either, account is correct. The present points are merely (a) that there are existing accounts of how justified beliefs can evidentially justify beliefs, and none, so far as I know, of how nondoxastic experiential states can do so, and (b) these accounts imply that nondoxastic experiential states cannot evidentially justify beliefs. So the experientialist has to produce not just one, but two, accounts. The one account has to explain why the evidential justifier's being justified is necessary (if the justifier is a belief), while the other has to explain why it is not necessary (if the justifier is not a belief), so there's little hope of a unified theory.

Now I realize that there is no shortage of printed *assertions* that nondoxastic states can evidentially justify beliefs, but this is not what is needed here. What is needed is an explanation of how this is possible, one that fits with some explanation of why unjustified beliefs cannot do so. What I am offering is an abductive argument for the claim that only beliefs can justify beliefs. I have offered an explanation for the fact that desires and unjustified beliefs and the like cannot evidentially justify beliefs, and this explanation implies that nondoxastic experiential states cannot do so either. One does *not* get to respond to such an argument by insisting that she still finds it intuitively plausible that experiential states evidentially justify; to undermine an abductive argument, one must offer a better explanation for the phenomenon in question.

Taking seriously the question of how justified beliefs confer justification, we get an argument for the Belief Principle: only beliefs can evidentially justify beliefs. The reason unjustified beliefs cannot evidentially justify beliefs is that only things that are themselves (epistemically) justified can evidentially justify anything else. And since only beliefs can be (epistemically) justified, only beliefs can evidentially justify beliefs.

Again, the Belief Principle is only part of doxasticism. So long as one rejects the Grounds Principle, one can endorse the Belief Principle without endorsing doxasticism. Even though only beliefs can evidentially justify beliefs, there are some beliefs that are justified but not evidentially justified; they are justified though ungrounded. In fact, since doxasticism just is the conjunction of the Belief Principle and the Grounds Principle, the argument against doxasticism in chapter 2, conjoined with the argument for the Belief Principle here, provides an argument against the Grounds Principle.

Another argument against the Grounds Principle has been interwoven throughout this chapter. Perceptual beliefs, if grounded at all, have either doxastic grounds or nondoxastic experiential grounds. Chapter 2 argued that they don't have doxastic grounds, and throughout the present chapter, I have been arguing that they cannot have experiential grounds. But they are sometimes justified. Therefore, there are justified but ungrounded beliefs.

5. Experiential States as Nonevidential Justifiers

I mentioned previously that one could endorse a "bare givenism," that is, givenism without experientialism, by claiming that experiential states nonevidentially justify perceptual beliefs. The bare givenist could retain much of the letter of experientialism, and could even continue to endorse the standard experientialist formulae, like the following:

> (EXP): If S is appeared to Φly, then S is prima facie justified in believing that Φ is exemplified nearby.

Also, the resulting theory would be immune to some of the previous objections, since again, there are no in-principle constraints on nonevidential justifiers.

Once again, the overarching goal here is to make room for a reliabilist theory that allows for justified though ungrounded beliefs; consequently, my immediate goal is to show that the Grounds Principle is false. Bare givenism as currently construed is compatible with the rejection of the Grounds Principle, and as such, I have no particular problem with it, although I will offer an alternative view in ensuing chapters. What I really need to resist here is a variety of bare givenism that would follow experientialism in *requiring* experiential states for the justification of perceptual beliefs. Such a theory, I think, would have very little going for it.

Most of what may appear to be defenses of givenism without experientialism are more likely defenses of a generic givenism, without adequate attention to the distinction between evidential and nonevidential justifiers. Steup (2000) and Alston (2002) each have recent responses to the Sellarsian dilemma, in which they seem to be flirting with the view that experiential states are nonevidential justifiers. In fact, both are more likely just failing to notice the distinction between evidential and nonevidential justification. Steup tries to evade the dilemma by claiming that experiential states are propositional, Alston by claiming that they are nonpropositional. Steup argues that despite their being propositional, experiences do not need to be justified in order to justify beliefs, because the justificatory relation in question is one of generation rather than transmission of justification. 'Justificatory generation', however, is still ambiguous between evidential and nonevidential readings, and Steup never explains how evidential generation could be possible.[47] His view that the supervenience thesis favors nondoxastic justification, endorsed here and elsewhere (e.g., 1996), only bears on nonevidential generation. But if nonevidential justification is what he has in mind, the states' being propositional is irrelevant; nonevidential justifiers obviously need not bear any logical relations to their justificanda.

Alston (2002) insists that the states are nonpropositional and thus need not be justified in order to justify beliefs. He admits that being nonpropositional prevents them from bearing logical or probabilistic relations to beliefs but claims that justifiers need not bear such relations to their justificanda—as the plausibility of reliabilism

---

47. If the arguments of the previous section are sound, then only justified things can evidentially justify. Therefore, the evidential generation of justification is impossible; all justificatory generation is ipso facto nonevidential.

illustrates. This is a bad example, however, for reliabilism is a theory of nonevidential justification. Though it is clearly true that nonevidential justifiers need not bear logical or probabilistic relations to their justificanda, this doesn't begin to show that the same is true of evidential justifiers. But if Alston intends experiential states to serve only as nonevidential justifiers, then their being nonpropositional is irrelevant; nonevidential justifiers—propositional or not—needn't be justified in order to justify beliefs.

Steup's appeal to supervenience establishes at best experiences' role as nonevidential justifiers, but his insistence that experiential states have propositional content suggests that he is really after evidential justification. Alston's enlisting reliabilism as showing that nondoxastic justification is possible suggests that his concern is with nonevidential justification, but then he has not responded to a Sellarsian objection to his own (1988) experientialist theory of evidential justification. Like the supervenience argument, both of these responses make claims about nonevidential justification where the real target was supposed to be evidential justification.

Whether the nondoxastic experiential states are propositional matters only if the Sellarsian argument is concerned with evidential justifiers, but then a response to the argument requires an explicit account of how nondoxastic states can serve as *evidence*, not merely how they can serve as justifiers. It is hard to find a coherent view behind Steup's and Alston's replies to the Sellarsian dilemma. The most likely account, however, is that the authors are simply conflating evidential and nonevidential justification; they probably mean to defend experientialism rather than bare givenism.

Bare givenism, as a serious view and not just an inadvertent slip, is quite unmotivated. Experientialism is motivated by its endorsement of the Grounds Principle, but bare givenism gets no such support, for it does not require experiences or anything else to serve as grounds. To the extent that bare givenism seems initially plausible, this is very likely the result of its superficial resemblance to experientialism. Take this away, and the resulting theory looks much less compelling. Because nonevidential justifiers need not bear any semantic relationship to their justificanda, the bare givenist might as well endorse schemas of the following form:

(PXE): If S is appeared to Φly, then S is prima facie justified in believing that Γ is exemplified nearby.

PXE, of course, does not have quite the intuitive resonance that EXP does.

The bare givenist might reply that EXP is superior to PXE in that the former but not the latter gets the cases right. Ordinary cases of perception are cases of justified belief, and the justified beliefs are ordinarily accompanied by the corresponding experiential state; thus perhaps the latter nonevidentially justifies the former. Getting the cases right is a significant virtue, but it is not obvious that bare givenism can claim any such virtue. To see whether a theory gets the cases right, we have to have generally necessary and sufficient conditions, which EXP doesn't offer. There are two clear reasons why these could not simply be obtained by turning EXP into a biconditional and claiming that S is prima facie justified in believing that Φ is exemplified nearby iff S is appeared to Φly. First, it is clear that not all justified beliefs are accompanied by the corresponding appearance state. I have the justified belief that two of the books on the table in front of me were bought used. Second, the view would be subject to zombie objections like those of previous sections.

It is important that what I am objecting to here is a bare givenism that *requires* experiential states for the justification of perceptual beliefs. I am not at this point denying that experiences can serve as nonevidential justifiers. By claiming that experiences are justifying evidence for perceptual beliefs, experientialism, like bare givenism, is committed to the claim that experiences are justifiers. Unlike bare givenism, however, experientialism embeds this claim in a more general theory of justification; thus the claim is far more principled in the context of experientialism than in the context of bare givenism. A reliabilist can claim that experiences figure into the (nonevidential) justification of perceptual or appearance beliefs, provided that experiences have a significant effect on the reliability of the relevant belief-forming processes. Again, there is nothing especially objectionable about the claim that experiences nonevidentially justify, in the context of an overarching theory of justification that explains how this is so. What is objectionable is an ad hoc stipulation that experiences nonevidentially justify, a stipulation that derives its spurious plausibility only from its superficial resemblance to experientialism. This is especially grievous if the proponent of bare givenism tries to follow her experientialist models in *requiring* experiential states for the justification of perceptual beliefs. Again, this requirement makes sense on an experientialist theory, but bare givenism offers us little or no reason to believe that such a requirement actually holds.

Mental state foundationalists sometimes reserve a crucial but obscure role for experiential states, claiming that these states justify the corresponding appearance beliefs in virtue of being directly present to the mind (e.g., BonJour 2001; Fumerton 2001). Thus, a representative claim from Fumerton (2001, p. 14): "When everything that is constitutive of a thought's being true is immediately before consciousness, there is nothing more that one could want or need to justify a belief." The metaphorical nature of talk about things being "immediately before consciousness" makes it quite hard to tell what is going on here. Recalling the discussion from chapter 1, section 2, the metaphor of x's being directly present to the mind most likely conveys the claim that x is directly known, that beliefs about x are basically justified.[48] This says nothing about whether these beliefs are grounded. If they are supposed to be grounded, then the objections already leveled against experientialism apply; if not, then nothing here stands in the way of my rejection of the Grounds Principle.[49]

One nonnegligible virtue that bare givenism may seem to possess is that it incorporates an internalist element. Even if experiential states aren't serving as evidence for beliefs, it is important that the justifiers are internally accessible. One influential reason for thinking an internalist component is necessary comes from Norman- and Truetemp-type cases.

48. Fumerton might claim that direct presence is a matter of acquaintance, which he insists is not an epistemic relation. Since, however, he says so little about what acquaintance *is* (save that it is sui generis), it is unclear whether we should believe him.

49. If these MSFists really do intend for nondoxastic states to serve as nonevidential justifiers, I won't be offering a direct refutation of the view here. Instead, I will simply offer an alternative incompatible view, which I think is superior.

Norman (BonJour 1985) is a completely reliable clairvoyant who has no idea that he has this power. One day, this clairvoyance power produces in him the belief that the president is in New York; though the belief is reliably produced, it is intuitively not justified, presumably because there is nothing available from the agent's perspective that might contribute to the justification of the belief. Truetemp (Lehrer 1990b) has recently had implanted in his head without his knowledge a tempucomp: a reliable device that registers the ambient temperature and produces the appropriate beliefs in him. The tempucomp produces the belief that it is 103° outside. Yet again, the agent is intuitively unjustified. Such cases have served as influential arguments against externalist theories.

In chapter 5, I will have a great deal to say about such cases and exactly what they show. For now, I want to point out that these cases are not the friends that the bare experientialist might think. The Truetemp case, in particular, offers a counterexample to bare givenism, for Truetemp clearly does have the relevant experiential state. He has not, after all, had the thermoreceptor neurons in his skin removed, and presumably he has the same kind of temperature sensations as we do. He is being appeared to in a certain way, and he forms the corresponding belief. It is easy to suppose that the way he's appeared to when it's 103° outside is different from the way he's appeared to when it's 102° or 104°. When it's 102°, it feels hot to him; when it's 103°, it feels hotter; and when it's 104°, hotter still. Obviously, the sensation in question is a state that does not represent the heat as being 103°; this is the sensation-perception gap again. But this shouldn't matter to bare givenism, which does not require that the sensation be evidence for the belief anyway. The Truetemp case is not just a problem for (certain) externalist theories; it is a problem for many other theories as well, including experientialism, bare givenism, and any other theory that endorses principles like EXP. Here is an agent who is appeared to Φly but who is not prima facie justified in believing that Φ is exemplified nearby.[50]

6. Intuitive Resistance

There is a great deal of initial appeal to the claim that our experiential states justify our perceptual and/or appearance beliefs; this is why I have spent so much time arguing against experientialism. In the end, I think the problems it faces are insuperable. Still, I expect a good deal of resistance, in part because experientialism has such intuitive plausibility. I want to briefly argue that at least some of that plausibility is specious, that the relevant intuitions are not experientialist-friendly intuitions after all.

The experientialist will likely insist that the negative conclusions here are only made possible by a militant and blinkered conception of evidence. I have repeatedly insisted that there are no prima facie constraints on what sorts of things can serve as nonevidential justifiers; why not say the same about evidential justifiers? I have even conceded in section 2.4 that the legal system and ordinary discourse operate with a

---

50. Certainly there are ad hoc restrictions the givenist might make to avoid this and similar counterexamples. Given the lack of independent motivation for the view, however, as well as the upcoming defense of a view I take to be superior anyhow, such prima facie objections are enough for the present purposes.

more liberal use of 'evidence' than I have been allowing here. If murder weapons, sagittal crests, and the like can serve as evidence, surely nondoxastic states can as well.

This point is well taken, and I cheerfully concede (a) that there is a sense in which murder weapons can serve as evidence and (b) that experiential states can serve as evidence in *that* sense. This, however, is not an epistemologically interesting claim. Experientialism is interesting precisely because it claims that experiences can serve as evidence in a way that murder weapons cannot, that they can serve as evidence in the way that beliefs serve as evidence and not merely in the way that sagittal crests can serve as evidence. This claim is what motivates the epistemologist's restrictive use of the term 'evidence'; experientialism is not the trivial claim that experiences can serve as evidence in a liberal sense of the term but the contentious claim that they can serve as evidence *in the epistemologist's sense of the term*. It is this contentious claim that I deny.

In a similar vein, an evidential appeal to nondoxastic experiential states seems to be embedded in our ordinary dialectical practices, and one might appeal to this as an argument for experientialism:

A: Why do you believe that the milk is in the fridge?
B: Because it was a minute ago.
A: And why do you believe it was a minute ago?
B: Because I saw it.
A: And what makes you think it was milk you saw?
B: I had a certain characteristic visual experience.

Such cases seem to indicate that in our ordinary practice of giving reasons, we appeal to experiential states. If so, this is at least presumptive evidence for thinking that experiential states can be reasons, that is, evidential justifiers. However, such an argument exploits the aforementioned ambiguity of the term 'evidence' (as does the previous sentence; the ambiguity is easy to overlook and difficult to avoid). We do in fact appeal to experiential states in defending our beliefs, but we appeal to footprints and DNA results as well. None of this means that any of these things themselves—as opposed to beliefs about them—can serve as justifying grounds. Our appeal to experiential states does not indicate that these states serve as evidence in the epistemologist's sense. B's third rejoinder might have been "It was in a white carton," but we certainly wouldn't conclude from that that being in a white carton is an evidential justifier, on a par with beliefs.

Perhaps epistemologists are not likely to be confused by this, but there is, I think, a real danger that our intuitions about the epistemological significance of experiential states trades on the present ambiguity. Surely experiential states are epistemologically significant; this was one of the lessons of the isolation objection. A theory is in trouble if it implies that my headache is irrelevant to the epistemic status of my belief that I don't have a headache. Surely the fact that I'm appeared to redly is relevant to my being justified in believing that I'm appeared to redly.

From the fact that they are epistemologically significant, we can conclude that experiences are evidence in some suitably broad sense of the term, but we cannot conclude that they are evidence in the epistemologist's restrictive sense. In chapter 7,

I will grant, indeed insist, that experiential states are epistemically relevant, but I argue that they are only relevant in the kind of way that murder weapons and sagittal crests are, namely, nonevidentially. The fact that I have a headache has a lot to do with the fact that I'm justified in believing that I have a headache and a lot to do with why I'm not justified in believing that I don't have a headache. Headaches are epistemologically significant without being evidentially significant.

It would, of course, be question-begging to use this way of formulating the epistemologist's sense of 'evidence' to argue that only beliefs can serve as evidential justifiers. This is why my argument for the Belief Principle (section 4) proceeded quite differently. The point here is merely that some nondoxastic states (sagittal crests, carton color, etc.) cannot literally serve as justifying grounds, so an argument against the Belief Principle that is based on the evidential status of *these very states* is a bad argument.

Another intuitive consideration in favor of experientialism is this. Perception produces beliefs, but it doesn't produce *just* beliefs; one of the most striking, salient features of perception is that it also produces experiential states, of a certain distinctive variety. And these experiences serve as signs by which we can distinguish genuine perception from mere arbitrary belief. There is an introspectible difference between beliefs that just pop into one's head and beliefs that result from perceptual processes: the latter but not the former have accompanying experiences. This, then, is the epistemic role of experiential states: they serve as signs that the beliefs have a perceptual cause, are thus to be trusted, and are not mere hunches. I tend to think that this line of reasoning is fairly plausible, but I think it has very little to do with experientialism. Even if this makes experiential states epistemically relevant, it does not mean that they serve as evidential justifiers for perceptual beliefs.

If the role of the experiential state is merely to serve as a sign to distinguish perceptual beliefs from mere hunches, any old experiential state would do. The existence of experiential states indicates to me that some of my beliefs are the results of perceptual processes and not some other source, and it indicates which ones are which. In that sense, experiential states are like little green lights that light up when the relevant belief has a certain source. But this is not really the role that experiential states were supposed to play for experientialism. A green light cannot by itself evidentially justify the belief that there's something red in front of me on some occasions and the belief that I'm hungry on other occasions.[51] The problem is that if the experiential states are supposed to play this green light role, then they apparently cannot serve as belief-independent evidence. But since the whole point of experiences was to terminate the justificatory regress, this is just what they need to do.

To make matters worse, the beliefs that the experiences justify on the experiences-as-signs view are not the perceptual beliefs they were supposed to justify but, rather, higher order beliefs about the source (and thus the reliability) of the first-order beliefs. The same is true even if the first-order beliefs are taken to be beliefs about

---

51. Obviously, we have different experiential states corresponding to different beliefs; it is not the same experiential state each time. However, the proposal being scouted here is that the experiential states play the role of indicating which beliefs have a perceptual etiology. Vis-à-vis such a role, the differences between experiential states serve only to bind them to their respective beliefs, to specify which beliefs are the perceptual ones; any semantic connection to the belief is evidentially incidental.

one's own current mental states, so this approach is little comfort to either EOF or MSF. My being appeared to redly would not directly justify my belief that I'm appeared to redly, but only the metabelief that my belief that I'm appeared to redly is an introspective belief. This and a good deal of additional information will justify the belief that I'm appeared to redly, but this appearance belief is now quite far from being basic.[52]

It may clarify matters to see how easily this green light story can be co-opted by the nonexperientialist. Consider a reliabilist who makes the following claims: I have the ungrounded but justified introspective belief that I'm appeared to kitchen sink-ly (introspection is a reliable process). Nothing about reliabilism precludes my being justified in believing that if I'm appeared to Φ-ly, there's probably something Φ nearby. So from these justified beliefs, I use a reliable inferential process to conclude that there is a kitchen sink nearby. The only substantial modification here is that the reliabilist will presumably present this inferential process as secondary; while the primary means of forming the justified belief that there's a kitchen sink nearby is perceptual and noninferential, use of this additional process is icing on the cake, as it were. The success of this account shows that the green light story does not provide an argument for experientialism. Experiences may indeed serve as signs in roughly the way suggested here, but this is really nothing like the role experientialism attributed to them.

In fact, I think that experiential states are epistemically relevant in very much this—nonevidential—way. To say that experiential states are epistemically relevant, however, is a far cry from saying that they are epistemically necessary. I will be defending a view that allows cognizers lacking in experiential states altogether to have justified beliefs. There is no reason I should also have to claim that cognizers that do have them lack any epistemic advantage over those who don't. On the contrary, because of the availability of the aforementioned inference, I can and on rare occasions do form perceptual beliefs that receive justification from two sources: (1) the reliability of the perceptual process and (2) the reliability of the inferential process of the aforementioned sort. A reliabilist is, of course, free to claim that a belief sustained by two reliable processes is more justified than one that is sustained by only one of these.

7. Recapitulation

This has been a long chapter, and a brief summary of the antiexperientialist argument is in order. Experientialism is a view that endorses the Grounds Principle and rejects the Belief Principle. Though it requires evidential justifiers for every justified belief, it allows nondoxastic experiential states to serve as evidential justifiers (i.e., justifying grounds) for beliefs. Because the basic beliefs involved in perception are not self-justifying, experientialism implies that these beliefs are justified only if grounded in the corresponding experiential state.

52. Reid ([1785] 1967) seems to endorse the experiences-as-signs view, and some (e.g., Lehrer 1989) have read him as endorsing a sort of coherentist theory on this account, despite the standard reading of him as an EOFist.

I began by distinguishing between high- and low-level experiential states. The low-level states (sensations) cannot justify the relevant beliefs in part because there is too big a gap between them and their justificanda for the normal agent to appreciate the former as evidence for the latter, and in part because their nonconceptual/non-propositional content prohibits them from serving as belief-independent evidence. For these reasons, the low-level states are not sufficient for the prima facie justification of the basic beliefs they are purported to justify. Nor are they necessary, for there are cases of justified perceptual beliefs without the corresponding low-level experiential state, cases of the philosophical zombie variety, the minor zombie variety, and cases where the sensation exists but the belief is not based on it.

We might turn to high-level representations (percepts), but then a dangerous dilemma arises: if the states are too high level, too belief-like, they are in danger of being too introspectively hunchlike to appease the internalist's scruples. The more like sensations they are, however, the more likely it is that they will be incapable of serving as evidential justifiers because of an analogue of the sensation-perception gap. In addition, if the states are too high level, it is quite likely that they will turn out simply to be beliefs, the very beliefs that the experiential states were purported to justify. Finally, a kind of zombie can arise even here, and it seems that the perceptual beliefs of these zombies can be justified, even though they lack percepts, so having percepts is not necessary for the justification of basic perceptual beliefs.

Next, I provided a general argument that was intended to show that nondoxastic experiential states could not possibly evidentially justify beliefs, because only justified beliefs can do that. I sketched a view about how justified beliefs evidentially justify beliefs, the main thesis of which was that what justifies a conclusion belief is whatever justified its premises. This account clearly implies that only things with justification can evidentially justify beliefs; therefore, nondoxastic states cannot evidentially justify beliefs.

Experiential states are neither necessary nor sufficient for the justification of perceptual or appearance beliefs. Their insufficiency provides one reason for thinking they are unnecessary (the zombie arguments provide another). There is no reason to require experiences to play the role of grounds for perceptual beliefs if they can't get the job done anyway. It is better, I think, to admit that grounds are not necessary for justification. Thus, while experientialism endorses the Grounds Principle and rejects the Belief Principle, I have been urging just the opposite: reject the Grounds Principle and embrace the Belief Principle. Only beliefs can serve as grounds, but beliefs can be justified even though ungrounded

4

Perceptual Systems and Perceptual Beliefs

Doxasticism and experientialism both face difficulties serious enough to motivate a kind of nonevidentialist nondoxasticism. Although I take this to be an important part of the overall argument for my view, the theory has more to recommend it than the failures of its rivals. It is common practice to defend philosophical positions by elimination: show that all the alternatives face insuperable difficulties, and the last theory standing wins. However, I want to defend a particular kind of nonevidentialist theory, and I don't want to have to eliminate all the possible nonevidentialist alternatives in order to settle on the one I prefer. So arguing by elimination has to stop somewhere. Here I want to articulate the theory of perceptual beliefs briefly mentioned in chapter 1 and offer some reasons for thinking it is true.

I will be working within the context of an external object foundationalism, for I think that the balance of considerations is in favor of this view. My primary goal is to defend a particular brand of EOF, but I take the main considerations in favor of a generic EOF to be the following:

1. As mentioned in chapter 1, EOF allows us to combine two problems into one. Solving the delineation problem (which beliefs are basic?) will go a long way toward specifying which beliefs are perceptual beliefs. More important, the converse is true as well; I will offer an EOF theory of perceptual beliefs and extract a solution to the delineation problem from that. Because of this tight connection between perception and basicality, EOF allows us to classify perceptual beliefs as noninferential, thus retaining the straightforward distinction between perception and inference.

2. Mental state foundationalism has always been plagued by the traditional skeptical problem of the external world: there seems to be no non-question-begging way of inferring beliefs about external objects from appearance beliefs. Obviously, several possible solutions have been vetted, but none strikes me as particularly plausible.

3. Finally and most important, there is simply no remaining motivation for MSF's restriction on basic beliefs within an externalist framework. MSF was most plausible in the context of a view according to which the basic beliefs had to be infallible, somewhat less so if they only had to be certain, and even less so otherwise. Even waiving all these requirements, there is perhaps some reason to prefer MSF if a doxastic or experientialist internalism is assumed. But I have argued against doxasticism and experientialism, and I am now ready to explore nonevidentialist options. In this context, there is no reason at all to suppose that the basic beliefs involved in perception will be limited to beliefs about one's own mental states.

Consequently, I will suppose that a generic EOF is true, that is, that some beliefs about external, physical objects are basic. In particular, I will suppose that perceptual beliefs are ipso facto basic. The full defense of EOF will be indirect and consists in the development of what I hope is a plausible and detailed version of EOF.

The epistemology that I want to defend is a type of reliabilism, but one that explicitly marks a distinction between basic and nonbasic beliefs. Though the details will be saved for later, the basic idea is that process reliability is necessary and sufficient for the justification of basic beliefs, though more is required for nonbasic beliefs. This means, of course, that we will need a nonreliabilist account of the distinction between basic and nonbasic beliefs, but this is exactly what I hope to provide.[1] Basicality has to be understood slightly differently in the context of a reliabilist framework than in an evidentialist one. The most important difference, discussed already in chapter 1, is that on a reliabilist theory, not all basic beliefs are even prima facie justified. To say that a belief is basic is, again, to say that its prima facie justification does not depend on evidential relations to other beliefs. Its prima facie justification might nevertheless depend on such nonevidentialist factors as process reliability and the like.

Reliabilism and the general account of basicality will be dealt with later. For now I want to tackle the question of which beliefs are perceptual beliefs, though it should be kept in mind throughout that I intend for a perceptual belief to be prima facie justified if and only if the process that produced it is reliable.

To return to some examples from chapter 1, which if any of the following are perceptual beliefs: that the dog is asleep? that the dog is lying down with her eyes closed? that there are people on the street below my window? that there are coats and hats moving below my window? that it's Smith that I see? that my sister is on the telephone?

1. By saying that the distinction between basic and nonbasic beliefs is a nonreliabilist distinction, I mean that the distinction itself is not drawn in terms of differential reliability, not, of course, that the resulting distinction is in any way at odds with reliabilism.

The theory I want to endorse could be called a perceptual system theory (PST). It is the view that a belief is a perceptual belief just in case it is the output of a perceptual system. This is a natural, I think intuitively obvious, suggestion—so much so that it might sound trivial. For some reason, however, PST is a minority view; to my knowledge I am the only one who holds it.[2] Though many epistemologists are regrettably silent on what they take perceptual beliefs to be, there does seem to be something of a received view, and it is a kind of experientialist view.

A natural and straightforward account of perceptual belief is this: my belief that p is a perceptual belief if and only if I believe that p because things look (sound, smell, etc.) as if p. My belief that it's cold in here counts as a perceptual belief if I hold it because it feels cold, but not if I hold it because someone I trust tells me it's cold. My belief that it's Jane on the phone is intuitively a perceptual belief, because it sounds like Jane; my belief that the youngest of my three sisters is on the phone is intuitively not a perceptual belief, because there is no obvious literal sense in which it *sounds* like the youngest of my three sisters on the phone. That is, my belief that p is a perceptual belief if and only if my belief that p is based on a perceptual experiential state with the content that p.[3] The restriction to perceptual experience is essential, as many epistemologists believe in nonperceptual experiences, such as mnemonic experiences (Audi 1998; Pollock 1986) or even purely intellectual experiences (Plantinga 1993; Pust 2000), and surely being based on nonperceptual experiences is not sufficient for being a perceptual belief. Distinguishing perceptual experiences from nonperceptual experiences would be a matter left for another discipline (e.g., psychology), or at least for another day.[4] In contrast to this general view, PST allows that one could have perceptual beliefs (and perhaps justified perceptual beliefs) even if one lacked experiential states altogether.

The challenge of experientialist theories of perceptual belief shows that PST is not so obviously true as to be unworthy of extended defense. There is, however, another sense in which PST might seem to be trivial: it looks circular. If a perceptual system is simply one that produces perceptual beliefs, then the account is indeed trivial. Thus we will need a nonepistemic way of distinguishing perceptual systems from nonperceptual systems. The solution to this is that 'perceptual', as it appears in

2. Fodor seems to be presupposing something like PST in a well-known exchange with Churchland concerning observation (1984, 1988). However: (1) it isn't a thesis he argues for, (2) his understanding of modularity differs from mine in important ways to be discussed later, (3) his main concern is theory neutrality rather than justification, and (4) on closer examination, it is probably not even PST that Fodor is presupposing. He thinks that "what one observes" is determined by one's perceptual modules. But this talk of observation might be intended as talk about one's experiential states, not one's beliefs. (Fodor's assumption, discussed later in section 1.2, that the outputs of perceptual systems are nondoxastic, makes this a rather plausible interpretation.) Even if Fodor does hold that "what one observes" is a matter of what one's perceptual beliefs are, his claims are all compatible with the view that there is (a) a constitutive connection between experiential states and what one sees (or what perceptual beliefs one has) and (b) a causal dependency between what modules one has and what experiential states one has. Such a view would be a kind of experientialism rather than a version of PST.

3. The proposal would have to be reformulated in terms of a "corresponding" sensation (and then this would have to be explicated) for the defenders of SE, since sensations don't have propositional contents.

4. There are tricky problems involving possible but nonactual cases: if Norman has a nondoxastic state accompanying his clairvoyance belief, would the belief count as a perceptual belief?

'perceptual belief', is a partly epistemic term, but as it appears in 'perceptual system', is a psychological/cognitive scientific term. In the end, I suspect that distinguishing perceptual from nonperceptual systems will be easier than distinguishing perceptual from nonperceptual experiential states, but I won't press the point.

For most of the following discussion, I focus on perceptual beliefs about the identities of objects, rather than their locations, positions, colors. The account I offer will easily accommodate these as well.

1. Perceptual Systems

It hardly illuminates the nature of perceptual belief to be told that perceptual beliefs are the doxastic outputs of perceptual systems, unless we know what perceptual systems are. Fortunately, the notion of cognitive systems and modules has received a good deal of attention in the cognitive sciences—especially cognitive neuroscience—and in the philosophy of these disciplines. There are two different questions that need to be answered: (a) what is a cognitive system, or module? and (b) which modules are perceptual modules?

1.1. Cognitive Systems/Modules

Fodor (1983), of course, has made the concept of a cognitive module a familiar one. According to this seminal view, modules are information-processing mechanisms that are innately specified, domain specific, informationally encapsulated (i.e., they lack access to the beliefs and goals of the larger organism), and introspectively opaque (their "interlevel" representations are not consciously accessible).[5] Fodor's own understanding of modularity, though setting the stage for most subsequent discussion, is quite restrictive, especially in its assumptions of innateness and informational encapsulation. Many authors opt instead for a kind of "weak modularity," which relaxes the more restrictive of Fodor's conditions.

I have tried elsewhere (2001) to clarify this notion of weak modularity: the conception in question is the cognitive neuroscientific understanding of a cognitive system. On this view, all modules in Fodor's sense are systems, but not all systems are modules in Fodor's restrictive sense. Some systems, for example, are assembled, in the sense of having a fairly elaborate virtual architecture; this is a feature Fodor's understanding of modularity prohibits (1983, p 37). Famously, and more important, some cognitive systems might very well fall short of total encapsulation (they may have partially but not fully restricted information trade with other systems), and some systems may result from, or at least be shaped by, learning (Elman et al. 1996)—again, features not had by Fodorian modules. Nor need cognitive systems be domain specific in any very robust sense. The term 'module' is a handy one, however, and

---

5. Fodor (1983) has either five (pp. 36–37) or nine (pp. 47–101) diagnostic criteria for modularity, depending on how (and where) you count. Many of these are quite controversial, and I have just listed a few of the more important. Fodor explicitly denies that he is defining the term 'module', and it is best to read him not as offering an account of what modules are but as propounding a high-level empirical theory: that cognitive capacities exhibiting some of these five or nine properties tend to have most or all of them.

I will retain it, though I will use it interchangeably with the term 'cognitive system' and will use it for this weak notion of modularity, rather than the strong Fodorian one. On my view, a cognitive system for some task is an isolable cognitive mechanism that specializes in that task and exhibits a kind of functional unity. I will summarize the basic view here; the argument for the view, along with a good deal of elaboration, can be found in my (2001) discussion.

A cognitive system is a virtual machine that is realized in some, presumably physical, substrate. In order to realize a cognitive system, a substrate must compute a cognitive function; that is, it must effect a mapping of representational states.[6] Now a function can be represented as a set of ordered input/output pairs, and this allows us to make an important distinction between subtasks and parts of a task. A subtask is a task (i.e., a function) that is performed as a step in a larger task; a part of a task is a subset of the ordered pairs that constitute the task. Suppose that visual object recognition requires a specification of retinotopic edge representations, which are fed into systems that extract higher level information from them. Edge detection is thus a *subtask* of visual object recognition. But visual object recognition effects a mapping from retinal irradiation arrays to object categorizations/identifications, and the pairs that make up this mapping do not include a pair whose first element is a retinal irradiation array and whose second element is an edge specification. So edge detection is not a *part* of visual object recognition.

Systems must be isolable in the sense of being independently capable of performing their tasks, in the absence of other mechanisms. This feature is illustrated by the cognitive neuroscientific methodology of double dissociation. If some disease or brain lesion produces an impairment with respect to task A but spared performance with respect to task B, that is some reason for thinking that A and B are subserved by distinct systems. However, such a single dissociation of A from B is compatible with A and B's being handled by the same system, if A is more difficult, the damaged system continuing to perform normally on the easy tasks but exhibiting deficits on the difficult ones. There are, for instance, patients with prosopagnosia: a selective deficit for recognizing faces, patients whose ordinary object identification is (relatively) unimpaired. Does this mean that there is a distinct face recognition system, or merely that face recognition is more difficult and thus more sensitive to injury? A double dissociation, where one population is impaired on A but not B and another population is impaired on B but not A, resolves this question. If A dissociates from B in some patients and B from A in others, it must be that different cognitive systems underlie performance of the different tasks, the one system being damaged in the one population, the other system in the other. I call a substrate S *isolable* with respect to task T iff S computes T and could do so even if nothing else computed any cognitive functions.

Cognitive systems are said to be systems, or modules, *for* something. There is a module *for* face recognition (equivalently: there is a face recognition module) only if there is a module that specializes in face recognition; that is, it does nothing else. If face recognition is performed by a more general-purpose visual module and not a separable component, then there is nothing that specializes in face recognition and

6. That is, the substrate must compute a function that has representational states as its range or domain (or both).

consequently no system *for* face recognition. We can say that *S specializes* in *T* iff *T* is an exhaustive specification of the input/output function that *S* computes.[7]

Finally, suppose there is a system for face recognition, and suppose also that there is a system for gustation. It clearly does not follow from this that there is a system for gustation-or-face-recognition. Cognitive systems must exhibit a certain functional unity; not just any gerrymandered collection of systems is itself a system. I say that a task *T* is *unitary* with respect to substrate *S* iff *S* computes *T* and no proper part of *S* both specializes in and is isolable with respect to any part of *T*. This requirement allows for the possibility of subsystems, provided that they compute subtasks rather than parts of tasks.

On my view, a substrate *S* realizes a cognitive system for *T* iff *S* is isolable with respect to *T*, *S* specializes in *T*, and *T* is unitary with respect to *S*. Technicalia aside, the intuitive idea is that a system for *T* is a virtual machine that does *T* and nothing else, is self-sufficient with respect to *T*, and is such that the *T* it does is a functionally cohesive task, rather than some gerrymandered collection of independent tasks.

1.2. Perceptual Modules

Clarifying the concept of a cognitive system, or module, takes us part of the way toward an understanding of perceptual systems, but we will need to know what the difference is between perceptual and nonperceptual modules. By 'perceptual system', or 'perceptual module', I intend whatever it is that contemporary cognitive science means by the terms. Thus the epistemological kind, *perceptual belief*, is fixed by the cognitive scientific kind, *perceptual system*. Thus an account of perceptual systems, like the account of cognitive systems more generally, should aim at capturing the conception operative in cognitive science.

Given the role I am reserving for perceptual systems, I clearly cannot delineate the class of perceptual systems in epistemological or phenomenological terms. The former would render the resulting theory of perceptual belief circular, and the latter would be hard to reconcile with my rejection of experientialism. Fortunately, cognitive science is notoriously unconcerned with either epistemology or phenomenology. A theory that captures cognitive science's assumptions about perceptual systems will be a theory that proceeds in terms of representations and computational processes, not in terms of reasons or raw feels.

It is an important part of my account of cognitive systems that they can be assembled out of simpler subsystems. Not only is this a conceptual possibility but it appears to be commonplace. Vision, for instance, seems to comprise a number of distinct systems, many of which sum together to form larger visual systems. Visual processing splits fairly early on into aforementioned "what" and "where" systems (Goodale

---

7. It may be convenient and acceptable to sometimes relax this constraint a bit, allowing, for example, talk about a face recognition system even if some of the outputs of this system are not face representations, so long as mostly what the system does is face recognition. Such a system would not, strictly speaking, be a face recognition system, but we might call it one anyway. This usage is a matter of pragmatics rather than semantics. Scientists probably never cite the exact input/output function, and it's fine to use the more relaxed way of speaking when it's not misleading.

and Milner 1992; Ungerleider and Mishkin 1982). These systems contain a number of subsystems, some in serial, some in parallel, including a system for the detection and analysis of motion, systems for computing object boundaries from surface disconti-nuities, and the like. Color vision is handled separately by a different system. Yet these systems "come together again" to bind object color, location, and identity into a single comprehensive representation.[8] Slightly different visual systems are known to exist in the different hemispheres, at least in the ventral pathways, with the left being thought to specialize in relatively abstract visual information and the right in relatively specific information; alternatively, the left may be engaged in "entry-level" categorization, while the right is engaged in subordinate-level categorization (Marsolek 1999). (The entry level is the level at which subjects tend to spontaneously identify perceptually presented objects, e.g., 'apple', 'chair' [Jolicoeur et al. 1984]. It is to be contrasted with subordinate levels, e.g., 'Granny Smith', 'Macintosh', and superordinate levels, e.g., 'fruit', 'furniture', 'object'.) Thus, face recognition is normally subserved by the right hemisphere, and general visual object recognition by the left.

Accurate boxologies of these things are exceedingly complex, but a (simpli-fied and fictionalized!) depiction appears in figure 4.1. Boxes are drawn to indicate some of the relevant systems. The upper box that takes retinal irradiation as input and returns object identifications as outputs corresponds (roughly) to one theory (Biederman 1990) about the computational nature of the left hemispheric ventral pathway, the location determination system corresponds to the dorsal pathway, and the color perception box corresponds to a system involving cortical area V4. The ventral system by itself computes object identities, but in conjunction with the dorsal system it produces representations of object-location pairs. These two, in conjunc-tion with color perception, yield object-color-location triples: for example, 'there is a red ball in front of me and to the left'.

Thus, several perceptual systems are represented in figure 4.1, including an edge detection system, a color perception system, and an object identification system. Just as separate subsystems can sum together to form a larger visual system, cross-modal interaction and integration are also possible. There may be a specific perceptual mod-ule responsible for the ventriloquism effect, that is, a module that takes auditory and visual location information and "corrects" the former in an effort to make plausible matches with the latter (Radeau 1994). Thus we hear the dummy's voice as coming from where we see the dummy's lips to be. The McGurk effect may involve a similar cross-modal module.[9]

My claim that perceptual beliefs are the doxastic outputs of perceptual systems embodies a commitment to the claim that the outputs of the perceptual systems are

8. Obviously such "coming together" need not involve any physical convergence of the various pathways; these neural pathways don't seem to reconverge again after that initial split. What matters is that after a certain point in processing, the whole mechanism has the kind of functional unity necessary for cognitive systems. This may be effected by means of synchronous oscillations (Crick and Koch 1990) or by some other means.

9. McGurk and Macdonald (1976) discovered that what phonemes subjects hear is affected by what lip movements they see. So when the sound |ma| is accompanied by a video of someone saying |ka|, what is heard is a |na|.

quite often beliefs. Though the term 'belief' is used very rarely in these areas of cognitive science, this is how I am reading the talk in the literature about object recognition and the like: to recognize an object, to categorize it, to identify it, is at least typically to *judge* it to be a member of a certain category. I suggested in the previous chapter that high-level perceptual representations with a certain functional role are beliefs, even though the same representations with a different functional role are not; they are mere percepts or something similar. I am now suggesting that these representations are the high-level outputs of perceptual systems.

Some seem to think that the outputs of perceptual systems are ipso facto nondoxastic. Fodor (1983), for example, thinks that belief fixation is under the purview of the central system. This, however, does not imply that the outputs of the modules are therefore nondoxastic states. There will be a temptation to think otherwise, if we are not careful to distinguish belief, the global property of an individual, from beliefs, occurrently tokened mental representations with a certain functional role. Whether, in the end, I believe that p might very well depend on how my central systems deal with some mental representation of p, but this is perfectly compatible with the claim that this representation of p is the output of some peripheral module.

The picture that emerges is one in which several smaller systems working relatively independently of each other add up to form larger perceptual systems. These systems may very well interact, despite their being independent of each other—no one doubts that it is possible to go blind without going deaf, the ventriloquism effect notwithstanding. The perceptual systems start with the transduction of energy by the sense organs and feed their outputs into more central, nonperceptual systems: practical and theoretical reasoning systems, the various memory systems, and so forth.

Even if the basic functional architecture of the perceptual systems is innately specified, the actual operation of such systems is patently affected by learning. My face recognition system can't identify someone as my mother unless it knows what my mother looks like, and this is clearly not innate. Expertise often brings with it changes in the outputs of perceptual systems. Though I am following convention in calling it a "face recognition system," it is very likely that the system in question is responsible for additional fine-grained judgments, not just those concerning faces (see note 7). An expert bird-watcher with prosopagnosia lost the ability to visually recognize bird species, and a farmer with the disorder could no longer tell which of his cows was which (Farah 1990). It is likely that such beliefs were also outputs of this perceptual system. Nor is it only this "face recognition" system that changes in response to experience; perceptual learning occurs in other modalities as well (Goldstone 1998).

A perceptual system is, in the first instance, a module that starts with the transduction of energy by some sense organ and produces beliefs or other relatively high-level representations as outputs.[10] This gives us a "lower bound": perceptual systems take transductions of sensory stimulation as inputs. Because larger systems can be composed of subsystems, however, not just any system that maps sensory stimulation onto beliefs will count as a perceptual system. Tacking a reasoning system onto the end of the system in figure 4.1 may very well result in another system, but this larger

10. There is a derivative sense in which any subsystem of such a system is also a perceptual system.

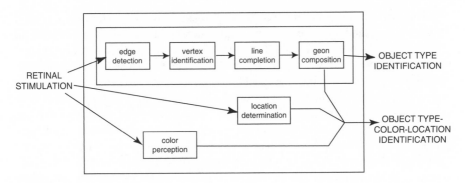

FIGURE 4.1

system would not therefore be a perceptual system. Whatever downstream processing occurs with the doxastic outputs of the system of figure 4.1 goes on outside the bounds of perception. We need to establish an upper bound, and one thing is clear: once beliefs are available to serve as inputs for some subsystems, the overarching system that results is no longer a perceptual system.

To take another, more concrete, example, consider our capacities for third-person mental state attribution, a process that has received a great deal of recent attention from the standpoint of psychology, neuroscience, and philosophy, though not epistemology. According to an older version of the simulation theory (Goldman 1992b; Gordon 1986), we "put ourselves in someone else's shoes," using our own belief-forming systems and behavior-generating mechanisms to ascribe mental states to others. We use these systems off-line by feeding in imagined beliefs, desires, perceptual states, and the like, so the output is ersatz beliefs, desires, and behavior instead of the real things. We then attribute real analogues of this ersatz output to anyone we take to have the real analogues of the inputs. A newer version of the simulation theory (Goldman 2006) distinguishes this kind of process (which is now referred to as "high-level mindreading") from the more automatic, sensory-driven "low-level mindreading." Although a high-level mindreading system is obviously not a perceptual system, a low-level mindreading system may be. Goldman proposes a face-based emotion recognition module, which produces outputs about the subject's emotional state from face representations.[11] This system presumably operates in parallel with a face recognition module that computes a person's identity from face representations. Both of these systems are automatic and operate below the level of consciousness, though their outputs are consciously accessible. Each system seems to qualify as a perceptual system. And if information from these two systems were bound together to yield outputs like 'Ann is angry' (from 'this is angry' and 'this is Ann'), the resulting system would be a perceptual system, and the output belief, that Ann is angry, would be a perceptual belief.

---

11. I am simplifying the proposal; rather than one overarching emotion recognition system, there are probably distinct systems for at least some different emotions.

This may strike some readers as a bit counterintuitive. There is a certain philosophical standpoint from which Ann's anger is a paradigmatic case of an unobservable. However, we should keep in mind that there is also a philosophical standpoint from which Ann is, too. It is not that Ann is supposed to be an immaterial thing but merely that being Ann and looking like Ann are two different things, just as being angry and having the external signs of anger are different. Such considerations show not that the mental states of others can't be delivered by perceptual systems but that a philosophical taxonomy that classifies persons and mental states as unobservables doesn't map nicely onto the psychological taxonomy or the philosophical taxonomy I endorse. I am happy with such a result. Cognitive scientific thinking has it that beliefs about the identities of persons are indeed sometimes the outputs of perceptual systems. There is no reason that beliefs about the mental states of persons couldn't also be. If cognitive science has learned anything, it is that perception would be impossible without ampliative inference, and if epistemology has learned anything, it is that the same holds for justification. Looking like an apple and being an apple are two different things, but this doesn't render apples unobservable in either the psychological or the epistemological sense of the term. The mental states of others don't seem to differ in any significant respects.

We have looked at two possible cognitive systems involved in mental state ascription. The low-level simulation system is pretty clearly perceptual, and the high-level simulation system is pretty clearly not. The high-level simulation system is nonperceptual not because its inputs are beliefs—they're not; rather, they are faux beliefs, desires, sensations, and the like. Still it is the nature of these inputs that makes the system a nonperceptual system. What it is, I think, is this: perceptual systems take their inputs from the world and not from the larger organism. *A perceptual system is a cognitive system that starts with the stimulation of sense organs by physical energy as input and processes information about the current environment, where none of the inputs to any of the subsystems are under the direct voluntary control of the larger organism.*[12] Thus we have both upper and lower bounds to distinguish the class of perceptual systems from cognitive systems more generally.

It might help to briefly compare and contrast perceptual systems as I understand them with modules as Fodor (1983) understands them. Fodor requires that his modules be informationally encapsulated (i.e., that they don't take the beliefs or goals of the larger organism as input). Though I don't lay it down as a requirement on modules more generally, I do require this of perceptual modules. Any point at which such inputs enter the picture is a point at which the module in question has ceased to be a *perceptual* module. Perceptual systems are, as Fodor calls them, input systems, though surely not all systems are input systems.

While Fodor's modules are innately specified, it is essential to my understanding of perceptual systems that perceptual learning is possible, and this involves

---

12. I intend for this view to be compatible with the claim that perceptual systems might share hardware with nonperceptual systems. Thus, a visual imagery system might be a nonperceptual system even if it shares hardware with some visual systems (Kosslyn 1994; Kosslyn et al. 1995).

changes to the perceptual system.[13] Perceptual systems develop through the interaction of genetic and environmental factors, a combination of innateness and learning. Experience fine-tunes discriminatory abilities and supplies concepts and the information necessary to match them with high-level perceptual representations. And even though the basic functional architecture may be innately specified, it is well known that some architectural details can be modified as the result of experience (Wiesel and Hubel 1963). In fact, not only can learning modify existing systems but also it can result in new ones. Because some tasks are more easily done separately, a connectionist network trained to do two different tasks can sometimes split into two functionally distinct networks as the result of training (Rueckl et al. 1989). Thus, whole new systems can apparently arise from learning.[14] On Fodor's view, the only way to acquire a new module (a fortiori a new perceptual module) is to *grow* one; on my view, it is also possible in principle to *learn* one. Some systems might be so rigidly hardwired that they never change in response to experience, but I take this to be the exception rather than the rule. It is certainly not built into my understanding of a perceptual module.

Fodor claims that modules are introspectively opaque, that their interlevel representations are not accessible to consciousness. Perceptual modules may count as opaque for Fodor because he thinks of their outputs as nondoxastic percepts, rather than beliefs. Perceptual systems are quite clearly not introspectively opaque if they are viewed as those larger systems that yield beliefs as outputs; with respect to such systems, virtually any nondoxastic experiential state will be an interlevel representation (assuming such states are indeed representational). Even if we think of the perceptual systems as having fairly high-level nondoxastic states as their final outputs, Fodor's claim is dubious, since we do have access to lower level representations, or at least some of their features. Marr (1982) explains certain psychophysical phenomena by appeal to our conscious access to certain features of the raw primal sketch, an interlevel representation if ever there was one. However, perceptual modules are what we might call *inferentially* opaque. That is, their doxastic outputs are cognitively spontaneous in BonJour's (1985) sense: they are not the result of an introspectible train of reasoning from earlier beliefs.[15] The only introspectibly accessible interlevel representations produced by perceptual systems are nondoxastic.

13. Whether my allowance for perceptual learning conflicts with Fodor's innateness constraint depends on just what Fodor means for innate specification to be. Some (e.g., Churchland 1988) have read modularity as precluding perceptual learning, though Fodor denies this.

14. In some cases of architectural change, especially the low-level architectural changes, as well as those occurring very early in ontogenesis, it is unclear whether it is experience per se or merely the environment that is doing the work, consequently, whether the phenomena in question involve learning or growth. Some prenatal wiring may be contingent on neural firing, for example, but this is presumably not a matter of learning, that is, *experience*-dependent change.

15. I mean that all—or nearly all—of their outputs are cognitively spontaneous. I am willing to accept a certain degree of vagueness in my account resulting from the fact that inferential opacity thus comes in degrees. This is unlikely to be of much practical consequence, since most systems seem to cluster at the extremes; they tend to be either such that all or very nearly all of their doxastic outputs are spontaneous, or such that none or very nearly none are.

The present understanding of perceptual systems is general enough that it applies to nonhuman perceptual systems as well, including some alien to us. Rattlesnakes and other pit vipers have temperature-sensing facial pits that give them a sort of three-dimensional "heat vision" that is sophisticated enough that they are able to hunt at night. Bats and dolphins have similar capacities for processing sound, as their echolocation abilities attest. Eels, alligators, and sharks all have perceptual modalities we lack. These capacities are underwritten by perceptual systems, and hosts of other perceptual systems are metaphysically possible even if unrealized in the actual world. Because my account of perceptual systems proceeds in nonphenomenological terms, it allows zombies to have perceptual systems as well. A creature could have perceptual systems in the present sense without there being anything it is like to be that creature, without the creature having anything that would count as *experiences* at all, and this seems to fit with the basic outlook of the cognitive sciences.

Which beliefs does PST count as perceptual beliefs? To begin with, it is clear that what gets counted as a perceptual belief or not is a belief token, rather than a proposition or a belief type. A belief token of the type 'it is raining' might be the output of a perceptual system, it might be the output of an inferential system, or it might just pop into one's head. Only in the first case would it be a perceptual belief. That said, there are certain propositions that are never the contents of the outputs of any of my perceptual systems, and other propositions that sometimes are. Let us call a proposition p a *perceptual proposition* for S at t iff p is a nomologically possible output of one of the perceptual systems of S at t. (The temporal index is meant to capture the fact that S's perceptual systems might change over time.)

What, then, are the perceptual propositions for normal people? I have provided part of the answer, and the remainder of the question is the empirical one of what beliefs the perceptual systems produce as output. The standard views in the empirical literature seem to suppose that propositions about chairs, desks, apples, and other entry-level categories, as well as their locations, colors, sizes, motions, and so on, but also more subordinate-level categories, like face identifications, individual objects, and the like, are all perceptual. 'There is something red in front of me', 'the book is on the desk', and 'Susan is wearing a blue shirt' are all the sorts of propositions that can be the outputs of the perceptual systems of normal people.

PST might have the result that superordinate category judgments (e.g., there is furniture nearby) are not actually perceptual judgments but are inferentially justified by judgments that are (e.g., there's a table nearby). Whether it does have this result depends on the empirical facts about the outputs of perceptual systems. If this is indeed a consequence of my view, I will take it to be an interesting finding, not particularly implausible, though not so obvious as to count in favor of my view.

It is crucial to my story that perceptual learning affects the outputs of perceptual systems, sometimes perhaps by resulting in new systems but often by altering the functions computed by existing systems. Expertise with a given domain has several well-known effects. One is that what counts as a subordinate-level category for ordinary people becomes an entry-level category for experts (Tanaka and Taylor 1991). This may very well translate into a difference in perceptual beliefs. Thus, where most people report seeing an airplane, the pilot reports seeing a DC-10. It is not implausible to think that the expert's visual systems differ from those of a nonexpert

by having more object models (the templates against which the high-level representations are matched in the final steps of identification). Thus, the belief that it is a
DC-10 might be a perceptual belief for the pilot and an inferential belief for the rest
of us. It is well known that chess experts are sensitive to the legality of chessboard
configurations (deGroot 1966), and there is reason to think that they use different
kinds of perceptual representations of board positions than do novices (Charness et
al. 2001). The beliefs of such experts about the legal status of a chessboard may very
well be the immediate outputs of their visual systems.

Perceptual learning is surely bounded and constrained, but in a way that is
impossible to delineate a priori. Churchland famously discusses a group of hypothetical properly trained perceivers, who, among other things, "do not observe the
western sky redden as the Sun sets. They observe the wavelength distribution of
incoming solar radiation shift towards the longer wavelengths (about 0.7×10^{-6} m)
as the shorter are increasingly scattered away from the lengthening atmospheric path
they must take as terrestrial rotation turns us slowly away from their source" (1979,
29). Though it is an empirical issue, I am doubtful of the nomological possibility of
such a scenario. It is important, however, to see exactly where the doubt lies.

One difference between Churchland and me is that his scenario is laid out in
terms of children being taught certain speech dispositions until the dispositions
become spontaneous. However, even if it is possible for children to be trained in
the way Churchland describes, this would not indicate a *perceptual* change. On
my view, the effect would not count as genuinely perceptual unless it occurred at
the level of the perceptual system and not merely at the level of spontaneous verbal reports. The latter would be a different kind of learning from perceptual learning, and I don't think we should classify its effects as altering the way they *see*; it
wouldn't change their perceptual beliefs but merely the way they spontaneously
reported these beliefs.

I am quite willing to grant—indeed, insist—that learning changes how/what
we see, in the sense that it changes what perceptual beliefs we are capable of.
Nonetheless, I want to reserve such a description for a particular kind of change, and
not just any old change that comes as a result of expertise and not just any change in
those beliefs that are caused by the stimulations of sense organs. It is an empirical
question as to which changes are perceptual and which are not, but my guess is that
in the end we will want to distinguish cases like the physicist "seeing" a proton in a
cloud chamber from cases like the histologist seeing an abnormal cell growth. As the
scare quotes indicate, I am predicting that it is not the output of the physicist's *visual*
system that has changed but some inferential capacity outside the visual system. In
the histologist's case, however, it is likely that the most important changes really
are changes to the outputs of the visual system; if so, the change is genuinely a
perceptual change.

It is impossible to provide an abstracted list of all and only perceptual beliefs.
This is partly because such a list can specify only types rather than tokens. More
important, even the list of perceptual propositions will vary from person to person
and will change over time even within an individual. Nonetheless, the account on
offer does fix a determinate set of perceptual propositions for any individual at a
time and implies that it is a relatively straightforward fact of the matter whether any

belief token is the output of a perceptual system or not, thus whether it is a perceptual belief or not.

2. The Plausibility of the Perceptual System Theory

I have tried to clarify what I mean by the claim that the perceptual beliefs are the ones that are produced by perceptual modules. But what reason is there for thinking that PST is true?

2.1. The "Grain Size" of Perceptual Beliefs

One initial reason for endorsing PST (the claim that a belief is a perceptual belief if and only if it is the output of a perceptual system) is that it gets the "grain size" right. The sorts of beliefs that are likely to be the outputs of the perceptual systems of normal humans are at the right level of generality for perceptual beliefs. They are beliefs about ordinary middle-sized physical objects—cups, tables, people, dogs, cats, cars, and the like—and some of their properties, such as spatial location, color, odor, and motion. Churchland's prophetic hopes notwithstanding, our perceptual systems do not currently deliver beliefs about the microstructural organization of objects or their mean molecular kinetic energy, just as they do not deliver beliefs about the historical or legal properties of objects (e.g., this coin was minted in Denver, is worth 25¢, and is mine).

The beliefs produced by the perceptual systems have a certain level of specificity and precision: generally, though not always, involving entry-level categorization. Here the individual variation is much more pronounced than elsewhere, but an ordinary person's perceptual systems will produce beliefs about cups, books, flowers, the identities of faces and voices, and the like. Superordinate category membership and extreme subordinate category membership must be inferred via some other system. When I look at my desk, I *see* pencils, a telephone, a computer mouse, and some paperclips. I *infer* that there are artifacts, that there are inorganic objects. I just discovered that my mechanical pencil is a Pentel P205, but it doesn't particularly *look* like that to me; I inferred it from the writing on the side. Similarly, I have the perceptual belief that it is a little below room temperature in this room (i.e., that is roughly the content of the output of my thermoceptive system); I look at a thermometer and *infer* that it is 65.3° F. Where individual differences are salient, PST gets the cases intuitively right. A decent mechanic can just *see* (a fortiori, perceptually believe) that a nut is a 17 mm nut; I have to either guess or figure it out by trying various wrenches. PST accounts for this by noting that the mechanic's perceptual systems produce identifications of nuts as 17 mm, whereas mine do not.

Some proponents of MSF have assumed the validity of a certain sort of test for nonbasicality: if one could cite the belief that p in (publicly) justifying one's belief that q, then the belief that q must be (partially) based on p and thus nonbasic (such a principle seems to be operative in Descartes, more explictly in Chisholm [1966, 1977]). An EOFist might be tempted to make a similar claim, though restricted to beliefs about physical objects. Thus, I believe that

(1) there is a coffee cup in front of me.

If pressed, I could defend this belief by appealing to my belief that

(2) there is in front of me a squat, upright, partly hollowed out cylinder with a curved vertical handle on its side.

My own view is that both beliefs are basic, in fact that both are perceptual beliefs (though perhaps the outputs of different perceptual systems). But someone may be tempted to invoke the test for nonbasicality just described and conclude that (1) is based at least in part on (2) and is therefore nonbasic.

One problem with this line of reasoning is that it is very unlikely that it could actually be adopted by a defender of EOF. If the fact that I can appeal to p to defend my belief that q indicates the nonbasicality of the belief that q, *when the belief that* p *is a physical object belief*, then why not in general? But the general principle—that if I can appeal to p in defending my belief that q, then the belief that q is nonbasic— leads quickly to MSF, for I can always invoke beliefs about my own mental states to defend any perceptual belief.

Second, the principle under consideration has little or no intrinsic merit. The fact that I could appeal to p in defending q shows at most that the belief that p bolsters my justification for q, not that the former is necessary for the prima facie justification of the latter. (Even then, what is shown is merely that the one belief *could* bolster the justification of the other, not that it actually *does*.) But there is nothing in the definition of basicality to preclude such bolstering. A basic belief is one that doesn't require evidential relations to any other beliefs for its justification, not one that couldn't admit of such evidential relations.

Most important, there is little or no reason to think that the beliefs I could actually appeal to in defending some higher level perceptual belief are going to be sufficient for its justification anyhow. Consider again Chisholm's description of face recognition:

In reply to the question, "What is your justification for counting it as evident that it is Mr. *Smith* whom you see?" a reasonable man would [respond with] something like this: "(It is evident that:) Mr. Smith is a tall man with dark glasses; I see such a man; no one else satisfying that description would be in *this* room now…etc." (1982a, p. 81; italics and ellipsis in original)

Chisholm must intend for the ellipsis to do a great deal of work, for the beliefs actually cited here do very little to justify the belief that it's Mr. Smith. However, it is doubtful that the ellipsis could be filled in with low-level perceptual beliefs that are at the same time sufficient to justify the belief that it's Smith. If 'Smith' or some other definite description known by the agent to denote Smith were used, then it might work—for example, 'there is a man who looks exactly like Smith'—but this is at best a temporary solution, for there are lower level beliefs the agent could appeal to if challenged on this claim. Yet it is extremely doubtful that any collection of low-level beliefs about nose shape, skin tone, glasses, hair color, or the like would come anywhere near singling out a unique individual, like Smith. This is true despite the fact that we can and sometimes do cite such low-level features in defending our perceptual beliefs. So it is not the case that if I can cite my belief that p in defending my belief that q then the former must make a positive and substantial contribution to the prima facie justification of the latter.

The point is not that the English language isn't rich enough to express the true contents of the low-level beliefs that would be required for face recognition, though this is obviously correct. The point is that the low-level beliefs, whether linguistically expressible or not, are insufficient for inferring the identity of the person, thus insufficient for the justification of the belief about the identity of the person. Chisholm offers the Smith story as an example of how a "reasonable man" would defend his beliefs; however, it is only victims of serious brain damage who actually form beliefs in this way. Prosopagnosics seem to have access to low-level features but, because their face-recognition systems are damaged, must resort to general-purpose inferential systems to try to identify faces.[16] Prosopagnosics can form beliefs about the identities of faces; they just can't use their face recognition systems to do so, and this is why they are so singularly bad at it. All they have to go on are the low-level perceptual beliefs delivered by the other perceptual systems and some general-purpose reasoning and memory systems.[17]

Yet we are presumably no different from prosopagnosics in this respect: the reason we can identify faces visually is not that we are better at inferring identity from low-level features but that we have face-recognition systems. But if I can't infer identity from the low-level features, then my beliefs about the low-level features aren't sufficient for the justification of my belief about the identity of the face. So my belief about the identity of the face must not get its justification from these low-level beliefs. Since there is no other apparent source for the justification of this belief, it must be basic if justified at all. So we must accept a rather ill-motivated skepticism or allow that face recognition yields basic beliefs.

Of course, if the beliefs about the identities of faces are basic, then many other beliefs will be, too, by parity of reasoning. It would be odd to claim that my belief that Susan is here is basic but my belief that there's a coffee cup on the table is not;

16. Compare Chisholm's epistemological reconstruction to an autobiographical anecdote of a self-described prosopagnosic:

I can recall one traumatic occasion when Mr. Strode, the principal, stuck his head out into the hall as I was passing and said, "Lois, if you're headed for the lunchroom, would you please ask Mrs. Romero to stop by my office for a moment?"

Mrs. Romero was my math teacher. She had brown hair and glasses. Miss Jacobis, my science teacher, also had brown hair and glasses. When I reached the cafeteria, two women with glasses and brown hair were sitting together at one of the tables. Despite the fact that I had taken classes from them for a whole semester, I couldn't tell them apart. (Duncan 1982, p. 32)

Similarly a famous anecdote tells of a patient who identified a random stranger as his father on the grounds that the person had a hooked nose.

17. The standard view among cognitive neuropsychologists is that face recognition involves a special system that computes configural information holistically, as opposed to a more general purpose feature-based recognition-by-components system (Moscovitch et al. 1997; Peterson and Rhodes 2003).

ordinary perceptual beliefs about desks and books and dogs and cats will be classified as basic for similar reasons.

So there is a class of beliefs that, for purely epistemological reasons, we want to treat as perceptual beliefs with the attendant epistemological status of basicality. This class happens to be coextensive, so far as we can at present tell, with a psychologically individuated class of beliefs: the outputs of perceptual systems.

2.2. Perception and Ungrounded Justified Belief

This last argument is reminiscent in obvious ways of the earlier arguments concerning sensationless perception and the sensation-perception gap. The main problems for experientialism involved its claim that perceptual beliefs were based on experiential states; many of the arguments against experientialism shared the claim that there are instances of justified perceptual belief where the agent lacks an experiential state that could serve to evidentially justify the belief. (This was for a variety of reasons: because the agent was a zombie, because the gap between the sensation and the belief was too great, because *no* experiential state can evidentially justify belief, etc.)

Much of the initial plausibility of experientialism derives from the simple observation that not every token of a given belief type will be basic. Sometimes I believe that it's warm outside because I'm outside and can feel that it's warm; sometimes I believe it because my calendar says it's June, and I know that it's usually warm outside in June. Having a perceptual proposition for its content does not make a belief (token) justified or basic or perceptual. It is natural at this point to be reminded of the Ground Principle's requirement that every justified belief have a ground; it had some independent (though I think mostly spurious) plausibility and might solve the present problem if experiential states could serve as grounds. Beliefs with perceptual propositional content would be prima facie justified and basic and perceptual just in case they are based on a corresponding perceptual experiential state. Because not every token of a given belief type is thus based, not every token will be basic.

If this move fails, as I have argued it does, then we should consider the other obvious move: to make the justification, basicality, and perceptuality of the belief a matter of the causal history of the token. One of the central insights of reliabilism is to employ this strategy to account of the justification of beliefs. What most epistemologists had been trying to accomplish via evidentialist means could be done instead—perhaps better—by adverting not to bodies of evidence but to generative and/or sustaining causal processes. I am now suggesting that the same general move be used to account for the basicality and perceptuality of beliefs as well. If the genesis of the belief determines both its justification and its basicality, then we need not appeal to the Grounds Principle. There are other, nonevidentialist ways to ensure that some tokens of a belief type will be basic and some not; we can, for instance, allow the outputs of some but not all cognitive systems to be basic and hold that different systems can produce tokens of the same belief type.

I argued in chapter 3 for the Belief Principle. It follows from this principle that all basic beliefs are ungrounded: only beliefs can serve as grounds, but a basic belief is one that's not grounded by another belief; thus a basic belief is not grounded at all. This is not to say that basic beliefs are arbitrary, of course. To say that a belief is ungrounded is to say that it does not have an evidential justifier; it is not to say that it is groundless in any pejorative sense, that it is not justified. By holding that basic beliefs are ipso facto ungrounded, I can avoid the problems I raised for experientialism, which all had to do with the absence of adequate justifying grounds. If, as I insist, basic beliefs are necessarily ungrounded, the absence of justifying grounds does not even begin to pose a problem. Zombies can have justified perceptual beliefs, even though they lack any experiential states that might serve as grounds for these beliefs, for zombies can still have perceptual modules, and if these modules are reliable, their doxastic outputs will be justified perceptual beliefs.

Even if it is granted that beliefs can be justified though ungrounded, it is obvious that some ungrounded beliefs are unjustified. We will need something to do the work that experiential states were supposed to do for experientialism, to account for which ones are which. Reliability is part of the answer. The problem behind the isolation argument was that epistemically arbitrary beliefs are not justified, and basic beliefs look to be in special danger of being epistemically arbitrary. The experientialist solution is to posit a special kind of nondoxastic ground to supply the nonarbitrariness; I will invoke the causal history of the belief to achieve the same end by nonevidentialist means. Reliability is an important feature of this causal history, but it is only part of the story, for I deny that all reliably formed ungrounded beliefs are prima facie justified. The argument so far indicates that all *basic* beliefs are ungrounded, not that all justified beliefs are. In fact, I think that some beliefs do require grounds, and it follows from the Belief Principle that these grounds must be doxastic. If some beliefs require—doxastic—grounds, a view that the experientialist presumably shares, then having a theory of perceptual beliefs and basic beliefs more generally becomes that much more important.

Perceptual beliefs on my view, though ungrounded, are epistemically nonarbitrary in two important ways. First, their being the outputs of perceptual systems is constitutive of their being perceptual beliefs and therefore among the privileged class of beliefs that are capable of being justified even though ungrounded. Second, because the overarching view endorsed here is a species of reliabilism, I will hold that a perceptual belief is justified only if it is reliably caused.

Sensationless perception becomes intelligible on my view: perception requires perceptual beliefs and hence perceptual systems, but neither of these requires experiential states of any sort. Sensationless perception also becomes epistemologically innocuous for analogous reasons. The sensation-perception gap is no threat to the justification of perceptual beliefs, for their justification never had much to do with the sensation anyway. Cognitive neuroscientific worries about basing, due to worries about the causal relations between experiential states and the beliefs, are simply irrelevant here, since perceptual beliefs aren't required to be based on anything. Sellarsian worries fail to touch PST for the same sorts of reasons.

2.3. Perceptual Learning and Nonexperiential 'Looks'

By denying that perceptual beliefs are grounded on experiential states, it may seem as if I am neglecting to allow a sufficient epistemological role for how things *look*. In a way, of course, I am denying that looks have any epistemic significance, but only if 'looks' is understood in a certain, experientialist sense. The term 'looks' is notoriously ambiguous, and I take it as a sort of virtue of the present theory that it reveals yet another sense of 'looks'. I think that there is a nonexperiential sense of 'look' and that this is the one that is genuinely epistemically significant.

Chisholm (1957, 1966) famously distinguished between comparative and noncomparative uses of 'x looks F to S'. To believe that x looks—in the comparative sense—F to me is to believe that x looks to me the way that F things normally look.[18] Such a belief cannot be basic, for it depends on additional beliefs, namely, beliefs about how x looks and how F things normally look. Chisholm argues that at least some of these additional beliefs must involve 'look' in the noncomparative sense, as a description of the intrinsic character of the state, not its relation to other states; thus such beliefs may be basic. It is common to add to these two senses epistemic and/or doxastic senses of 'looks' (e.g., Alston 2002), but we must be careful to distinguish purely epistemic or doxastic senses from those that make an essential reference to an experiential state. According to the experiential-epistemic sense, x looks F to S iff the way x looks to S prima facie justifies S in believing that x is F; the purely epistemic sense allows that x looks F to S iff S is prima facie justified in believing that x is F. Similarly, according to the experiential-doxastic sense, x looks F to S iff the way x looks to S disposes S to believe that x is F, while according to the purely doxastic sense, x looks F to S iff S is disposed to believe that x is F.[19] The difference between the pure and the experiential senses is that the latter explicitly involve the agent's perceptual phenomenology. Thus, the reference to "the way x looks to S" is to be read as picking out a particular experiential state.

The comparative, noncomparative, experiential-doxastic, and experiential-epistemic senses of 'looks' are all experiential senses; they make essential reference to the agent's experiential states. They are literally about how things look. It is clear that the purely epistemic and doxastic senses of 'look', 'appear', and the like, on the other hand, are metaphorical and really have little if anything to do with looking or appearing. If I say that it looks as if the Republicans are going to win the upcoming election, I'm using either the purely epistemic or the purely doxastic sense; I am clearly not making any claims about *vision*.[20] What makes these metaphorical senses metaphorical, however, is *not* that they make no essential reference to visual *experience* but, rather, that they make no essential reference to vision. There is another sense of 'looks', one that makes no essential reference to experiential states either but is a literal sense nonetheless.

According to what I will call the "perceptual output sense" of 'looks', x looks F to S iff one of S's visual systems is outputting an identification of x as F (likewise,

---

18. In this discussion, 'x' occurs transparently and is not taken to have ontological import. Nor do I mean to be making any substantive commitments to the metaphysics of perception. This might have been more clear in the 'appeared-to' idiom, but 'looks' talk will be less obtrusive.

19. This is not, of course, intended to be an exhaustive classification of 'looks' locutions.

20. Of course, these metaphorical senses are generally compatible with the literal senses. If I say, in the purely doxastic sense, that the tower looks round from here, this doesn't rule out the tower's looking round to me in one or more of the experiential senses.

mutatis mutandis, for perceptual output senses of 'sounds', 'smells', etc.).[21] This is an important sense of 'looks', and it describes neither the intrinsic nature of an experiential state nor a relationally characterized fact about the experiential state. The other literal senses of 'looks' are all concerned with the experiential state, described in terms of its intrinsic nature, how it compares with other experiential states, what beliefs it tends to produce, or what beliefs it justifies. The perceptual output sense is divorced from all of this, for something can (perceptual-output-)look a certain way to an agent who has no visual experiences, and something can (perceptual-output-)look different ways to different agents who have the same visual experience.

To some extent, my introduction of a new sense of 'looks' is a matter of stipulation, but I think that the perceptual output sense is one that we all implicitly recognize, and experientialism derives a good deal of spurious plausibility from the general failure to explicitly recognize a nonexperiential sense of 'looks'. Perceptual learning provides a useful illustration, for learning frequently results in a change in how things look in the perceptual output sense, without necessarily changing how they look in any experiential sense. Now perceptual learning does sometimes affect what nondoxastic experiential states one has: what used to sound (in some experiential sense or other of the term) like an uninterrupted stream of phonemes now sounds (in this same sense) like a sequence of words, with pauses in between them that weren't heard before. This is such a striking and fascinating phenomenon that it is easy to lose sight of a point crucial to the present concerns, however: that learning need not and does not always affect the experiential state. Thus, two agents (or the same agent at different times) can have identical experiential states but different perceptual outputs. Consider a few representative examples:

(a) You and I have identical visual experiences, but the face looks like Joe to you and just looks like a face to me.

(b) Walking through a field, you and I come across a copperhead. I'm a professional herpetologist, and it looks like a copperhead to me, though only like a snake to you. (It also, of course, looks like a snake to me.) Nonetheless, you and I have identical visual experiences.

(c) I can now hear the difference between a melodic minor scale and a diminished scale; they sound quite different to me. Several years ago, they sounded the same as each other to me (i.e., I couldn't tell the difference), though neither sounds any different now than it ever did (i.e., the experiential state itself seems to be the same).

(d) X is an expert chicken sexer. Some chicks look male to X and some look female, even though the visual states do not differ in any articulable way, nor do they differ from those of a novice.

Here (c) and (d) are paradigm cases of what a psychologist would count as perceptual learning; (a) involves learning, but it differs from the more interesting kinds of perceptual learning in that it doesn't require repeated exposure and subsequent

---

21. I am not sure whether something's looking a particular way to me is necessarily something of which I am aware. If so, we can add the requirement that this identification is consciously available to S.

enhancement of discriminatory abilities; (b) is a sort of intermediate case, though I suspect it's closer to (c) and (d) than to (a).

In each case, the experiential states are the same, despite the fact that things *look* different. Consequently, there must be a nonexperiential sense of 'look'. This, I suggest, is the perceptual output sense. The claim that it *looks* like Joe to you but not me in (a) amounts to the claim that your face recognition system produces an 'it's Joe' output, while mine does not. Its looking like a copperhead to me but a snake to you in (b) is a matter of my visual system delivering the belief that there's a copperhead in our path, while yours delivers the belief that there's a snake in the path. To say that minor and diminished scales sound different to me, though they used to sound the same (c), is to say that my auditory system now yields identifications of diminished scales and of minor scales, where it used to output identifications of "dark-sounding" scales. And if the chicken sexer and the novice have identical experiential states, yet a particular chick looks male to the expert and not to the novice (d), then the best explanation for this is that the expert's visual system classifies distal stimuli as male or female, while the novice's does not.

Note that the sense of 'look' that is being evoked here is not a purely doxastic or purely epistemic sense. Nor is it in any way metaphorical. The examples crucially involve a particular sense modality. Even the experiential-doxastic and experiential-epistemic senses of 'look' are less strictly concerned with vision than the current examples. My current visual experience might dispose me to (justifiably) believe that I'm confronted with Bruce's favorite venomous reptile, but clearly it is only in a relatively extended and metaphorical sense that anything could *look* to me like Bruce's favorite venomous reptile. Even if the snake in (b) looks in an experiential-epistemic or experiential-doxastic sense like a copperhead, it also looks like a copperhead in some important, more restrictive sense of 'looks'. This is the perceptual output sense.

My argument requires only that cases (a)–(d) are possible, but I think a stronger claim can be supported. I think that cases like this are not only possible but also actual, and in fact quite common. Some of the cases might require a more careful formulation before this is at all obvious. In the face-recognition case, for instance, it is clear enough that faces don't look—experientially—any different on becoming familiar ones, but it is tempting to think that whatever learning occurs does so outside the perceptual system. If the belief glossed as 'it's Joe' is the belief that the person here *is named* 'Joe', then of course this is not the output of a perceptual system, and the learning involved does indeed take place outside the perceptual system. However, to count as a face-recognition system, the system must in some sense attribute identities to faces. Any minimal representation of an individual will suffice for this; the representation need not contain any other information about the individual but may function like one of the "instance units" of McClelland's (1981) famous Jets and Sharks network, which can acquire links to information about the person but contains no such information in itself.[22] To visually recognize or identify someone is not necessarily to be able to specify the person's name (or occupation or connection

---

22. This connectionist network consists of several groups of similar units, with mutually inhibitory connections within each group and mutually excitatory connections between units in different

to oneself, etc.), which presumably takes place outside the face-recognition system, but rather to activate some minimal representation of the individual. This must occur within the face-recognition system for it to count as a face-recognition system.

What, though, is my evidence for thinking that the experiences are the same in the sorts of examples under discussion? In the chicken sexing case, it is mostly conjecture, based on the fact that chicken sexers are unable to specify what cues they are using. They will certainly claim that males "look different" from females, but it would be question-begging to infer from this alone that males cause different experiential states than females. In the other cases, I have introspection to go on, in diachronic, within-agent versions of the relevant sorts of cases. Introspection is a dubious source of information about the workings of the mind, but here the issue is how things seem, and it is unlikely that we will get more reliable information from some other source. And cases (a)–(c) represent the way it seems to me that things seem to me. The people I met yesterday don't look (experientially) different than they did yesterday when I saw them for the first time, though now I recognize them and then I didn't. Copperheads don't look any different to me now than they used to, but now they look copperheady, and before they just looked snaky. Likewise with the musical/auditory case, and it seems that similar phenomena occur in other modalities as well. Developing a more discriminating palate does not, as far as I can introspect, alter the gustatory qualia in the way that, say, quitting smoking does; it alters one's psychological responses—including one's classificatory and discriminatory responses—to the relevant stimuli.

One might insist that the experiential aspects do change in the kinds of cases at issue. Even if this is true, it is clear that they change very little, not enough to fully account for the drastic change in classificatory capacity. These sorts of cases are, after all, quite different from the case of learning a new language. Even if copperheads somehow produce in me a different experiential state than they used to, this experiential difference is too slight to amount to much; the difference that really matters and that perceptual learning produces is the higher level change in identification capacities. If distal stimuli were suddenly to begin causing in me the same kinds of experiential states they do in an ornithologist, I doubt I would notice the difference. But even if I did, without an accompanying change in identifications (i.e., a change in the doxastic/classificatory outputs of my perceptual systems), there would be no epistemologically significant sense in which some object suddenly now *looks* like a two-year-old ivory-billed woodpecker.

I should also point out that my claim is a claim about the visual (or auditory, etc.) experience, not about the whole subjective experience of the agent. Patients with Capgras delusion continue to recognize close acquaintances but have the unshakeable conviction that these people are actually imposters; they insist that the person in front of them looks exactly like Mom but isn't. Now perhaps there is something about the experiential states of Capgras patients that is different than it was before the onset of

---

groups. One group has a number of age units (each unit representing some age); another has a number of name units; there are units for gang affiliation, occupation, marital status, and so on. Each individual unit is a minimal representation of the individual person in the sense that it carries no information in itself about that person. But this individual node has excitatory connections to that person's age, name, marital status, occupation, and the like.

the syndrome; perhaps they no longer experience a sensation of familiarity, and this is why the person seems to be an imposter. This now-absent "sensation" of familiarity (if it deserves to be called that), however, is not a component of the visual experience. After all, the patient's visual system is by all accounts intact, and the patient insists that the person looks exactly like Mom. In addition, it is hard to understand how one could have a visual experience of familiarity; familiarity, after all, doesn't *look* like anything. The sensation of familiarity is one that (normally) accompanies the visual experience, but it is not a part of that experience. So there is no obstacle to the claim that even Capgras patients have visual experiences just like ours.[23]

Again, it is worth repeating that all that's really needed here is that cases like (a) through (d) are possible, and they clearly are. In fact, far more extreme possibilities obtain. Suppose two *zombies* (in the proprietary sense of the previous chapter) are walking through a field. A snake in the grass reflects photons into the eyes of both zombies, activating their perceptual systems, all of which produces in one of them the cognitively spontaneous belief that there's a snake, and in the other (a professional herpetologist zombie) the cognitively spontaneous belief that there's a copperhead. The latter zombie would be inclined, despite the fact that she has no experiential states, to say that it looked copperheady to her. And, I submit, she would be right. A slight air of paradox is bound to still attend the claim that things look certain ways to zombies or that there are nonexperiential senses of 'sound', 'taste', and the like. This air is dispelled, however, by the essential role of perceptual systems. To say that *x* looks—in this sense of 'looks'—red to me, to repeat, is to say that the belief that *x* is red (or something very much like a belief) is the output of one of my perceptual systems, in particular, one of my visual systems. There is nothing metaphorical about this use of 'look'. Even subtracting out the experiential component, there is a vast difference between 'that looks like Joe' and 'it looks like someone has broken into your house and stolen your VCR'. When I say that something sounds like a diminished scale, I don't (typically) mean merely that I think it's a diminished scale or that I have some reason to think it is a diminished scale, and I am not (or not merely) reporting the contents of my experience. I am describing a belief, but a certain kind of belief, one that has a very tight connection with perception, in particular, audition. That connection is that the belief is the output of an auditory system.

Finally, crucially, this perceptual output sense of 'looks' is epistemically significant. You are justified in believing that Joe's here because the face looks—in the perceptual output sense—like Joe to you; I am justified in believing that a diminished scale is being played because it sounds—in the perceptual output sense—like a diminished scale to me. If it hadn't (perceptual-output-)sounded that way, I wouldn't be justified in believing it was a diminished scale.

While the experientialist and I will agree that its looking copperheady (at least partially) justifies me in believing there's a copperhead, we will mean very different things by this claim. The experientialist's appeals to looks are appeals to nondoxastic experiential states; the claim is that there is a copperheady experiential state, which is different from mere snaky experiential states, and the copperheady experience

---

23. For a more detailed defense of these claims and a discussion of clashing intuitions from other introspectors (e.g., Kelly 1999; Siegel 2006; Siewert 1998), see my (2005) article.

grounds my belief that there is a copperhead. This is implausible in light of the present cases. On my own view, however, how things look is not to be construed as something distinct from and causally antecedent to the perceptual belief; it is not a ground on which the belief is based. To say that the look justifies the belief is merely to say that the belief's being the output of a perceptual system is (a part of) what justifies the belief.[24]

The notion of justification at issue in the two formulations is also quite different. Whereas experiential looks are intended to serve as evidential justifiers for beliefs, my nonexperiential looks serve as nonevidential justifiers. My belief that there is a copperhead is not *based on* that belief's being the output of a perceptual system. The causal history of the belief justifies the belief, but it does not ground it, any more than reliability does.

Not only is the perceptual output sense of 'look' and its ilk an epistemically significant sense but also it is more epistemically relevant, or at least more directly epistemically relevant, than any experiential sense. The present cases show that while there is no necessary or even very close connection between nondoxastic experiential states and prima facie justified perceptual beliefs, there may yet be a tight, and perhaps even necessary, connection between perceptual system outputs and prima facie justified perceptual beliefs.

Among the arguments for experientialism is what we might call the "Looks Principle": our perceptual beliefs are epistemically justified, at least in part, because of how things look, sound, taste, smell, or feel to us. The intuitive appeal of this principle can lend a specious plausibility to experientialism. It is natural to take the Looks Principle as claiming that perceptual beliefs receive their justification from the corresponding experiential states. This latter claim, however, does not follow from the Looks Principle, for the Looks Principle, as stated, does not distinguish between experiential looks and perceptual output looks. Thus I can accept the Looks Principle without accepting any kind of experientialism.

2.4. Percept Experientialism Revisited

I have argued that the perceptual output sense of 'look' allows PST to accommodate the view that perceptual beliefs are justified at least partly in virtue of how things look. In so arguing, have I not conceded too much to PE (percept experientialism)? Is the view I am endorsing not itself a version of PE? There is at least one kind of argument that might suggest it is.

The very notion of perceptual output looks opens up a new line of reasoning to the proponent of PE. In chapter 3, I suggested that percepts and beliefs be identified with representations. In the typical case, it is numerically the same representation to which I stand in both the percept and the belief relation, so the percept is not in such cases numerically distinct from the belief. However, the experientialist could insist that percepts and beliefs be identified not with particular representations but with the

---

24. The look only partly justifies the belief on my view because I hold that the belief must also be reliably caused; its looking to me as if *p* is not sufficient for my being prima facie justified in believing that *p*.

instantiated relations to those representations. The functional relations are, as I have conceded, different; thus the token instantiations of those relations are numerically distinct. My standing in the percept relation to S at t is distinct from my standing in the belief relation to S at t, even though the relata (myself and S) are numerically the same; in fact, my standing in the belief relation is caused by my standing in the percept relation. Thus the distinctness of the percept and the belief, and even causal relations between them, can be preserved.

PE could now even appropriate my PST here to lend substance to this line of response, claiming that having a representation of p as the output of a perceptual system is simply what it is to have the percept that p. PST could thus be invoked to explicate the percept relation. What I have said about the epistemic status of the outputs of perceptual systems could be accepted but now framed in terms of percepts and their epistemological consequences. My belief that p is justified because a representation with the content that p is the output of one of my perceptual systems; that is, my belief that p derives its justification from my having the percept that p. In this way, PE could accept the bulk of my proposal, but as a version of PE rather than as an alternative to it.

I think that the view I am articulating here on behalf of the experientialist is a very plausible view. This, however, is because it is actually my own view, and it is plausible largely because it is not genuinely a version of experientialism, despite its use of the term 'percept'. Adopting the present proposal would amount to the experientialist's coming over to my side, not my going over to hers.

'Percept' is a term of art, and I have no objection to its being used in the way just now suggested. But if it is, then my earlier comments about perceptual output looks apply to percepts as well, most notably, (a) that "percepts" are not experiential states—zombies can have them, after all, and zombies by definition lack experiential states—and (b) that they serve as nonevidential justifiers, rather than as grounds. Experientialism, however, is the view that experiential states serve as grounds, so the view now on the table is not in fact an experientialist view. The argument just given for (b) is now complicated by the fact that percepts are construed as relations instead of representations. Nonetheless, it seems clear that if the only thing that justifies my belief is the fact that this belief is the output of a perceptual system—most obviously in a case where this fact is completely beyond my ken—this belief would be ungrounded. I might lack introspective access to anything except this belief; if the belief is still justified by the percept (i.e., by the belief's having the causal history it does), this is a matter of nonevidential justification. One could use the term 'percept' in the way suggested, but this would offer no assistance to the percept experientialist.

3. Perceptual Beliefs and Basic Beliefs

The examples from section 2.3 strongly suggest not only that the outputs of perceptual systems are prima facie justified but also that they are basic. Part of the argument for this is the one already given concerning face recognition in section 2.1, but the view has a good deal of independent intuitive plausibility. Again, this is brought out well by the perceptual output sense of 'looks'. Suppose you have just read and memorized the following description of copperheads from a field guide:

> A *coppery-red head* and an hourglass pattern. Viewed from above, the dark chestnut crossbands are wide on the sides and narrow at the center of the back. Small, dark spots are frequently present between crossbands. Dark, rounded spots at sides of belly. Scales *weakly keeled*; anal *single*; a single row of scales under tail, at least anteriorly. (Conant and Collins 1998, p. 397)

You notice a number of these features, and with this description in mind, you conclude that the thing before us is a copperhead. And perhaps you're justified in this belief. But if so, your justification is very different from mine. I don't notice these features, nor do I appreciate their diagnostic significance—it just looks like a copperhead to me. Intuitively, your belief is inferentially justified, while mine is basic. Perhaps my visual system uses similar cues (though probably not); to find out, we would have to do experiments involving painting over the lateral spots and the like and find out whether the object still looked like a copperhead. In any case, *I* don't use such cues; I wouldn't have been able to come up with such a list without having a specimen or a field guide in front of me.

In this way, my belief that it's a copperhead, unlike yours, is similar to my belief that it's a snake: both are cognitively spontaneous outputs of perceptual systems, and both are, intuitively, basic beliefs. This is plausible even if the more general belief is more highly justified than the latter. My copperhead judgment depends in a negative way on my snake judgment, whereas yours depends positively. If I were to (consciously) cease to believe that it's really a snake, that would undermine my belief that it's a copperhead, but your belief that it's a copperhead is based on your belief that it's a snake (with a certain pattern of coloration).

I have concentrated on a small handful of examples, but similar cases are legion. My brother can identify tree species from several hundred yards away, in the winter, and he can say little more about it than that the tree looked like a white oak. The different varieties of orchid all have a certain look to those who know how to identify them, but they don't cause different experiential states in these people than they do in the rest of us. Similar points could be made for the ability of some people but not others to identify at a glance certain makes of car or certain geological formations, to identify voices of familiar callers or singers, or to recognize various types of perfume. I have concentrated on relatively fine-grained subordinate-level category judgments, because these are the ones where the reader is most likely to be able to remember acquiring an analogous perceptual capacity. But the same points hold for what are for all of us entry-level categories like *book*, *cup*, *desk*, *dog*, *hand*, and the like. Some of these are more like faces than like diminished scales, but all seem to require at least minimal learning.

I have focused on cases where learning does not affect the experiential state because I wanted to draw attention to an important disconnect between how things look in an experiential sense and how things look in a nonexperiential sense. I also wanted to point out differences between agents regarding which of their beliefs are basic, which could not be traced to differences in experiential states. Yet cases where learning also affects the experiential state are certainly no trouble for my view. In these cases, it is especially likely that the relevant changes have occurred within the perceptual system, and the output beliefs are still intuitively basic and intuitively perceptual.

All of these cases support the central contention of this chapter: that a belief is a perceptual belief just in case it is the output of a perceptual system. It is a largely empirical issue which beliefs are perceptual beliefs, because it is an empirical issue which beliefs are produced by perceptual systems. I have made some informed guesses here, but the sciences may prove me wrong. As things now stand, however, is looks as though the sciences will specify the outputs of our perceptual systems in such a way that the class of such outputs is roughly coextensive with the class of beliefs we intuitively thought were perceptual beliefs. I am betting on the empirical research discovering enough, but not too many, perceptual beliefs. There will be some, but there will be plenty of nonperceptual beliefs as well.

Finally, PST is the claim that the doxastic outputs of perceptual systems are perceptual beliefs, where part of what this entails is that they are basic. Although my primary concerns are justification and perceptual belief, it is a short step from this to a theory about claims of the form 'S sees that x is F'. For it seems quite plausible that S sees that x is F iff S has the visual belief that x is F, and this belief satisfies whatever the requirements are for knowledge. Although I don't propose to try to say what those requirements are here, it is worth noting that PST can be used as a core element of a theory of perception (S sees that x is F) and not just of perceptual belief.

5

Perception, Clairvoyance,
and Reliability

Standard varieties of reliabilism allow beliefs to be justified even though ungrounded; what the Grounds Principle denies, the reliabilist warmly embraces. There are some well-known counterexamples to reliabilism that seem to show that this is a problem for the theory. I want to argue that the real issue, however, is basicality rather than groundedness. The counterexamples to reliabilism stem not from its rejection of the Grounds Principle but from its insufficient attention to nonbasic beliefs.

I stated at the beginning of the last chapter that the overarching epistemology I endorse is a kind of reliabilism but one that differs from standard versions of reliabilism in explicitly insisting on a distinction between basic and nonbasic beliefs. Although reliability is sufficient for the prima facie justification of *basic* beliefs, I want to endorse a view I will call "Inferentialist Reliabilism," one that requires inferential support for nonbasic beliefs. A first approximation is as follows:

> (IR) (i) a basic belief is prima facie justified iff it is the result of a reliable cognitive process; and (ii) a nonbasic belief is prima facie justified iff it is the result of a reliable *inferential* process, the inputs to which are themselves (prima facie) justified.

IR is clearly a form of (externalist) foundationalism; applied recursively, IR entails that every justified belief is either basic or derives its justification from a set of basic beliefs. Most reliabilist theories are versions of foundationalism, though unlike IR they tend to satisfy the definition of foundationalism in a degenerate way, as I will soon argue, by making all beliefs basic.

To flesh out IR and to make it more than merely degenerately foundationalist, we will also need an account of which beliefs are basic and which are nonbasic. That, of course, is where we are eventually headed; it is the subject of the next chapter. Even without that piece yet in place, IR is important, for it provides an answer to a famous class of objections to reliabilism that purport to show that reliability is not sufficient for the justification of beliefs.

1. Simple Reliabilism and the Norman/Truetemp Objections

The objections I want to address here are aimed at an unadorned version of relia-bilism, though the general sentiment is that they affect a larger group of theories as well. Despite its prevalence in the literature, I'm not sure that anyone has ever inten-tionally defended the following view, which I'll call "Simple Reliabilism":

(SR): A belief is prima facie justified iff it is the result of a reliable cognitive process.

SR is a simpler view than the one defended in Goldman's first, seminal paper on reliabilism (1979), but it is already a significant improvement over an even simpler view, which we might call "Kindergarten Reliabilism":

(KR): A belief is justified iff it is the result of a reliable cognitive process.

One problem with KR is that it fails utterly to handle epistemic defeat. Vision is gener-ally reliable, but I currently happen to know that I'm in a hall of mirrors. We certainly wouldn't want to say that my reliably formed belief that there's a person in front of me is justified. Such examples pose no problem for SR, which can maintain that the belief is merely prima facie justified but defeated by my knowledge that I'm surrounded by mirrors. (The reliabilist may prefer to claim that what defeats the target belief is the *process* in virtue of which my belief that I'm in a hall of mirrors is justified.)

I will assume in what follows that any reliabilist theory worth discussing is first and foremost a theory about prima facie, not ultima facie, justification. Of course, one might cash out defeat in reliabilist terms as well (e.g., Goldman 1979) and combine the two to form a theory of ultima facie justification, but the heart of the theory is the theory of prima facie justification. Hence, I will often omit the 'prima facie' qualifier in what follows, though it will be assumed throughout. It will often appear as a reminder, and whenever I have ultima facie justification in mind, I will explicitly say so.

The earliest versions of the objection currently under investigation are due to BonJour (1980, 1985). After three objections to KR, objections where the agent in question clearly has defeaters for the intuitively unjustified belief, he offers the now famous case of Norman:

Norman, under certain conditions which usually obtain, is a completely reliable clairvoyant with respect to certain kinds of subject matter. He possesses no evidence or reasons of any kind for or against the general possibility of such a cognitive power or for or against the thesis that he possesses it. One day Norman comes to believe that the President is in New York City, though he has no evidence for or against this belief. In fact the belief is true and results from his clairvoyant power under circumstances in which it is completely reliable. (1985, p. 41)

Intuitively, Norman's belief is not ultima facie justified, and the case is so laid out as to render it intuitively unlikely that he has any defeaters. Thus the belief is not even prime facie justified, and thus the case is a counterexample to SR.

Lehrer (1990b) offers a similar though in some ways more compelling example. Mr. Truetemp has had a device surgically implanted in his head without his knowledge: a tempucomp, which registers the ambient temperature and produces very precise and reliable beliefs about the temperature. He has no information one way or the other about this tempucomp but simply unreflectively accepts its outputs. His resulting belief that the ambient temperature is 104° (Lehrer was living in southern Arizona when he wrote this) is, intuitively, unjustified. Yet the process was stipulated to be reliable; therefore, reliability is not sufficient for even prima facie justification; therefore, SR is false.

Though I find the Truetemp example more convincing than the Norman example, the latter is more standardly discussed, and I'll refer to any such example as an instance of "the clairvoyance objection." Such examples seem to show that reliability is not by itself sufficient for justification. Perhaps they show even more than that. Perhaps they show that every justified belief is based on some justifying ground. Lehrer and BonJour (that is, BonJour circa 1985) seem to think that they also show that every belief requires for its justification a metabelief: a belief to the effect that the first-order belief is reliably formed, highly likely to be true, formed in a trustworthy manner, or the like. Sosa (1991) calls the clairvoyance objection the "meta-incoherence problem," a phrase that implies a similar diagnosis. My own view is that the clairvoyance objection is a sound objection to SR but that it does not serve the more ambitious aims of establishing the Grounds Principle and certainly not a general metabelief requirement.

One possible line of response to the clairvoyance objection is simply to concede that SR has counterintuitive results but to insist that Norman and Truetemp really are nonetheless justified and that SR is still acceptable. Some have argued that such intuitions have little or no role to play in serious epistemological theorizing (e.g., Kitcher 1992; Kornblith 2002). I actually have some sympathy for this approach, but it is not the approach I will take, at least not at this point. I do have the intuition that Norman is unjustified and an even stronger intuition that Truetemp is unjustified, and I want a theory that captures these intuitions. If in the end there are good reasons for thinking we *shouldn't* have these intuitions, then that is another matter, though it is hoped that these reasons will have something to do with why we have these particular intuitions, rather than simply proceeding from a blanket dismissal of intuitions tout court.[1]

Instead, I want to respond to the objection by abandoning SR in favor of IR, which is immune to the clairvoyance objection.

---

1. I will have a bit to say later, in chapter 6, section 2, about revisionist epistemology, though I won't be adopting either Kitcher's or Kornblith's approach.

2. Clairvoyance and Basicality

How does IR handle the clairvoyance objection? Recall that IR does not claim that reliability is sufficient for justification; it holds that reliability is sufficient for the justification of a belief only if that belief is basic. But IR also allows that there are nonbasic beliefs, and mere reliability is explicitly not sufficient for the justification of these. Since IR does not claim that reliability is sufficient for justification, Norman- and Truetemp-type cases cannot serve as counterexamples. Unlike SR, IR does not imply that Norman or Truetemp is justified.

2.1. Underspecification and the "Clairvoyance Challenge"

One might reasonably think that there's something cheap, something evasive, about this response; it can be argued at this point that IR avoids the clairvoyance objection only by failing to offer a full epistemology. IR doesn't imply that Truetemp is justified, but it doesn't imply that he *isn't*, either. Since IR per se says nothing about which beliefs are basic, it says nothing about which beliefs can be justified in virtue of mere reliability, and this may very well be the only reason it is not subject to the clairvoyance objection. IR says too little about what justification is to be susceptible to counterexample, but this is hardly a theoretical virtue.

I hope the reader does feel dissatisfied by this response to the clairvoyance objection. SR loses to IR in these cases only because SR is ambitious enough to offer necessary and sufficient conditions for justification, and absent necessary and sufficient conditions for basicality, IR does not do this. This is a genuine shortcoming on the part of IR, but it is a shortcoming that is shared by many other theories, which is why I am addressing the issue before having fleshed out my proposed theory of basicality. The problem that has just arisen for IR arises for several other epistemologies as well, though this is almost never noticed. The problem is that even if IR is immune to clairvoyance objections, it is open to a "clairvoyance challenge," the challenge being to actually solve the problem rather than simply avoid it by underspecification. The challenge is to offer a theory of basicality that doesn't invite Norman- or Truetemp-style counterexamples and also to embed that theory of basicality in an overall epistemology that implies that Norman and Truetemp are *unjustified*. This, however, is a challenge for *any* version of foundationalism, not just reliabilist versions.

Pollock and Cruz (1999), for example, offer a fairly standard experientialist version of EOF. They provide a list of sufficient conditions for (prima facie) justification (and in the process, sufficient conditions for basicality) of the following sort:

- *x*'s looking red to S is a reason for S to believe that *x* is red.
- S's seeming to remember *p* is a reason for S to believe that *p*.

Their theory also avoids the clairvoyance objection only by underspecification. Surely there is a sense in which it seems to Norman that the president is in New York. Why isn't this enough to justify Norman's belief that the president is in New York? Truetemp has, as noted in chapter 3, a certain experiential state. Why doesn't that give him a prima facie reason to believe that it's 104°? Pollock and

Cruz's theory doesn't imply that Norman and Truetemp are justified, but, like IR, it doesn't imply that they aren't, either. Pollock and Cruz offer a few sufficient conditions for basicality, but to respond fully to the clairvoyance challenge, a theory also needs to provide necessary conditions as well. It needs to offer a solution to what I called in chapter 1 the delineation problem.

We can come up with other examples quite easily. I have an overwhelming, visceral feeling of dread and conclude that something bad is going to happen. The nondoxastic and the doxastic states seem to be about as closely linked as in standard perceptual cases, though surely we would not want to say that my pessimistic belief is prima facie justified. The reliabilist has an easy response here in terms of reliability, but the internalist experientialist will need to find some principled means of excluding the belief in question from the class of basic beliefs, perhaps by excluding the nondoxastic state in question from the class of potential justifiers.

I argued in chapter 1 that any version of foundationalism needs a full theory of basicality anyway. There are two reasons for reiterating this here. The first is that it helps to show that the Norman-type cases really have very little to do with reliability per se. Internalist EOF makes no mention of reliability and is subject to exactly the same clairvoyance worries as IR is (though admittedly not the same as SR). The second reason is that it helps to emphasize that the real issue here is basicality. Internalist EOF will want to respond to the clairvoyance objection in the way that MSF surely will: by denying that Norman's belief is a basic belief and pointing out that he has no other beliefs that would support it. The best move for the experientialist here is to be clear about what kinds of experiential states can serve as justifiers, what counts as such a state, and what the contents of these states can be. My nonexperientialist theory will have to get at basicality in a different way, one foreshadowed by the discussion of perceptual belief in the previous chapter, but the point is that if internalist EOF can deal with Norman by arguing that his belief is unjustified because it is nonbasic, then a reliabilist EOF should be able to do so as well. This, of course, is just what IR does.

It is not just EOF that has to contend with the clairvoyance challenge; MSF does as well, and even certain versions of coherentism might have to. We saw in chapter 1 that the problems that arose for EOF regarding the basic beliefs have close analogues for MSF. Where EOF had to say whether my belief that there's a dog is basic, MSF had to specify whether my belief that I'm appeared to dogly is basic. For the standard—nondoxastic—versions of MSF, it is the same entity doing the evidential work as it would be for EOF: the agent's being appeared to dogly; the only difference relevant to the present issue is which belief gets basically justified by this state. But then the same issues arise for the clairvoyance belief. Whereas EOF has to explain why Truetemp's belief that it's 104° outside is unjustified, MSF has to explain why he's unjustified in his belief that he's appeared to 104°-ly. If one holds that this belief *is* justified, we will need an explanation of why Truetemp is not justified in inferring from this that it's 104°.

This last point leads to a difficulty even for Lehrer's own coherentism. Mr. Truetemp, like the rest of us, presumably accepts an instance of Lehrer's Trustworthiness Principle; that is, Truetemp accepts that he is trustworthy in what he accepts. Lehrer claims that our acceptance of our own trustworthiness plays a crucial role in the justification of our beliefs (1990b, pp. 121ff.), but then why isn't Truetemp justified in his belief that it's 104° outside? He needs a metabelief, perhaps, but he has one: he's trustworthy in what he accepts. The answer must be that he needs a more specific metabelief than this, but now Lehrer faces the unenviable task of having to specify the relevant metabelief, and it is unlikely that he could do so in a principled manner without first developing a general theory of induction. For my perceptual belief that there's a coffee cup nearby to be justified, is it enough that I accept my general cognitive trustworthiness, or must I have metabeliefs specifically about the trustworthiness of my perceptual faculties? my visual faculties? in these lighting conditions? on Tuesdays? concerning pottery? Once again, we have a theory that doesn't imply that Norman and Truetemp *are* justified, but only by underspecification, since it doesn't imply that they *aren't*, either. So IR seems to be in quite good company so far.

2.2. Perception and Other Cognitive Abilities

The parallel between IR and other theories, especially other versions of EOF, is an illustrative one. I want to press this a bit further by incorporating into IR the theory of perceptual belief from chapter 4. Recall that the claim endorsed there was a perceptual system theory of perceptual belief (PST): a belief is a perceptual belief iff it is the output of a perceptual system. I think that perceptual systems constitute a natural kind (a cognitive neuroscientific kind), and I want to leave it up to the sciences to empirically discover exactly what perceptual systems are, and what perceptual systems there are, without a priori interference from philosophy. Nonetheless, I offered a characterization of perceptual systems in chapter 4, based on what I currently know about what science currently knows. All of this is subject to emendation.

Let us press on in the meantime, taking the characterization from the previous chapter and codifying it as a tentative definition of a perceptual system and thus of perceptual belief. Then, since I insist that perceptual beliefs are ipso facto basic, we will have a relatively precisely stated sufficient condition for basicality (though, of course, not yet a necessary condition), and we can see how it fares vis-à-vis the clairvoyance objection. The two features of a perceptual system most prominent in chapter 4 were these:

(a) Its lowest level inputs are energy transductions across sense organs.
(b) None of the inputs to any of its subsystems are under the voluntary control of the larger organism.

Yet, I also mentioned two other features, which will come to be quite important:

(c) It's inferentially opaque (i.e., its doxastic outputs are cognitively spontaneous in BonJour's [1985] sense).
(d) The system has developed as the result of some combination of learning and innate constraints.

(As mentioned in chapter 4, I mean for wholly hardwired systems to count as having this last feature; they constitute a limiting case where the contribution of learning is nil.) Consequently, we can define for the present purposes a perceptual system as any cognitive system that satisfies (a)–(d). Not only is this the picture that we get from cognitive science but it is also fairly intuitive, even though probably far more precise than our ordinary folk understanding of perceptual system or perceptual belief.

We can add this theory of perceptual systems to IR to get the view that reliability is sufficient for the justification of a belief that is the output of a system that satisfies (a)–(d), but perhaps not sufficient for the justification of other beliefs. Again, this parallels the degree of underspecification typical of foundationalist theories more generally; we have sufficient but not necessary and sufficient conditions for basicality and for prima facie justification.[2]

The resulting theory, which I will continue to refer to as inferentialist reliabilism (IR), handles the clairvoyance objection by noting that neither Norman's nor Truetemp's belief is the output of a perceptual system. The beliefs may be the results of cognitive systems, and systems that are similar in many important respects to perceptual systems, but the systems are not perceptual systems.

We can assume that the capacities are manifested in the existence of actual cognitive systems, in the sense of the previous chapter; otherwise, it is clear that IR yields no counterintuitive implications. Still, the intuitive force of the objections depends on how we are understanding the relevant systems. I think a standard understanding of clairvoyance, for instance, sees it as a nonperceptual capacity par excellence; this is one reason that we don't think there could be a reliable such capacity. The problem with clairvoyance is that there is no mechanism, and there is no mechanism because there is no energy transduction. There is no energy transduction because there is no energy of the relevant sort to transduce. Thus, Norman's clairvoyance system fails to count as a perceptual system because it fails to satisfy (a). Such a response, however, will take us only so far, for one might simply stipulate that the relevant kind of energy does exist and is transduced by some clairvoyance organ. At this point, however, the intuitions become a bit hazy. Was Norman born with some funnel-shaped organ on his head that collects C-waves? Does he have some special brain structure that the rest of us lack? If so, it is not so obvious that he's *not* (prima facie) justified.

Even if Norman's clairvoyance system does satisfy (a), however, it would have to also satisfy (b)–(d) to count as a perceptual system, and it is far from obvious that the system in question satisfies (d). Although the description of the case doesn't absolutely mandate this interpretation, the natural assumption to make is that Norman's ability has some unusual—and recent—etiology; perhaps it is the result of a recent encounter with radioactive waste, a neurosurgical prank, or the like. Norman, we are told, has "no evidence or reasons of any kind for or against the general possibility of such a cognitive power or for or against the thesis that he possesses it" (1985, p. 41). This would be quite unusual if this capacity is one that he's had for a long time. Unless Norman is unusually unreflective—and we're not told that he is—the most likely reason for his lacking any evidence is that the capacity is new.[3]

---

2. MSF does offer necessary conditions for basicality: an empirical belief is basic only if it is about one's own (existence and/or) current mental states. It also offers sufficient conditions: my belief that I'm appeared to redly is basic. However, it does not provide individually necessary and jointly sufficient conditions: few if any MSFists give us enough details to know whether my belief that I'm appeared to dogly is basic or not.

3. BonJour claims that Norman has no "evidence" or "reasons" concerning the reliability of clairvoyance. These terms are ambiguous, and BonJour's claim might be that Norman has no (justified) *beliefs* about his clairvoyance, or it might be that Norman has no data from which he could relatively easily infer that he has a reliable clairvoyant power. Either way, the claim seems most plausible on the assumption that Norman's clairvoyance capacity is novel.

A comparison here with the Truetemp case is instructive; Truetemp's system (assuming that's what it is) satisfies (a)–(c) but explicitly violates (d). This, I submit, is part of why our intuitive verdict of unjustified belief is clearer in the Truetemp case than in the Norman case. Truetemp's belief is more obviously not a perceptual belief in the present sense.

To bring out the nonperceptual nature of the relevant systems, it is helpful to contrast these cases with otherwise similar cases where the system in question satisfies the present definition of a perceptual system. As a point of departure, let us elaborate on the original Norman case; let us stipulate that his clairvoyance system does not involve any kind of energy-transducing organ and that it has just arisen overnight. Call this "the Norman* case," and contrast it with the following:

> Nyrmoon is a member of an alien species for whom clairvoyance is a normal cognitive capacity, which develops in much the same way as vision does for humans. Members of Nyrmoon's species have specialized internal organs that are receptive to the highly attenuated energy signals from distant events; as an infant, all was a "blooming buzzing confusion" for Nyrmoon, until, like everyone else, he learned to attend selectively, recognize various objects, and filter out coherent distant events. Nyrmoon, however, is so extremely unreflective that he has no beliefs (a fortiori, no justified beliefs) about the reliability of his clairvoyance. One day he forms, as the result of clairvoyance, the belief that his house is on fire (which it is).

This case differs dramatically from the Norman* case. Though I'm very much inclined to say that Norman*'s belief is unjustified, I have no intuitive problem at all with the claim that Nyrmoon's belief is justified. In fact, my own intuition is positively in favor of his being justified. But note that Nyrmoon's clairvoyance system satisfies the present definition of a perceptual system. How the original Norman case is interpreted substantially affects the resulting intuitions. The more similar it is assumed to be to the Norman* case, the stronger the intuitions of unjustifiedness; the more similar it is thought to be to the Nyrmoon case, the weaker, even to the point of reversing them.

Similar points can be made about the Truetemp case. We can easily imagine a Mr. Vipertemp, a member of an alien species that has, like our own pit vipers, evolved a sensitive and highly reliable heat-detection faculty, complete with specialized thermoception organs. If Vipertemp is sufficiently unreflective, he may lack any specific metabeliefs about the reliability of his thermoception, but still his belief that it is 104° outside is intuitively justified. Although it's not entirely obvious that a reliable, perceptual system for clairvoyance is even possible, a heat-detection faculty like Vipertemp's is clearly possible and would count as a perceptual system in just the way that our visual and auditory systems do. This fits well with the intuition that Vipertemp's beliefs are justified.

Nyrmoon and Vipertemp, unlike Norman and Truetemp, are in all relevant respects just like an extremely unreflective, though otherwise normal, human. Consider one more case:

> Normina is an otherwise normal human, with normal, reliable perceptual systems, but she is quite unconcerned with anything other than what's immediately in front of her and so extremely unreflective that she has no metabeliefs about the reliability

of her perceptual faculties. One day, she forms the (visual) belief that there's a chair in front of her.

Normina may be statistically unusual, but her belief is intuitively justified.

In case the strength of the Norman example is thought to derive from his not having any evidence for the reliability of his clairvoyance, not just in the sense of his not having any metabeliefs but in the sense of his not possessing any evidence from which he could readily infer the reliability of clairvoyance (see note 3), we can suppose that Normina has a memory deficit that prevents her from having any reasonable data concerning the reliability of perception. Thus, she has no evidence for the reliability of perception in either sense of 'evidence'. Still she seems intuitively to be justified in her perceptual beliefs. Similar considerations apply to the Nyrmoon and Vipertemp cases.

Nyrmoon, Vipertemp, and Normina are of a piece in that they all seem intuitively to be justified despite their lacking the requisite metabeliefs. If their beliefs are justified, but not in virtue of any evidential relations to other beliefs, they must be basic. IR accounts for this by noting that the beliefs are the outputs of reliable perceptual systems, and that being the output of a reliable perceptual system is sufficient for prima facie justification. So a reliabilist theory that invokes the basic-nonbasic distinction can capture the intuitions that these three are justified while avoiding the counterintuitive results concerning Norman and Truetemp.

There has been no mention, in either the original Norman and Truetemp cases or my variations, of any experiential states. Our intuitions seem to be independent of these. In fact, we can easily elaborate the cases so that Truetemp and Vipertemp are doxastically and phenomenologically identical (this requires only further specification rather than any modification), and this does little or nothing to change our intuition that Vipertemp is justified and Truetemp not. Similarly with Norman and Nyrmoon. It is not the presence or absence of an experiential state that distinguishes these cases but the nature of the cognitive system responsible for the beliefs. Zombie versions of Normina and the others seem to have the same intuitive consequences as the zombie cases of the previous chapters.

Underspecification worries still loom and will continue to do so for any kind of foundationalism that doesn't offer a solution to the delineation problem, and so the clairvoyance *challenge* remains. However, the addition of my perceptual system theory to IR adds content to the latter without making the resulting view susceptible to the clairvoyance *objection*, because the compelling examples of unjustified belief do not involve perceptual systems. When otherwise analogous scenarios are described in such a way that the responsible systems clearly are perceptual systems, we lose the intuition that the agent was unjustified.

2.3. "Meta-Incoherence"

I have been insisting that all of foundationalism faces the same problems as IR concerning clairvoyance-type cases, and this is because the clairvoyance problems really concern basicality rather than reliability. Clairvoyance cases motivate a challenge to the foundationalist to provide a theory that implies that Norman and Truetemp are not justified. But clairvoyance cases pose another threat to all foundationalist theories: these cases are often taken to show that no beliefs are basic.

I mentioned before that the clairvoyance objection is often thought to establish a general metabelief requirement to the effect that no belief is justified unless the agent is justified in a metabelief attesting to the reliability of the process that produced it, or to its probable truth, or something similar. If this is true, then internalist foundationalists should be just as worried as reliabilists, for, supposing that this metabelief plays an evidential role, such a requirement clearly precludes the possibility of basic beliefs.

It is fortunate for foundationalists that the clairvoyance objection fails to establish a general metabelief requirement. At most, the cases show that *some* beliefs require metabeliefs. It is not clear that they even do this much, but granting for the moment that they do, showing that some beliefs require metabeliefs for their justification is a very far cry from showing that all do. To show that all do, one would have to pose counterexamples involving beliefs that serve as intuitively good candidates for basicality. The antifoundationalist would need an argument that takes a belief that is intuitively or plausibly basic and shows that it really requires a metabelief for its justification. But this is patently not what is done. It is no coincidence that the counterexamples involve bizarre belief-producing mechanisms; Norman's and Truetemp's beliefs were never on anyone's list of putatively basic beliefs. On the contrary, imagine someone arguing against reliabilism on the grounds that it implies that *Normina* is justified. This would be a lot like objecting to reliabilism by pointing out that it allows animals and children to have justified beliefs. Reliabilists are typically *proud* of such results; these are certainly not embarrassments.

Obviously it is asking too much to require a theorist to go through every possible belief and show that it couldn't be justified in the absence of metabeliefs. But if one wants to generalize from a small number of cases, those cases need to be *typical* cases, *representative* cases, or cases that represent foundationalism's best shot at basicality. Instead, the examples are chosen precisely for their atypicality, their unrepresentativeness, their dissimilarity to the kinds of beliefs foundationalists standardly take to be basic.

BonJour seems to be sensitive to this problem. After presenting the Norman objection, he mentions a "restricted externalism," which could claim that reliability is sufficient for the justification of some beliefs, including perceptual beliefs, without being sufficient for the justification of all beliefs (1985, pp. 49 ff.). He concedes that such a view is intuitively plausible but objects on the grounds that the restriction is ad hoc: "The restricted externalist must explain clearly why [the clairvoyance objection] does not apply equally well to the more familiar cases with which he is concerned. If mere external reliability is not sufficient to epistemically justify a clairvoyant belief, *why* does it somehow become adequate in the case of a sensory belief or an introspective one? What is the difference between the two sorts of cases?" (p. 50). What is most puzzling here is BonJour's apparent puzzlement. Given that this discussion appears in a chapter titled "Externalist Versions of *Foundationalism*" (my emphasis), the answer should be clear. Perceptual beliefs are basic; clairvoyant beliefs (for us) are not. Perceptual beliefs are the outputs of a certain kind of cognitive system; clairvoyant beliefs are not. BonJour's concession to the intuitive plausibility of the view indicates that even he doesn't think that Normina-type cases pose any kind of threat to reliabilism.

3. Reliability and Basicality

I have been arguing for a particular diagnosis of the clairvoyance objection to simple reliabilism, one that motivates inferentialist reliabilism. The reason Norman and Truetemp are unjustified is that the beliefs in question are nonbasic. IR avoids this problem by drawing an explicit distinction between basic and nonbasic beliefs, claiming the sufficiency of reliability only for the former.

The problem with SR, then, is that it makes too many beliefs basic. How many? To a very close first approximation, *all of them*: SR implies that all beliefs are basic. If reliability is sufficient for justification, then the agent's having evidential justifiers for a given belief is not necessary, since there is always a possible reliable process that will produce the belief without the agent's having any evidential justifiers. (Even if there are beliefs that just couldn't be arrived at reliably and noninferentially, it is possible that the relevant inferential process happens outside the head of the agent in question; the process would be reliable and noninferential *for that agent*.) But a nonbasic belief is one that requires evidential relations for its justification, and consequently, mere reliability is not sufficient for its justification. So if reliability is sufficient for justification, then no belief is nonbasic; in other words, all beliefs are basic.[4]

If this diagnosis of the problem is on target, it ought to be relatively easy to generate many Norman-type counterexamples to SR. Take any belief that is intuitively nonbasic (any hard-won bit of science or philosophy makes a good example), stipulate an agent with a doxastic structure that guarantees that the belief is not evidentially justified, and concoct a scenario that makes the belief the result of a reliable process without thereby making the operative process so perception-like as to alter the initial intuition of nonbasicality.

Thus, *S* is under the influence of an officious demon, who really wants to ensure that *S*'s philosophical beliefs are correct and inserts in *S*'s mind the belief that four-dimensionalism is true. If the demon is right most of the time, this belief will be the result of a reliable process, even though this belief is clearly nonbasic and thus unjustified. Or perhaps the demon rewires *S* so that every time she is in the presence of someone with the blood type O+, the belief that this is so pops into *S*'s head. I suggest that the reason reliability is not sufficient for the justification of such beliefs is that they are nonbasic. If you want to know whether four-dimensionalism is true, what blood type someone is, the age of the earth, or the proper cladistic tree for primate

---

4. There is a slight hitch, which motivates the first approximation qualification here, concerning the individuation of belief tokens. If a given token is the result of an inferential process, one might argue that no noninferential process could justify that belief, because if the causal process were different, it would no longer be *that* belief. I'm not sure how plausible this is, especially given that it's really sustaining causes that are supposed to do the work for reliabilism, not initiating causes, and certainly the numerically same belief token can have different actual or counterfactual sustaining causes. In any case, the conclusion might be reformulated as the claim that SR implies that, for any proposition *p*, it is possible to be basically justified in believing that *p*, and this is grounds enough to reject SR.

phylogeny, you will have to engage in some inference. Vampires might detect blood types in much the way we detect conspecifics—though perhaps using scent instead of vision—in which case, the belief that someone is O+ might be basic for them. But it wouldn't be basic for any creature very similar to a normal human. For a cognizer built like us, there are simply some propositions that can't be justified without evidential support from other beliefs. These are the nonbasic beliefs for us.

SR is not the only version of reliabilism that faces this problem. In fact, I think that some version of it arises for every reliabilist theory except IR and for the simple reason that none of these theories requires that any belief have evidential support (or not the right sort of evidential support). Though I can't address every reliabilist theory, I want to examine some representative and influential examples. Each of these theories requires something other than mere reliability for prima facie justification, though what these theories require is not evidential support, and consequently they all fail.

Before looking at these theories, however, I want to make sure the issue really is one of prima facie justification.

3.1. Clairvoyance and Defeat

Goldman has endorsed several solutions to the clairvoyance problem over the years. One is to embrace the result that Norman is prima facie justified but to capture the intuitions by denying that he is ultima facie justified. That is, Goldman argues that Norman is unjustified because the clairvoyance belief is defeated:

> Norman *ought* to reason along the following lines: "If I had a clairvoyant power, I would surely find *some* evidence for this. I would find myself believing things in otherwise inexplicable ways, and when these things were checked by other reliable processes, they would usually check out positively. Since I lack any such signs, I apparently do not possess reliable clairvoyant processes." Since Norman ought to reason this way, he is *ex ante* justified in believing that he does not possess reliable clairvoyant processes. This undermines his belief....(1986, p. 112)

Ex ante justification is the kind that applies to propositions the agent does not actually (occurrently) believe; it is contrasted with *ex post* justification, which is the ordinary notion of justification and attaches to occurrent beliefs. Goldman's notion of undermining is the same, or at least very similar to, the present notion of defeat.

As initially plausible as this solution is, Goldman's appeal to epistemic obligation fits rather poorly with the overall spirit of reliabilism. Surely Goldman doesn't want to say that Normina is under some similar obligation, or that you and I are under an epistemic obligation to reason about the reliability of our belief-forming processes. Are children and animals under such obligations? It is better, I think, to use this general line of reasoning in the context of Goldman's older (1979) theory of defeat, omitting any mention of such deontological-sounding concepts of obligation.

Because our intuitions about justifiedness are primarily intuitions about ultima facie justification, it is always tempting to take what looks like a counterexample to one's theory of prima facie justification and let one's theory of defeat handle it. Such a move is legitimate if one can also specify a general and satisfactory theory of defeat. In "What Is Justified Belief?" (1979), Goldman endorses an alternative reliable process theory of defeat.

> (ARP): S's belief that p is defeated iff there is available to S an alternative reliable process, the use of which, in addition to or instead of the one actually used, would have resulted in S's not believing that p.[5]

I think that ARP is basically on the right track, though it will have to be amended to handle defeater-defeaters (Pollock 1986). Suppose vision produces in me the belief that the thing in front of me is red, even though you have just told me that the thing is illuminated by a red light. I happen to know that you *always* lie about red lights. Intuitively, my belief remains justified, even though there is an alternate reliable process available to me (testimony), which if used in addition to vision would have resulted in my not believing that the thing was red. This of course is because the defeater is itself defeated. The basic proposal here will have to be modified, perhaps generally along the lines suggested by Pollock (1986), though he conceives of defeat in evidential terms, where Goldman does not. In any case, I will assume for now that this is merely a matter of detail and that it can be relatively easily patched up, and I will stick with ARP for the sake of simplicity.

Thus, Goldman's (1986) response to the clairvoyance objection can be viewed as the claim that, though Norman's belief is prima facie justified, there is an alternative reliable process, the use of which would have resulted in Norman's not believing that the president was in New York. Namely, Norman had available to him the aforementioned line of reasoning and thus the cognitive processes that would produce such reasoning. Consequently, Norman's belief is defeated, hence not (ultima facie) justified.

Thus stripped of its deontological veneer, this strikes me as a fairly plausible reply. Unfortunately, it provides a response to only certain versions of the clairvoyance objection, and it is not difficult to modify the counterexample so that it precludes such a reply. We can just stipulate that Norman is so bad at reasoning about such matters that there is no such process that is both reliable and available to him. This doesn't seem to change the intuitive verdict. Instead, I think that the best solution to the clairvoyance objection will be one that, like the one I have offered, gives the result that Norman and Truetemp are not even prima facie justified. If so, then for some beliefs, something other than reliability will have to be required for justification. But what?

3.2. Experientialist Reliabilism

One approach is to add an internalist—perhaps an experientialist—element. Thus, Alston (1988) develops a reliable indicator theory, according to which a belief is (prima facie) justified iff it is based on a ground, and that ground is a reliable indicator of the truth of the belief. The existence of the ground must be accessible to the

---

5. This differs somewhat from the theory of defeat he endorses in his later book (1986), but the difference won't matter for the present purposes, since his response to the Norman objection only utilizes that part of the theory that was already in place in 1979. The 1986 version allows the possibility of unjustified beliefs serving as defeaters. I'm not sure what to make of this, and so I'm just leaving it out.

agent, but its adequacy (the reliability of its connection to the justificandum belief) need not be.

Some problems for Alston's view were already discussed in chapter 3. We can now see how they tend to work. I gave the examples of the belief that the moon is 2,187 miles in diameter and the belief that bats are more closely related to primates than to rodents. These are beliefs that are intuitively nonbasic (for creatures remotely like us). Following the recipe for generating counterexamples to reliabilism, all we have to do is stipulate that such beliefs are reliably produced in an agent whose doxastic structure precludes her from having any evidential justification for said beliefs. This is what we got in chapter 3. Another example given there involved a perceptual *proposition* where the causal history of the belief makes it not a perceptual belief. Pressure to my right big toe causes a sensation of warmth on my left cheek, and from this sensation I infer that there's pressure on my toe. Such a belief is not the output of a perceptual system and is not, intuitively, a basic belief, even though this time it is the sort of proposition that could be basic. It is not the content, but the etiology, of the belief that makes it nonbasic on this occasion.

Furthermore, Alston's internalist externalism fails to deflect the original clairvoyance objections to simple reliabilism, or at least very slight elaborations of the original objections. As we saw, Truetemp surely continues to have normal heat sensations; the tempucomp adds without taking anything away. Suppose then that the tempucomp is fashioned so as to take these sensations as input, causing him to form his temperature beliefs *on their basis*. Still the belief is unjustified. Suppose that Norman has an experiential state that causally grounds and reliably indicates his belief that the president is in New York. To ensure that the case does not sound perceptual enough to ruin the intuitions, suppose that the experiential state in question is produced directly in Norman by the spirit of his dead grandmother, who is quite excited about the president's appearance in New York. Again, Norman has no idea that there is a reliable connection, but Alston's view is that no such knowledge is necessary. Intuitively, Norman is unjustified, though Alston's account predicts otherwise.

3.3. Early Reliabilism

The earliest worked-out reliabilist theory of justification is still in many ways the best. It is also perhaps the most similar to the one I am endorsing, and it is important to be clear on the differences. My distinction between basic and nonbasic beliefs, though familiar enough from foundationalism, is bound to sound a bit like Goldman's (1979) distinction between belief-dependent and belief-independent processes. Reliability (as opposed to conditional reliability) is sufficient for the justification only of the former.

Goldman's early reliabilism distinguishes between belief-dependent processes (those that take beliefs as inputs) and belief-independent processes (those processes none of whose inputs are beliefs) and draws a corresponding distinction between reliability, which is a matter of truth-ratio or truth-propensity, and conditional reliability, which is reliability *given* true beliefs as inputs. He adds ARP as a no-undermining clause, but the focus is on the recursively specified theory of prima facie justification:

(ER): (1) S's belief that p is prima facie justified if the belief results from a reliable belief-independent cognitive process.
(2) S's belief that p is prima facie justified if the belief results from a conditionally reliable belief-dependent process, all the doxastic inputs to which are themselves justified.
(3) No other beliefs are prima facie justified.

It is an important feature of (ER) that it does not make reliability sufficient for the justification of all beliefs. Clause 2 makes a requirement that is in a way stronger, and in a way weaker, than mere reliability. My deductive processes may be unreliable simply because most of my premise beliefs are false; this doesn't change the fact that deduction is conditionally reliable, and deduction ought to be considered a justification-preserving process as long as it is conditionally reliable, even if its unconditional reliability is fairly low. Requiring merely conditional reliability in this way weakens the epistemic requirements to a more reasonable level. Requiring justified inputs, on the other hand, strengthens the requirements for justification. Goldman cites memory as a paradigmatically belief-dependent process (it takes beliefs at earlier times as inputs and yields beliefs at later times as outputs). A result of this, and a consequence Senor (1995) has emphasized, is that my current memory belief that p is justified only if my earlier belief that p was justified. This claim, which I will refer to again as the Goldman-Senor thesis, is a contentious but important claim. For the moment, we need only note that this thesis imposes a stronger requirement on memory beliefs than does a more standard EOF, according to which any belief that is based on a seeming-to-remember state is prima facie justified (Audi 1998; Pollock 1986).

Once again, however, we have complications to simple reliabilism that don't yield the requirement that nonbasic beliefs be the result of an inferential process. Consequently, clairvoyance and similar objections are bound to cause trouble. Recall that ER was the theory that generated the original Norman and Truetemp cases. The fact that the beliefs are nonbasic has nothing to do with the fact that the processes that produce them are belief-independent. The counterexamples offered in opposition to Alston's and Plantinga's theories apply equally well here, since again, the processes in question are belief-independent. Having a belief-independent etiology does not make a belief basic; if it did, reliability would suffice for the belief's justification, and such counterexamples wouldn't arise.

Belief-dependent processes cause trouble for ER as well. Suppose that while you slept recently, a group of logicians implanted a device in your head that contains a list of abstruse theorems of the predicate calculus; the device is designed to take particularly sudden and decisive olfactory appearance beliefs as inputs and respond by selecting a random theorem from the lookup table and producing belief in that theorem as output. On driving by a chicken house, you form the characteristic olfactory appearance belief and immediately afterward, the belief that $(x)(y)(z)((Fxy \& Fxz) \supset Fyz) \supset (x)(y)(z)((Fxy \& Fxz) \supset Fzy)$. The process is belief-dependent, but it is intuitively not an *inferential* process; this and the fact that the output belief is intuitively nonbasic explain why the belief is intuitively unjustified.

The distinction between beliefs that are arrived at via belief-dependent processes and those arrived at via belief-independent processes does not map onto the distinction between basic and nonbasic beliefs. Clairvoyance beliefs and perceptual beliefs alike result from belief-independent processes, but only the latter are basic. Introspection is a belief-dependent process, in that some of the inputs are beliefs (i.e., we can intro-spect beliefs), but introspective beliefs are basic.[6] Memory beliefs also result from belief-dependent processes but are intuitively basic. Far from denying that memory is belief-dependent, or that belief-dependent processes require justified inputs, this claim is actually compatible with the Goldman-Senor thesis.[7] A basic belief is one that does not depend evidentially on other beliefs; the epistemic dependence here is not an evidential one. The justifiedness of the prior belief that p is necessary for the justification of the memory belief, but it serves as a nonevidential justifier for the later memory belief that p, rather than, say, a premise in an inference to the conclusion that p. Although I don't want my claiming that memory beliefs are basic to commit me to denying the Goldman-Senor thesis, I don't intend to endorse the thesis either. My own intuitions about whether the earlier belief must be justified are unclear, so I'll leave the requirement out, content with the fact that it could easily be added without disrupting the rest of my theory. I will, however, return to this issue in chapter 6, section 1.

Neither the belief-dependent–belief-independent distinction nor the distinc-tion between reliable and conditionally reliable processes maps onto the distinction between reliable processes and reliable inferential processes. I take Goldman's point about deduction seriously and want to demand only conditional reliability from the inferential processes, but a process can be belief-dependent without being an inferential process. We will need—eventually—a better characterization of inferential processes.

3.4. Teleological Reliabilism

Plantinga (1993) endorses a view he calls "proper functionalism," but a more descrip-tive title is "teleological reliabilism."[8] Roughly, Plantinga claims that, in addition to the belief's being reliably produced, the cognitive faculties responsible for the belief must be (a) functioning properly, (b) designed with the aim of truth, and (c) operat-ing in the sort of environment for which they were designed.[9] It must be noted here that proper functioning is a roughly biological (or perhaps theological) notion, not an epistemic one. Here is another reliabilist view that denies the sufficiency of reli-ability, without explicitly invoking a basic-nonbasic distinction.

Consequently, the theory is vulnerable to the same sorts of examples. In fact, the Truetemp objection, published three years before Plantinga's book, already offers

6. I make more out of this point in chapter 6, section 1.2.

7. I will eventually deny the claim that belief-dependent processes require justified beliefs to yield justified outputs, though not for reasons that have to do with memory.

8. This phrase is due to Tom Senor.

9. This is rough, partly because Plantinga adds further complications, which won't affect the present discussion, and partly because the theory he offers is a theory of warrant (i.e., that which, when added to true belief, yields knowledge), not of justification. I am treating it as a theory of justification because that's what the present topic is. I think that its failures as a theory of justification make it a failure as a theory of warrant, as well; because the agents of the counterexamples fail to be justified in their beliefs, they fail to know.

a compelling counterexample. Not only is Truetemp's faculty reliable but also it is designed to produce true beliefs, it is designed for the sort of environment in which Truetemp finds himself, and it is functioning properly.[10]

Consider an example a little closer to Plantinga's own heart. Plantinga offers the example of the epistemically serendipitous brain lesion to argue against certain reliabilist theories of knowledge. This is a brain lesion that makes its possessor think she has a brain lesion. Consequently, it is perfectly reliable, but nonetheless the belief in question is not an instance of knowledge or justification. But the same intuitive consequences result from the case of the God-given brain lesion: God, working in mysterious ways as he is wont to do, gives someone a brain lesion with the express intention of causing him to truly believe that he has a brain lesion. The lesion thus serves as a reliable cognitive capacity that produces the belief that the subject has a brain lesion. It is functioning properly, in the right environment, and it is aimed at the truth. Nonetheless, the resulting belief is unjustified.

I think Plantinga has gotten one thing very nearly right. He thinks—correctly, in my view—that the etiology of the faculty is relevant. However, he fails to distinguish between something's being innate and something's having a function, and I suspect that his teleological intuitions are really just misplaced nativist intuitions. Perhaps many of our innate faculties are *for* something, in some suitably anemic, evolutionary biological sense of the phrase. But there could be adventitious faculties, which satisfy Plantinga's teleological constraint without satisfying my etiological constraint (d), faculties realized by God-given brain lesions or tempucomps. The converse is probably true as well: learned systems and some innate ones may not be *for* anything but may nonetheless be justification-conferring.[11]

Unlike most other reliabilists—unlike most *epistemologists*—Plantinga has a theory of basicality. He seems to hold that a belief is basic for S iff S is functioning properly in taking it as basic (1993, p. 183). Presumably, "taking a belief as basic" is a matter of accepting the belief in the absence of inferential support from other beliefs. For some beliefs, the agent's design plan will require both a ground for the belief in question and the further belief that the ground is an adequate one. Perhaps the design plan will require other kinds of inferential support as well. For other beliefs, the design plan will not require any doxastic evidence (though Plantinga seems to think our design plans always require at least an experiential ground). This theory of basicality follows directly from the more general theory of justification. If justification is a matter of proper functioning, and S is functioning properly in accepting p without any doxastic support, then S is justified in accepting p without any doxastic support, and thus S's belief that p is basic.

10. There are also some well-known objections designed to show that Plantinga's conditions—in particular, proper functioning—are not necessary for justification. Since the worry at hand is one about the beliefs for which reliability is sufficient, I won't address these worries here.

11. The debates over adaptationism in the philosophy of biology and evolutionary psychology are far from settled. If Gould and Lewontin (1979) are right, many of our cognitive capacities may be "spandrels": unintended by-products that do not have functions in the teleological sense. They may be the result of genetic drift, of general "*Baupläne*," or as exaptations, which piggyback on genuinely functional concomitants. If so, this would combine with a Plantingan theory of justification to have skeptical consequences. Not so with my own theory, since I do not make any teleological requirements on the systems.

Plantinga's theory of basicality thus doesn't really add anything to his already existing theory, and it takes very little further elaboration of the present counterexamples to
show that this theory won't work. We need merely also suppose that the tempucomp
was designed to produce temperature beliefs *without the agent's having any evidence
of or beliefs about reliability* or that God intended the brain lesion to produce the lesion
belief directly, without inference. Similarly, the objections to experientialist reliabilism noted previously can be easily extended to Plantinga's teleological experientialist
reliabilism as well.

I have examined a few reliabilist proposals that don't distinguish between basic and
nonbasic beliefs, as well as one that does but draws the distinction in the wrong way.
All except the last one imply that all beliefs are basic, and even that one is too lax
about which beliefs it allows to be noninferentially justified. Consequently, all are
susceptible to clairvoyance-type counterexamples. This lends support to the diagnosis offered at the beginning of this chapter: that the real problem brought out by
Norman-type examples is one of basicality rather than reliability. If we can offer the
right distinction between basic and nonbasic beliefs, we will see that reliability really
is sufficient for the prima facie justification of basic beliefs. The classic internalist
objections to reliabilism can be met.

6

Basic Beliefs

In the previous chapter, I sketched a kind of reliabilism that explicitly marks the distinction between basic and nonbasic beliefs, making reliability sufficient for the prima facie justification of the former but not the latter. The account, of course, was incomplete. Though I proposed sufficient conditions for basicality, I have not yet offered necessary and sufficient conditions.

Recall the discussion from chapter 1 of two problems concerning basic beliefs. The source problem is that of specifying where the justification of basic beliefs might come from, since it is by definition not from other beliefs. The delineation problem is that of specifying in substantive terms which beliefs are basic and which are not. I have argued against doxastic and experientialist solutions to the source problem, concluding that what makes basic beliefs justified is the nature of the process that produces them, the obvious factor here being the reliability of such processes. Although clairvoyance-type problems have been taken to show that reliabilism cannot provide an adequate solution to the source problem, I have argued that they show no such thing, since the source problem only concerns *basic* beliefs, and the putative counterexamples all involve intuitively nonbasic beliefs. Nothing about the clairvoyance cases poses any real problem to a reliabilist account of basic beliefs.

We still need a theory about which beliefs are basic; the present task is to provide one and thereby offer a solution to the delineation problem.

1. The Delineation Problem

Part of my solution to the delineation problem has already been given. Perceptual beliefs are basic, and to be a perceptual belief is to be the doxastic output of a certain kind of cognitive system. An obvious suggestion presents itself: a theory of basicality can be constructed by simply generalizing from the theory of perceptual beliefs already developed. This is the approach I will take. Of course, there are indefinitely many sets that contain the set of perceptual beliefs as a subset, and we will need to choose among these.

Let me emphasize from the start that my intention, at least for the time being, is to maintain reasonable contact with our intuitions. In section 2, I will examine the methodological consequences of such an intention, making suggestions for how a more revisionist epistemology might go. For the time being, however, I want intuitions about basicality to serve as the data points a theory of basicality needs to capture.

1.1. The Desiderata

What are these intuitions of basicality? Which beliefs do we want a theory of basicality to classify as basic, and which as nonbasic? Concerning those beliefs that originate with the stimulation of sensory organs, chapter 5 offers a fairly clear distinction between basic and inferential beliefs. When I look at my desk, my visual system (or one of my visual systems) outputs the belief that there is a pencil on the desk. It also outputs the belief that there is a yellow object on the desk. Perhaps the belief that there is an object on the desk is the output of a perceptual system. More likely, however, such a belief is the result of some other cognitive system, one that takes the belief that there is a pencil on the desk, or the belief that there is a yellow object on the desk, as input. If this second possibility obtained, the belief in question would pretty clearly not be a basic belief, nor would it satisfy the requirements for perceptual belief, since the system in question is hypothesized to take beliefs as inputs.

Consider another example, of a sort that was discussed in chapter 4. I look at Jane and form the belief that Jane is in front of me. Again, this belief is distinct from the belief that the person in front of me is *named* 'Jane'. The former belief is, intuitively, both basic and perceptual; the latter is presumably neither. The latter belief is based in part on the belief that Jane is named 'Jane'. Consequently, it is held partly on the basis of perception and partly on the basis of semantic memory. From the (perceptual) belief that Jane is in front of me and the (mnemonic) belief that Jane is named 'Jane', I conclude that the person in front of me is named 'Jane'. I may draw this inference so habitually and rapidly that it does not seem like an inference to me, but it is an inference nevertheless, and the resulting belief is nonbasic.

When looking at Jane (who happens to be my sister), I also form the belief that a sibling of mine is in front of me. My personal guess is that the sibling belief is not the output of any perceptual system but is instead in the same camp with the belief that the person in front of me is named 'Jane'. If so, the belief will count as inferential rather than perceptual. On the other hand, my belief that there's a conspecific in front of me might be the output of a perceptual system and thus count as a perceptual belief. The idea, roughly, is that while *conspecific* might be a perceptual kind, *sibling* most likely isn't.[1] Things *look* like conspecifics (in the perceptual output sense), but they don't *look* like siblings to me. Rather, they look like Pat, Ann, Jane, or Mike, whom I know to be my siblings, thus allowing me to infer that one of my sibs is nearby. I don't need to identify someone first, however, to be justified in believing he or she is a conspecific.[2]

Now I don't mean to suggest that *sibling* couldn't be a perceptual kind. For all I know some species recognize siblings by scent, for instance: some mice might, as it were, "smell like a brother" to other mice. Even the claim that things don't look like sibs to me is intended merely as a fact about *my* siblings; yours may be different, and some visual systems may have access to that fact.

In saying all this, I am expressing my hunch about how the science is going to turn out, about how the perceptual systems actually work. My guess is that our perceptual systems classify things as humans, and even as particular individuals, though not as siblings. This guess is based in part on the fact that there is a set of visually accessible features that reliably, even if imperfectly, distinguishes humans from other things and a set of visually accessible properties that the different views of an individual person have in common, which pretty reliably distinguishes that individual from others, but there is not a set of visually accessible features that reliably distinguishes siblings from other things.

There is also an important epistemological assumption embedded in this discussion. A number of authors (e.g., Greco 2000; Plantinga 1993; Pollock 1986) assume that if a belief B_1 is not introspectibly inferred from belief B_2—perhaps because B_2 wasn't consciously tokened—then B_1 cannot be based on or otherwise epistemically dependent on B_2. I deny this. I see no good principled reason to hold that basing relations are always transparent to introspection (especially in the context of the kind of externalism already endorsed), and the examples currently under investigation strongly suggest that some basing does not involve consciously introspectible inferential moves. Suppose that the psychological account I have suggested is correct, that this particular belief that there's a sib in front of me, though relatively spontaneous, is causally dependent on the outputs of semantic memory (in this case, the belief that Jane is one of my siblings) and face recognition (the belief that Jane is here). If, in this particular instance, I am unjustified in believing that Jane is nearby, or that Jane is one of my siblings, then I am similarly unjustified in believing that one of my siblings is nearby. The only natural explanation for this is that the sibling belief

1. I leave the notion of a perceptual kind unexplicated here, as I think the rough, intuitive notion is clear enough for the present purposes. For a detailed account, however, see my (2005).

2. Translating the outputs of perceptual systems into English is a difficult matter, as is the case with translating any beliefs into English, though the difficulty may be more a matter of getting the pragmatics right than of getting the semantics right. Perhaps it would be better to say that the visual system classifies distal stimuli as humans, or better yet people, rather than conspecifics. One need not have a concept answering exactly to *conspecific* in order to engage in the relevant classification. Nothing hinges on my describing the output as conspecific detection; I do so only because this is how the cognitive scientists are prone to talk, ethologists especially, even though nonhumans presumably lack the concept *conspecific*. Nonetheless, it should be perfectly clear what is meant by saying that the pigeon or its visual system classifies some distal object as a conspecific but not as a sib.

was based on the Jane beliefs, despite the fact that I didn't have any introspective awareness of explicitly inferring the one from the others. Suppose, for example, that I am at a large gathering of my extended family, and I need to find one of my siblings. Because I'm on the lookout for one of my siblings, when I see Jane, what pops into my head is something like 'there's one of my siblings now'. Though I certainly wouldn't consciously rehash my belief that Jane is one of my siblings, this belief is clearly part of my evidence for my belief that one of my siblings is here.

This example also illustrates an important distinction between systems and processes (see also Goldman 1979). Although the *process* involved here is intuitively an inferential process, neither of the two relevant *systems* is inferential in any interesting sense. Both of these systems (face recognition and semantic memory) are inferentially opaque. The belief that one of my sibs is in front of me is not the output of either of these systems; rather, the causal history of this belief spans more than one system. Though there may be a larger system that includes visual and memory systems as subsystems, this larger system would not necessarily be inferentially opaque just because its components are. Nor would such a system be inferentially opaque merely because *some* of its outputs are cognitively spontaneous. A system must at least approximate total opacity to count as inferentially opaque: all or nearly all of its outputs must be cognitively spontaneous.

It is important to distinguish inferential processes from mere belief-dependent processes. A belief-dependent process, again, is one that takes beliefs as inputs (Goldman 1979). Goldman explicitly cites memory as a belief-dependent process. Memory takes beliefs at t as input and delivers beliefs at $t + n$ as outputs, where n is typically a long interval (in the case of long-term memory, anyhow) and the outputs are typically (though, alas, not always) the same as the inputs. Despite this, memory is intuitively not an *inferential* process. Though all inferential processes are belief-dependent, not all belief-dependent processes are inferential.

Memory beliefs, despite being the result of belief-dependent processes, are commonly taken by external object foundationalists to be basic beliefs. Since standard versions of EOF are experientialist theories, the standard view is that memory beliefs are justified by seeming-to-remember states (Audi 1998; Huemer 2001; Pollock 1986). My own view being a nonexperientialist one, of course, I will be claiming that what justifies memory beliefs is the nature of the memory process, rather than any kind of phenomenology. (Given the controversial status of seeming-to-remember states, it is a nontrivial virtue of my view that it gets by without them.) Still, I want memory beliefs to turn out to be basic.[3] (I will have more to say on the distinction between inferential and belief-dependent processes in section 1.2.)

It is well known that there are different kinds of memories and different memory systems: a standard taxonomy distinguishes between procedural and declarative memory (remembering how vs. remembering that), and within declarative memory between episodic memory (memory for first-person autobiographical events) and semantic memory (memory of general facts). There is also implicit memory, which,

---

3. As argued in chapter 5, this claim is compatible with, though does not require, the Goldman-Senor thesis. Intuitively, neither does memory seem to be an inferential process, nor does a current memory belief seem to be in any ordinary sense *based on* the old belief.

though unconscious, reveals itself on certain priming tasks and the like, but since it is unconscious, I won't worry about it here. Like procedural memory, it is not the sort of thing that epistemologists are concerned with. I take it that it is intuitively plausible (at least from the standpoint of EOF) to claim that both semantic memories, such as 'there are 5,280 feet in a mile', and episodic memories, such as 'I ate breakfast this morning', are basic beliefs.

Again, to say that a belief is basic is merely to say that its prima facie justification does not depend on evidential connections to other beliefs; it does not imply that all basic beliefs are equally justified or that they are all highly justified, nor does it preclude other justificatory requirements, like reliability of the sustaining process, or even the justification of some earlier token of the same belief type.

Because virtually any proposition can be the object of semantic memory, it is impossible to develop a very rigid notion of a basic proposition, analogous with the notion of a perceptual proposition introduced in chapter 3. However, it is convenient to treat certain propositions as nonbasic, or certain beliefs, whose etiology is unspecified, as nonbasic. I will occasionally do so, assuming that the beliefs in question are not semantic memory beliefs.[4]

I also take it that those beliefs that are standardly classified as a priori intuitions are basic. So beliefs like '$1 + 1 = 2$', 'if something is red all over it is not green all over', and 'bachelors are unmarried' are basic. By saying this, I don't mean to deny even the most radical empiricism (though I don't mean to endorse it either). Whether the beliefs are genuinely independent of experience in the requisite way doesn't matter for the present purposes; basicality is the more important epistemic property here. I will continue to refer to such beliefs as a priori, though officially I will remain neutral on the larger issues of rationalism and empiricism. What is important for the present purposes is that the beliefs in question are intuitions (in the narrow, historical, sense of the term), not that they are a priori.

Belief in the Pythagorean theorem is a priori, but it's not an intuition: it's not basic—at least not for us or creatures cognitively similar to us.[5] Obviously a very difficult question arises, analogous to the one that arose for perceptual beliefs. For perceptual beliefs, the question was: which of those beliefs that begin with sensory stimulation count as basic and which do not? For a priori beliefs, the question is: which of those beliefs that begin with reason alone count as basic and which do not? Some particular instances are intuitively very clearly nonbasic, some very clearly basic, and some uncertain. It is difficult to give a theory-neutral description of which ones are which, but I presume that there is at least rough uniformity of intuitions among readers.

The set of empirical beliefs counted as basic by EOF will include those taken by MSF to be basic, though not, of course, vice versa. In particular, though EOF denies

4. A basic proposition, relative to a certain class of cognizers, would be a proposition such that those cognizers could have a basic belief with that proposition as its content. The force of 'could', here, though fairly intuitive, is difficult to make very clear. Perceptual learning would result in certain propositions that are not now basic for me becoming basic, as would certain counterfactual histories. In any case, the notion of basic propositions serves only a heuristic function here.

5. That is, taking into account the aforementioned possibility of semantic memory, the belief is nonbasic *when* it is not the result of semantic memory. One might say that any particular token of the belief that $a^2 + b^2 = c^2$ is either basic or a priori, but never both.

that perceptual beliefs are based on appearance beliefs, we will still want to insist that appearance beliefs are basic. Introspective beliefs in general are good candidates for basicality, so my belief that I'm hungry, that I'm in pain, that my current visual sensation differs in certain ways from an earlier one: all these are basic beliefs. Of course, the claim of basicality is only intended when these beliefs result from introspection. If I believe that I'm hungry because it's after noon, and I haven't eaten yet, and I'm generally hungry under such circumstances, that's a different story.

The status of some other beliefs is much more controversial. Some authors think that testimony is a basic source of justification (e.g., Coady 1992; Lackey 2003); this view is compatible with the claim that testimony is a source of basic justification as well, while a reductionist theory of testimony (Fricker 1994; Lyons 1997) implies that testimonial beliefs are nonbasic. Perhaps our beliefs about the mental states of others ought to count as basic, perhaps not. Neither sort of belief is obviously a perceptual belief in any direct sense, though they may be sufficiently like perceptual beliefs to count as basic. Some beliefs about the speech of others are clearly perceptual. My auditory belief that so-and-so just said "The cat is on the mat" is a straightforwardly perceptual belief. My belief that so-and-so just said *that* the cat is on the mat will be a perceptual belief only if the language comprehension system counts as a perceptual system; it very well might on the present understanding of perceptual systems, and I have no problem with this result.

Moral beliefs are sometimes classified as basic because they are held to be a priori intuitions (this is most plausible if the beliefs in question are general beliefs, like 'murder is wrong'). Some theorists deny this but hold that moral judgments are basic nonetheless because they are in fact perceptual beliefs, or at least perception-like (this is most plausible if the beliefs in question are particular beliefs, like 'what X is doing right now is wrong'). I have fairly liberal intuitions about basicality and thus wouldn't mind if some moral judgments ended up being basic. Along with my belief that so-and-so just said that the cat is on the mat, or my testimonial belief that the cat is indeed on the mat, these are controversial examples, and I will put them aside and use the more standard cases, the cases of intuitively basic beliefs, to argue for my view.

There is also, however, a class of beliefs that are intuitively nonbasic. Some of these have played an important role in arguing against various versions of reliabilism. In fact, a good intuitive test for nonbasicality is to stipulate that the belief is the result of a reliable process, even though the agent has nothing like an argument for the belief; those that are intuitively unjustified are nonbasic. It is thus quite easy to come up with belief types, standard tokens of which are typically intuitively nonbasic. Some of these we have already seen:

- the president is in New York
- it's 104° outside
- bats are more closely related to primates than to rodents
- the moon is 2,187 miles in diameter
- there are 5,280 feet in a mile
- proper psychological taxonomy individuates states by their wide contents
- the hippocampus is responsible for the formation of new long-term memories
- the fall of the Roman Empire was caused partly by the military's having too much influence on the government

Most of these may be appropriate objects of semantic memory, and when they are, they are basic, but otherwise, they are paradigmatic examples of nonbasic beliefs.

So what we are looking for is a theory that counts these and similar beliefs as nonbasic but counts perceptual beliefs, memory beliefs, introspective beliefs, and some—but not all—a priori beliefs as basic.

1.2. A Systems Theory of Basicality

Being a perceptual belief is a sufficient but not necessary condition for basicality, and we already have an account of what a perceptual belief is: a perceptual belief is a belief that is the output of a perceptual system, where the notion of a perceptual system is to be understood in cognitive architectural terms, rather than, for example, phenomenological, semantic, or epistemic terms. The most obvious approach to the delineation problem is to take this sort of account and simply remove whatever requirements on perceptual beliefs are particular to them and speak to their perceptuality rather than their basicality. Two ends would thereby be accomplished. If it is plausible to think that it is the architectural features of the generating system that make a given belief a perceptual belief, it is plausible to think the same is true of memory beliefs, a priori intuitions, introspective beliefs, and the like. What makes a belief an introspective belief, for example, is the fact that the cognitive system that produced it is an introspection system; it is not, for instance, the content of the belief (surely I can have nonintrospective beliefs about my current mental states) or some attendant phenomenology (surely zombies can have introspective beliefs). Second, such an approach will offer a unified solution to the delineation problem by offering a system-oriented theory for all basic beliefs, not just for perceptual beliefs.

I suggested in chapter 5 a tentative analysis of perceptual systemhood, which, conjoined with the overarching theory, resulted in the following sufficient condition for basicality:

A belief is basic if it is the output of a cognitive system such that

(a) its lowest level representational inputs are the results of energy transduction across sense organs,

(b) none of the inputs to any of its subsystems are under the voluntary control of the larger organism,

(c) it's inferentially opaque (i.e., its doxastic outputs are cognitively spontaneous in BonJour's [1985] sense), and

(d) the system has developed as the result of the interplay of learning and innate constraints.

The first two conditions are intended to capture the fact that perceptual systems take their inputs from the world and not from the larger organism. Since these are particular to perceptual systems, they should not be demanded of all systems whose doxastic outputs are basic.

Call any system that satisfies (c) and (d) a *primal system*. This terminology is intended to reflect the etiology of the system as well as its inferential opacity. A system need not be simple, nonassembled, or even *introspectively* opaque to count as primal in the present sense. Nor, since a primal system can result from or be shaped by learning, need a primal system be ontogenetically prior to other systems, although a system that just came into being overnight would fail to satisfy the etiological constraint (d) and thus not be a primal system.

I think that all basic beliefs are the outputs of primal systems, but it is clearly not the case that any doxastic output of a primal system is therefore basic. I might have an "AND-elimination system," which takes beliefs like 'p & q' and returns beliefs like 'q' as output. Obviously, if such is the origin of my belief that q, the belief is nonbasic, even if this AND-elimination system is primal. What is needed is an additional criterion that will separate the basic-belief-producing primal systems from the rest.

Although the particular input restriction required by (b) had to be dropped to allow for nonperceptual systems, perhaps some other input restriction is necessary to delineate the class of systems whose doxastic outputs are basic. Cognitive systems can take various sorts of inputs. Beliefs and sensory transductions are the most salient candidates, but other possibilities abound. A visual imagery system might take pairs of pictorial representations as inputs and deliver as outputs judgments as to whether one can be rotated to match the other (Shepard and Metzler 1971). A mental state simulator could take ersatz beliefs and desires and yield beliefs about how people with the corresponding beliefs and desires are prone to act (Goldman 2006; Harris 1992). Though such systems might well take inputs that are under the direct voluntary control of the larger organism, the inputs are not beliefs, and it is reasonable to hold that the output beliefs are basic. So we might be tempted to conclude that the basic-belief-producing systems are those primal systems that don't take beliefs as inputs.

This won't work, however, for memory can take beliefs as inputs, and we want to say that its outputs are still basic. Perhaps the requirement should instead be that none of the *synchronic* inputs to the system are beliefs. Even this, however, runs up against difficulties. Introspection systems presumably take not only sensations and the like, but beliefs, as inputs, and as synchronic inputs. Nonetheless, the results of introspection are intuitively basic; they are surely not inferentially justified by the beliefs that serve as inputs to them.

It is worth pausing for a moment to note an important consequence of this. Goldman (1979) insists that the results of belief-dependent processes are justified only if the beliefs used as input are justified, where a belief-dependent process is one some of the inputs to which are beliefs. The case of introspection shows that this cannot be right. Surely my belief that I believe that p can be justified on the basis of introspection—a belief-dependent process in just the way that memory is—even if my belief that p is unjustified.[6] Again, the distinction between belief-dependent and inferential processes needs to be made explicit.[7]

6. Goldman concedes in footnote 7 of "What Is Justified Belief?" that introspection satisfies his definition of a belief-dependent process, even though it shouldn't. The problem he notes there is that we want to require more than conditional reliability of introspection; that is, the resulting analysis is too weak. The problem I am pointing out is that the analysis is also too strong, for it has the result that introspective beliefs about unjustified beliefs cannot themselves be justified.

7. In this vein, it turns out that nondoxastic justification—an essential element in any nondoxastic theory that endorses the Grounds Principle—is harder to specify than we might have initially thought. It

One might take a perceptual model of introspection very seriously here and deny that beliefs per se are ever really inputs to introspection mechanisms. What serves as input to my visual system is not the chair but some representation of some proximal stimulus caused by the chair; similarly, it may be some more proximal representation of the belief, rather than the belief itself, that serves as input to the introspection system. There is, however, an important difference between introspection and perception in that the objects of perception, being distal phenomena, *couldn't be* inputs to the system; the objects of introspection could be. One might simply insist that introspection doesn't take actual beliefs as inputs, but this seems more like an ad hoc posit than an independently motivated view. In addition, such an argument for the claim that introspection is not belief-dependent could by parity of reasoning be used to argue that memory isn't either, that is, that memory doesn't take old beliefs as inputs, but only representations of them. This would amount to dismissing the Goldman-Senor thesis out of hand. I won't want to take this way out.

We may be better off changing our focus from the input class to the system to the way the system processes these inputs. Intuitively, an AND-elimination system, or a more general reasoning system, would be *inferential* in a way that a memory or introspection system would not, even if the latter take beliefs as inputs. The difference involves the notion of basing. If the notion of basing can be extended from the individual level to the level of the modules, it seems intuitively clear that some belief-dependent modules base their outputs on their inputs, while others do not. The belief that p may be directly input to the introspection system, without the introspective belief—my belief that I believe that p—being in any way *based on* it.

To base a belief on e is to take e as evidence for that belief. Taking as evidence is a psychological, not an epistemological, relation. We can take something as evidence for a belief even though it's not actually evidence for the belief; we could ground beliefs on other things even if no epistemic properties were instantiated. I don't claim to know exactly what psychological relation basing—taking as evidence—is, but do think that the relation is partly causal. It is well known even to proponents of such causal views (Alston 1988; Pollock 1986) that not all causal relations are ipso facto basing relations, so something else must be required. It is doubtful, however, that this something else must involve the subject's having a metabelief to the effect that e is evidence for the relevant belief.[8] Intuitively, it is possible to take something as evidence without being aware that this is what I am doing, in fact, without even

---

is tempting to claim that doxastic justification is what happens when a belief evidentially justifies a belief, and nondoxastic justification is what happens when a nonbelief justifies a belief. But this would inappropriately distinguish my nondoxastic justification for my introspective belief that I hope it's Tuesday from what would then have to be doxastic justification for my introspective belief that I believe it's Tuesday, at the same time inappropriately classifying the latter together with the genuinely doxastic justification enjoyed by my belief that it really is Tuesday.

8. Kvanvig (2003b) does defend a metabelief account of the basing relation, which I am denying, although I can't argue against it here. My extension of the notion of basing to subpersonal modules will look substantially less plausible on a view like his.

having the concept of evidence. Animals and small children base some beliefs on others, but lacking the concept of evidence, they lack the metabelief that the ground is evidence for the target belief. Although I lack a careful analysis of 'taking as evidence', there is no reason to doubt that it can be cashed out in naturalistic terms, presumably in some kind of counterfactual, dispositional, and/or functional terms.[9] The basing relation is a naturalistically specifiable relation, a psychological relation, a species of causal relation; thus there is no reason it couldn't apply to modules as well as persons.

It is obviously nonsensical to claim that modules are aware of what they are doing, and they surely don't have beliefs in any literal sense, let alone beliefs about evidence. Still, modules take some things as evidence for the conclusions they output.[10] The visual system takes shading as evidence for shape; it takes discontinuities as evidence for object boundaries. Though a ground needs to be accessible to whatever is basing a conclusion on it, the grounds that are used by my visual system need not be used by or even accessible to me. An aforementioned assumption on which the visual system bases its conclusions is that distal objects are lit from above, an assumption that I might not share and thus might not have accessible to me. The system that calculates depth from eye convergence may base its outputs on facts about trigonometry and the distance between the eyes, facts which it "knows" but I do not.[11]

I think that the standard view, that perception and cognition more generally are species of unconscious inference, actually requires something like this.[12] I tend to think that 'inference', at least in the psychological sense, is univocal, that perception is genuinely inferential and not just in some unusually broad sense of the term. My perceptual modules engage in inference in more or less the sense that I do, although I have additional capacities to reflect on my inference, and so forth. The main difference, noted in chapter 3, is that modules can take as premises items that are not beliefs, at least not beliefs of the larger organism. This is consistent with there being a univocal concept of basing in play. One need not agree with all this, however. One who insists that 'inference' really must be construed in an artificially lax sense

9. Keith Korcz (1997, 2000) has a sophisticated theory of basing, and it is a naturalistic one. I don't want to endorse the particulars, however, for he allows metabeliefs to substitute for causal relations, in part because he wants to capture the intuition that Lehrer's (1974) gypsy lawyer is justified in believing in his client's innocence. My own intuition is that the gypsy lawyer is not justified, so I take gypsy lawyer types of cases to militate *against* such a role for metabeliefs, rather than in favor of them. Korcz's view, however, once purged of metabeliefs, strikes me as fairly plausible on independent grounds, and it would also suit the present purposes quite nicely.

10. These outputs/conclusions will not always be beliefs. The basing relation can have some other kind of mental state as the downstream relatum. Nonetheless, I will typically use 'belief' rather than some more general term for the sake of exposition.

11. The basing relation will have to be construed as a three-place relation: a set of grounds, a set of conclusions, and the thing that is basing the conclusions on those grounds. Thus a particular belief might be grounded for my visual system on the rigidity assumption (Ullman 1979) but not grounded for *me* on anything.

12. Though it relies on a dramatically overhauled conception of inference, connectionism is not necessarily a challenge to this. There is nothing about connectionism per se that favors, say, Gibson over Helmholtz.

when applied to modules will read 'basing' in a correspondingly broad sense in those contexts. I can accept this so long as it is agreed that the relation in question is both intelligible and naturalistic.

Some systems base their outputs on beliefs—that is, beliefs belonging to the larger organism. The AND-elimination system hypothesized previously bases the conclusion that p on the belief that p & q. Any reasoning system would base its outputs on the premises it takes as inputs. Importantly, however, not all belief-dependent processes use the input beliefs as grounds. My introspective mechanism doesn't base its outputs on the beliefs that it takes as inputs: it doesn't take the belief that p as evidence for the belief that I believe that p. To take a belief as evidence for another is to take the content of the first as evidence for the content of the second, and this certainly isn't the case with belief introspection.

Similarly, the belief dependence of memory is not one that involves basing; the beliefs on which memory is dependent are not beliefs on which the outputs are based. In the simplest case, what happens is that I believe that p at time t, and this belief serves as a diachronic input to a memory system that yields as output the belief that p. In such a case, the output belief (that p) is clearly not based on the input belief (that p).

Memory is quite a bit more complicated than this simple case suggests, however, for memory is surely a constructive process (Bartlett 1932; Loftus and Palmer 1974) and not—or not always—a mere passive recorder. Consider a standard example (Roediger and McDermott 1995). Subjects are presented with a list including the following words: 'bed', 'dream', 'snooze', 'awake', 'blanket', 'tired'. When tested later and after a number of distracting intervening tasks, they falsely "remember" having heard the word 'sleep'. I think we want to say that this belief, though false, is justified, assuming that such phenomena are not so pervasive as to undermine the overall reliability of memory. However, there is presumably some kind of inferential process responsible for the belief that 'sleep' was on the list. The question is whether this output belief is based on the relevant input beliefs, whether the process is inferential in a sense that would undermine the basicality of the belief.

Memory consists of encoding, storage, and retrieval. Where in this might the constructive/inferential part occur? A memory system Σ can engage in inference (in the psychologically relevant sense of the term) either at the time of encoding (t_e) or at the time of retrieval (t_r); storage, I take it, really is a matter of passive retention. At t_r, Σ may base its outputs on stored representations that were encoded at t_e; that is, the occurrent memories of the larger organism may be constructed at the time of retrieval on the basis of stored representations, the content of which is nonidentical with that of the resulting occurrent memory. These stored representations may in turn have been constructed by Σ on the basis of beliefs of the agent that were occurrent at t_e. But despite all this construction, it does not follow that Σ's conclusions at t_r are based on the nonconstructed input beliefs that were occurrent at t_e. The stored representations may have been based for Σ on the old belief tokens, and the new belief tokens may be based for Σ on these, but it does not follow that the new tokens are based on the old tokens. The basing relation is not transitive. If an output is based for an agent on e at t, then e is accessible at t to that agent, and the same holds for modules. In an ordinary memory case, the belief tokens occurrent at t_e no longer exist and thus are not accessible to the system at t_r; thus they cannot be part of the system's grounds for its outputs. (If the belief tokens were still accessible, the long-term memory system would be superfluous, and the case in question would not be a pure memory case of the sort that concerns us here.) Basing is thus necessarily synchronic, even though dynamic, and because diachronically persistent mental states are possible, basing is nontransitive. So in a standard case of memory, the output beliefs are not based on the input beliefs, *even for* Σ.

It is even more obvious that the output beliefs are not based on the input beliefs *for the larger organism that possesses* Σ. Just as my visual system—unlike myself—has access to the rigidity assumption and the like, Σ has access to those stored representations on which it bases its outputs, though I, the larger organism, do not. All I know about these representations I must either piece together from the outputs of Σ, which, by hypothesis, have a different content from those representations, or discover by way of empirical research in the psychology of memory. So my occurrent memories are not based for me on the stored representations, and even if basing were transitive, this would not provide an argument for the claim that memory beliefs are based on old input beliefs. Nor is there any more direct reason for thinking that the new beliefs are based on the old; to reapply the earlier argument, since the old belief tokens are not now accessible to me, the new tokens cannot be based for me on them.

A more direct argument for this same conclusion can be found by returning to the Roediger and McDermott example. At the time of encoding, I believe that I have just heard 'bed', that I have just heard 'dream', and so forth. Presumably, at no time *prior to retrieval* do I believe that I've heard 'sleep'. My memory belief that I've heard 'sleep' could not be based on an earlier occurrent belief unless it is the belief that I've just heard 'bed' or the like. But surely it is not plausible that my belief at t_r that I heard 'sleep' at t_e is based on my belief at t_e that I've just heard 'bed'. Misremembering may constitute an epistemic failing, but surely not one so egregious as this.

I have belabored the case of memory and the less direct argument for the claim that memory beliefs are not based on older tokens because it highlights a very important issue concerning the notion of inference. There is a prima facie tension between foundationalism and the received view in contemporary cognitive psychology, for the received view holds that perception, memory, and perhaps even introspection involve unconscious inference in good Helmholtzian fashion. Perceptual and memory beliefs are thus inferential. Yet the foundationalist (the external object foundationalist, at least) holds that these beliefs are noninferential. I have been trying to resolve this tension by relativizing the notion of basing, and thus the notion of inference, to a system or entity doing the basing. The fact that certain of my subpersonal modules base their outputs on certain premises does not mean that these outputs are based *for me* on these premises, or on anything else. Perceptual beliefs are inferential in the sense that perceptual systems base their outputs on other states; they are noninferential in the sense that the person who holds these perceptual beliefs does not base them on other states, in particular, does not base them on other beliefs.[13]

13. Where exactly to draw the boundaries between the agent and her subpersonal systems, where to draw the line between beliefs of the agent and assumptions of the perceptual and other modules, are difficult questions, and I have nothing very precise or illuminating to say about them. There is a genuine

There is another way to frame all this. I have been claiming that 'inference', at least in the psychological sense of the term, is univocal, that the inferential processes engaged in by whole persons are of a piece with the inferential processes engaged in by smaller cognitive modules. In addition to this psychological sense of 'inference', however, there is an epistemological sense. Psychological inference is a matter of moving from one cognitive state to another, but the connection between this and a belief's being inferential in the epistemological sense is far from straightforward. As 'inferential' is used in epistemological circles, for a belief to be *epistemically* inferential is for it to be nonbasic. But a belief's being epistemically noninferential is compatible with the belief's being psychologically inferential, at least so long as the entities for which the belief is (psychologically) inferential are subpersonal.

Although perception and memory and the like are inferential processes in the psychological sense, they are not inferential in the epistemological sense. I will say that *a process is (epistemically) inferential* if and only if (i) the synchronic inputs to the process are beliefs and (ii) the outputs it produces in response to such inputs are not only caused by, but based on, these beliefs.[14] Introspection is (epistemically) noninferential in this sense because the outputs are not based on their doxastic inputs; memory is (epistemically) noninferential for the same reason, but also because beliefs are diachronic rather than synchronic inputs to memory processes; perception, imagery, and simulation as discussed previously are noninferential because their inputs are not beliefs.

Some cognitive systems, including primal systems, can take beliefs of the larger organism as inputs. But they can do so in one of two ways: these beliefs can either serve as grounds for the system or not. If they do, then the system is operating inferentially; otherwise, it is operating noninferentially.[15] Let us make the temporary simplifying assumption that any system that ever operates inferentially always does; similarly, one that ever operates noninferentially always does so. Then an inferential system would be one that operates inferentially and a noninferential system is one that operates noninferentially. Note that a noninferential system is not necessarily an inferentially opaque system, nor is an inferential system necessarily nonopaque. Opacity is a matter of accessibility to doxastic interlevel representations; inferentiality is a matter of what the inputs are and whether the system actually bases its outputs on them. Thus, there can be inferential, as well as noninferential, primal systems.

The operation of an inferential primal system, like the AND-elimination system, results in a nonbasic belief, but one that is arrived at by means of what I will call a *basic inference*, a notion that will be important in chapter 7. The operation of a noninferential primal system is the concern here, for this results in a basic belief; a

---

problem here, and though it is perhaps made more salient by the present discussion, it is certainly not a problem created by or limited to my view. These are questions any epistemological theory must eventually answer; claims of the form '*S* believes that *p*', though central to epistemology, need to be understood much better than they currently are.

14. Because basing is necessarily synchronic, the reference in (i) to synchronic inputs doesn't really add anything to (ii). I include it just to be explicit.

15. I am construing the inputs to the system in such a way that inputs even to downstream subsystems will count as inputs to the whole system. Thus, the (whole) visual system may include among its inputs primal sketches and the like, not just retinal stimulation.

basic belief is one that is the output of a noninferential primal system. More formally, though still working with a simplifying assumption,

(B*) A belief B is basic for S at t iff B is the output at t of one of S's cognitive systems that (i) is inferentially opaque, (ii) has resulted from learning and innate constraints, and (iii) does not base its outputs on any doxastic inputs.

(B*) claims that a belief is basic if and only if it is the doxastic output of a noninferential primal system. The examples of intuitively basic beliefs all seem to come from such systems, and the examples of intuitively nonbasic beliefs all seem not to. Perceptual systems, for example, seem to satisfy these requirements, as do memory and introspection systems.

Our a priori intuitions don't come from nowhere; they are presumably the outputs of some cognitive system or other, and whatever system it is must be inferentially opaque, or we would likely know otherwise. Folk psychology tends to classify such intuitions as the output of a faculty of reason—not to be confused with a nonopaque faculty of reason*ing*—but there may very well be different systems involved in different kinds of a priori intuitions: a pictorial representational system for spatial/geometrical intuitions (deSoto et al. 1965; Knauff et al. 2003), a separate "accumulator" system for simple arithmetical intuitions (Wynn 1992), and so on. Any such system seems to satisfy (B*).

It is important that the aforementioned examples of intuitively nonbasic beliefs are also examples of beliefs that are very plausibly never the outputs of (noninferential) primal systems. Semantic memory aside, I doubt that I have any noninferential primal systems that yield the belief that bats are more closely related to primates than to rodents. I do have such systems that are capable of producing the belief that there's a desk nearby or that the shortest distance between two points is a straight line. But given my current cognitive architecture and setting aside memory and the belief's simply popping into my head, the only way for me to form the belief that bats are more closely related to primates than to rodents is to reason it out, on the basis of premises about dentition or the like. Any system that produced the belief in that way would be an inferential system and would very likely fail to be inferentially opaque as well.

The simplifying assumption, that a given system operates either always inferentially or always noninferentially, should be dropped. It is important to leave room for the possibility of a system that bases some, but not all, of its outputs on beliefs of the larger organism. There may still be many inferential systems (whose operation is always inferential) and many noninferential systems (whose operation is always noninferential), but some systems may be neither, operating inferentially on some occasions and noninferentially on others. We would not want to ignore the important epistemological difference between the inferential and noninferential operations of such systems. Take, for instance, some primal reasoning system that basis its doxastic output, q, on the input belief that p. Perhaps the system could be used for hypothetical reasoning as well; it might produce the belief 'if p then q' when fed the *supposition* that p as input. Intuitively, we would want to count 'if p then q' as a basic belief but the belief that q as a nonbasic belief, inferentially justified on the basis of the belief that p. (B*) can be modified accordingly:

(B) A belief B is basic for S at t iff B is the output at t of one of S's cognitive systems that (i) is inferentially opaque, (ii) has resulted from learning and innate constraints, and (iii) does not base B on any doxastic inputs at t.

Thus amended, I think that (B) gets things right: a basic belief is one that results from the noninferential operation of a primal system.

I began the discussion of basicality in chapter 1 with the definition of a basic belief as one whose prima facie justification does not depend on evidential connections to other beliefs. I have been trying to provide reasons for thinking that the beliefs that satisfy (B) are, to a pretty close approximation at least, the same as the beliefs that satisfy this definition.

1.3. Counterexamples and Replies

In the previous chapter, I distinguished between the clairvoyance objection and the clairvoyance challenge. The former is supposed to show that reliabilism is false, because it falsely entails that Norman is justified. The latter shows that reliabilism, like so many other theories, is incomplete in that it does not entail that Norman is not justified. I was able to reply to the clairvoyance objection in chapter 5, but it is only now, with a full account of basicality, that I can answer the clairvoyance challenge.

The clairvoyance-type cases that need to be taken most seriously all suppose that the agent has neither defeaters nor independent evidence for the belief in question but that the belief was reliably produced. In such conditions, a belief will be justified if and only if it is basic. I claim that a belief is basic only if it is the noninferential output of a primal system. Norman's clairvoyance belief, as argued in chapter 5, is intuitively not the result of a system that satisfies the etiological constraint on primal systems. Truetemp's belief is, *ex hypothesi*, not the result of such a system. Though the relevant systems are noninferential, they are not primal, and this is why their outputs are nonbasic.

Recall the Nyrmoon case as contrasted with the Norman case. There were two differences between Nyrmoon's clairvoyance system and Norman's, as BonJour's description invites us to conceive the latter. The first difference is that Nyrmoon's system is stipulated to take sense organ transductions as inputs, while Norman's presumably does not. This makes Nyrmoon's belief a candidate for being a perceptual belief (though obviously in a sense modality foreign to us) where Norman's is not. The second difference is that Nyrmoon's system is stipulated to have the same developmental trajectory as our perceptual systems, while the description of the Norman case invites us to assume that the system (if there even is a system responsible for the belief) has just recently popped into existence. Although the perceptual or nonperceptual nature of the belief is no longer the topic, the second difference speaks to the etiological constraint on cognitive systems. Even without the stipulation that Nyrmoon's belief utilizes energy transduction across a sense organ, our intuition is that his belief is (at least prima facie) justified. (If no such transduction occurs, the belief is basic though nonperceptual.) But now the only remaining difference between his case and the Norman case is the etiology of the system. If Norman's system is assumed to violate the etiological constraint for primal systems, my theory implies that his belief is nonbasic, hence unjustified. If Norman's system does satisfy the etiological constraint, then I see no difference between his case and the Nyrmoon case, and I, at least, cease to have the intuition that Norman's belief is not prima facie justified.

Thus the clairvoyance *challenge*—and not merely the clairvoyance *objection*—is addressed. Not only does the present theory not imply that Norman and his ilk are justified; it positively implies (at least for the intuitively compelling versions of the cases) that they are unjustified. Clairvoyance problems are not, as on most views, merely avoided by underspecification; they are actually solved. Again, Lehrer's Truetemp case makes the same points, but even more clearly. By stipulation of the case, the system fails to satisfy the etiological constraint. Thus my account straightforwardly implies that the belief is nonbasic.

What about the other sorts of cases that caused problems for other reliabilist theories? My cognitively spontaneous belief that the moon is 2,178 miles in diameter is presumably not the result of a primal system, so it is not basic. Semantic memory aside, it is doubtful whether any of my cognitive systems are capable of producing such a belief via any kind of reliable process. So any such belief must either not be the output of any (reliable) cognitive system, or the system must have just recently arisen. Similarly for any of the beliefs on the list of intuitively nonbasic beliefs from section 1.1.

How about the officious demon, who produces mostly true philosophical beliefs in me? Such beliefs are not the results of any of my cognitive systems, thus not the results of any of my primal systems. Hence the beliefs are nonbasic. And since I don't have any other argument for them, they are unjustified. The God-given brain lesion results in a cognitive capacity, but not every capacity involves an actual system. The lesion intuitively does not constitute a system; it certainly does not constitute a primal system, again because of the etiological constraint.

Perhaps, however, there are other primal, noninferential systems that intuitively don't produce justified beliefs. Take any of the beliefs on the previous list of intuitively nonbasic beliefs. Surely there could be some creature whose cognitive architecture were such that some of these beliefs are noninferential outputs of primal systems of that creature. The scope and the resolution of our primal systems is obviously a contingent matter. There could certainly be creatures for whom the belief that the moon is 2,178 miles in diameter *is* the output of a primal system, or for whom the belief in the Pythagorean theorem is.

This all seems quite right to me, and I take it to be a virtue of my theory rather than an objection to it that creatures with very different cognitive architectures would have basic beliefs concerning propositions that are nonbasic for us. The tree outside my window looks to me to be somewhere in the neighborhood of fifteen to twenty feet tall. The output of my perceptual system is a rough height estimate, but with a good deal of training, my visual system might come to make more fine-grained classifications. Recall the mechanic who can tell by looking whether a given nut takes a 17 mm or 19 mm wrench. I find it quite plausible to claim that the belief that there's a 17 mm nut is a basic, perceptual belief for the mechanic, even if not for the average philosopher. There are certainly limits to the fineness of grain possible for *our* perceptual systems, but a creature for whom the belief that the moon is 2,178 miles in diameter is the output of a primal system would be one whose perceptual systems are very different from ours, different enough, perhaps, to be capable of producing basic beliefs of this sort.

Similarly, if the Pythagorean theorem were the output of a noninferential primal system of some creature, then it seems that the truth of the Pythagorean theorem would strike that creature as being as obvious as the fact that $1 + 1 = 2$ is for us. Though I am suspicious of appeals to "intellectual experience" (Plantinga 1993; Pust 2000), there is a sense of "seeming true" that parallels the nonexperiential sense of "looks" discussed in chapter 4; in this sense, the Pythagorean theorem would seem true to this creature in just the way that the law of noncontradiction does to us. Provided that the belief is reliably caused, I see no reason to deny that it is basic for that creature. In fact, that same creature might not have any noninferential primal systems that output the belief that $1 + 1 = 2$, in which case, this belief would be non-basic for that creature. This all strikes me as quite intuitively acceptable.

Suppose, however, that some creature had an innate wishful thinking module; surely the outputs of such a system could not be prima facie justified in the absence of evidential support from other beliefs? Since the inputs to the system are desires rather than beliefs, its operation is noninferential, and stipulating it to be innate and inferentially opaque, it would be a primal system. Why, then, are its outputs not basic? I have to answer that they would indeed be basic. I hasten to point out, however, that basicality does not by itself imply justification, or even prima facie justification. A basic belief, on my view, is one that is prima facie justified *if* it is reliably produced. What is distinctive about basic beliefs is that reliability is sufficient for their prima facie justification. However, it is also necessary for their justification, and it is highly doubtful that a wishful thinking module—if that is genuinely what it is—could really be reliable.

If these responses are adequate, then being the noninferential output of a primal system may really be sufficient for basicality. But is it also necessary?

One well-known counterexample to Plantinga's theory involves the Swampman (Sosa 1993). The Swampman comes into being fully formed, as the result of a random convergence of particles of swamp gas, and by an amazing coincidence, happens to be molecularly identical to some ordinary person. The Swampman, being the result of a fully random process, cannot be functioning properly or improperly, so his beliefs cannot, on Plantinga's theory, be justified/warranted. But intuitively, the Swampman is justified.[16] Though I posit no teleological requirement, an analogous problem might be thought to arise for my view. If the Swampman has just popped into existence, none of his systems satisfy the etiological constraint, and thus none of his beliefs are basic. But this is surely wrong.

---

16. The Swampman first entered the philosophical literature in Davidson's (1987) paper and has been the source of wildly conflicting intuitions ever since. The intuition Davidson wanted from us was that, because of his strange history (or lack of history), the Swampman doesn't have contentful mental states. I am talking and thinking about the Queen of England; the Swampman is merely blabbering sounds that happen to be acoustically indistinguishable from mine. Others have invoked the Swampman to support the exact opposite conclusion; Millikan's (1984) theory of content is sometimes criticized for implying that the Swampman has no contentful states. Consensus among epistemologists seems to be that the Swampman has not only contentful beliefs but also justified beliefs.

However, I think that the Swampman's systems do in fact satisfy the etiological constraint. If innateness is understood to require presence at birth, and the notion of birth is taken in a certain way, then the Swampman doesn't have any innate traits, since he wasn't, strictly speaking, born. But there is no good reason to embrace such a flat-footed conception of either innateness or birth. I don't have a worked-out theory of innateness to offer, but no one in either biology or psychology thinks that all innate traits are present at birth. Nor is literal birth of any consequence anyhow. Trees have innate as well as acquired traits, but plants aren't literally born any more than the Swampman was. To say that a trait is innate is—very roughly—to say that its presence in an entity was more or less determined by the *initial state* of that entity. The moment of birth is an arbitrary point at which we conveniently and frequently agree to count as the initial state of animals; germination provides a convenient place to fix the initial state for plants. For an artificial intelligence, its initial state is the state it is in when it comes online: what it knows then is innate knowledge; what cognitive systems it has then it has innately. The Swampman's initial state is the state he is in when he comes into existence. What systems he has at that time, he has innately, so the Swampman is guaranteed to have systems that satisfy the etiological constraint if he has any systems at all.

Must a cognizer have opaque systems in order to have basic beliefs? Because my view is a foundationalist view, it is committed to the claim that a cognizer that lacks basic beliefs therefore lacks any justified beliefs at all. Some[17] have suggested to me that God might not have any opaque cognitive systems (perhaps opacity would conflict with omniscience), thus no primal systems, thus no basic beliefs, thus no justified beliefs.

I have three responses to this objection; I arrange them in order of decreasing glibness. The first response is that if such a result is good enough for Plantinga, it's good enough for me. God doesn't have a design plan, and so, on Plantinga's theory, doesn't know anything. If Plantinga can live with it, I surely can. The more serious point behind this response brings me to a second response, which is that, as Plantinga is likely to reply, epistemology for God is different. God is so radically different from finite creatures, it never was very likely that we would find an epistemology that covered both. Presumably, for an omniscient S, S knows that p iff S believes that p. This is just one example of how different divine epistemology would be from epistemology for ordinary, finite cognizers. Thus the fact that an epistemology for finite creatures fails to transfer well to omniscient beings is perhaps little argument against that epistemology.

A third response is that omniscience does not guarantee nonopacity. Let an *introspectively omniscient* agent be one that has conscious access to all interlevel representations tokened by any of its cognitive systems. The most that would follow from introspective omniscience is that none of that agent's systems *that token interlevel representations* is introspectively opaque. Even this is not the claim that these systems fail to be *inferentially* opaque, because systems all of whose interlevel representations are nondoxastic will still be inferentially opaque, even if these interlevel representations are consciously accessible. However, any system that does not

---

17. Including, I think, Alvin Goldman, in conversation.

token any interlevel representations is ipso facto inferentially opaque, omniscience or no. Our visual systems are opaque because we lack introspective access to certain interlevel representations. If we had greater introspective access, and if some of these interlevel representations were beliefs, it would only be certain subsystems of our current visual system that were opaque, rather than the larger system. The outputs of what now counts as our visual system would no longer be basic, and they would no longer be perceptual. An increase in introspective capacities along these lines would increase the territory of inference and reduce that of perception. But it would not threaten the very existence of either perception or basic beliefs.

A more serious threat to inferential opacity involves not introspective omniscience but a failure of modularity. If some form of modularity is true of us, that is surely but a contingent fact about us and not necessarily of any possible cognizer. Lashley's holism (1929) could be true of some possible creatures, even if not of us. If a creature's cognitive processes are so interconnected as to constitute only one large, undifferentiated system, and that system happens not to be inferentially opaque, then that creature will have no basic beliefs and thus no justified beliefs. I think this is a real possibility, and I will have to deny that such a creature has any justified beliefs.

It is well worth noticing, however, just how different from us such a creature would be. The kind of modularity required by the present account is far weaker than, say, Fodorian modularity (Fodor 1983). Though Fodor's conception of modularity is quite controversial, failure of even the weaker sort of modularity required here would be quite surprising. A creature with one undifferentiated system would be very different from us in its cognitive architecture; to exhibit so much homogeneity that it fails to have isolable systems, the creature's cognitive systems would have to be remarkably interdependent. The creature couldn't go blind without also going deaf— or at least suffering some auditory impairment; otherwise audition would be isolable from vision. It couldn't suffer an impairment with respect to thermoception without thereby having new difficulty finding its way home. Any deficit with respect to task *A* that spares performance with respect to task *B* indicates that different, though possibly highly overlapping, systems are responsible for *A* and *B*.[18]

The subjectively available mental life of such a creature would also be very much unlike ours. Suppose our various perceptual mechanisms were not isolable from each other but were interdependent in the way required for a failure of even weak modularity. It is hard to imagine the kind of synesthesia that would result. Oddities like the McGurk effect result where two systems interface; to fail to be distinct systems, the two mechanisms would have to interface *all over*, in which case closing one's eyes would almost invariably affect audition. Worse, higher cognitive processes would have unrestricted access to perceptual mechanisms, making the results of perceptual processes subject to the vagaries of occurrent thought. Changing one's mind would literally change how things look. Such a truly Lashleyan cognizer has, I think, no business forming beliefs. My theory implies that a cognizer of this

---

18. There are methodological worries here, having to do with the fact that an immeasurable deficit is a deficit nonetheless. I address these in my (2001, 2003) articles. The use here of 'spared performance' means 'genuinely spared performance', not 'performance that is not measurably impaired'.

sort would have no basic beliefs, and thus, because I embrace foundationalism, no justified beliefs. So be it.[19]

The response just given is likely to sound like biting the bullet, but I think it actually embodies one of the fundamental intuitive rationales behind foundationalism. It is only because we are passive recipients of what is given to us in perception that we are capable of having justified beliefs; were all of our beliefs of our own making, we would have no right to them. This general sentiment has, of course, been elaborated in certain famously discredited ways, but the failure of these elaborations does not subvert the ultimate plausibility of the view. In claiming that we are passive recipients, I don't mean to deny any Kantian or Helmholtzian insights about the role of the cognitive makeup of the perceiver; in fact, I have insisted on taking these insights seriously. I mean merely that our contribution here is neither deliberate nor optional; it is out of our control. Our perceptual systems are active, though *we* are passive.[20] In claiming that things are "given" to us in perception, I do not, of course, mean to suggest any kind of infallibility, incorrigibility, or the like, nor is my intentional use of this unfortunate word intended to implicate any interesting role to experiential states. What is given to us in perception is belief, and beliefs are given merely in the sense that they are cognitively spontaneous and justified independently of their relations to other beliefs.

2. Intuitions and Beyond

The theory developed thus far is intended in large measure to capture our intuitions about basicality and justified belief. What else, one might ask, could a philosophical theory hope to do? In recent years, a number of authors have distinguished between two broadly different epistemological projects. One project, which Goldman (1992a) calls the 'descriptive project', attempts to capture and systematize our intuitions about justification, and another project, the 'normative project', aims to improve on these intuitions, to tell us not how we intuitively think we should form beliefs, but how we *really should* form beliefs.[21] Obviously, fidelity to our intuitions is of paramount importance to the former project, though its relevance to the latter project is far from clear.

---

19. The argument here implies that some very weak notion of modularity is mandated by introspectively available facts, without any need for empirical findings in cognitive neuroscience. I think this is true, but empirical findings will be necessary to support stronger notions of modularity, like Fodorian modularity, and they will be necessary to justify any detailed claims about the nature of even the weakly modular systems. Nor is introspection likely to be able to indicate very decisively whether a given belief token is the output of a given module. If I'm endorsing a kind of armchair cognitive neuroscience here, I'm not endorsing much of one.

20. Of course, this is not to deny the even more obvious fact that we are active in certain ways: I open my eyes and move my head, look behind doors and under rocks and through microscopes, and so on. Nonetheless, I have little or no control over which beliefs (or identifications) spontaneously result.

21. Kitcher (1992) makes a very similar—perhaps the same—distinction, though his is between the "analytic project" and the "meliorative project," respectively. In a similar but more contentious spirit, Kornblith (2002) contrasts giving a theory of our concept of justification/knowledge with giving a theory about the natural kind, knowledge itself.

2.1. Descriptive and Normative Epistemology

Several years before drawing the distinction in these terms, Goldman had already tacitly recognized the difference between these two projects. Thus, after considering the question of whether wishful thinking produces justified beliefs in worlds in which wishful thinking is reliable, Goldman sets aside the "standard format" of conceptual analysis and claims that "what we really want is an explanation of why we count, or would count, certain beliefs as justified and others as unjustified. Such an explanation must refer to our beliefs about reliability, not to the actual facts. The reason we count beliefs as justified is that they are formed by what we believe to be reliable belief-forming processes" (1979, reprinted in Goldman 1992c, p. 121).

This general approach evolves into the well-known normal worlds analysis in his (1986) book: here justification is a matter of reliability in normal worlds, where a normal world is one that satisfies our general beliefs about the actual world. As Goldman himself later admits (1992a), this seems to make for an unacceptably idiosyncratic account of justification. Someone like Kornblith might ask why our general beliefs about the world should have any influence on what justification is. They don't, after all, have any influence on what aluminum is.

A normal worlds type of analysis is inadequate qua theory of justification *itself*. This, however, does not imply that it has any significant failings as a theory about our *concept* of justification. That is, something in the neighborhood of a normal worlds approach might be just what descriptive epistemology requires, even if it is inappropriate for a normative epistemology. In fact, in the very same (1992a) paper in which he rejects his earlier normal worlds analysis, Goldman offers his two-component reliabilism as a descriptive epistemological theory; as such, it is not an analysis of justification but an account of why we have the epistemic intuitions we do. Simplifying somewhat, two-component reliabilism holds that our intuitive judgments of justifiedness are made on the basis of whether we take the target belief to result from a cognitive process represented on a stored mental list of virtuous processes; a process gets onto my virtue list by way of my deeming that process to be reliable in the actual world. This is quite similar to the normal worlds account; those processes that I take to be reliable in the actual world are by and large those that are reliable in normal worlds.

Among the virtues of this theory is that it handles the famous demon-world case: victims of a Cartesian demon use the same kinds of belief-forming processes that we do, though these processes are highly unreliable in their demon world. Our intuition, however, is that their beliefs are nonetheless justified. Thus reliability is not necessary for justification. Two-component reliabilism's treatment of this issue is complex, but the bottom line is that it is our beliefs about real-world reliability that determine our intuitions about whether a given belief is justified, and we don't believe the real world to be a demon world. Our beliefs about the world influence our epistemic intuitions.[22] Descriptive epistemology aims to account for these intuitions and thus needs to advert to these beliefs.

---

22. The influence intended here is diachronic, rather than synchronic. Compare chapter 4, section 1. People do have differing intuitions about justification, though this is less prominent among professional epistemologists, perhaps partly because of a selection bias. These differences might be explained in terms of differences in beliefs about the world.

It is plain to see how a descriptive epistemology of this sort would serve as a basis for a normative epistemology that hoped to transcend or improve on our intuitions. If we have the intuitions we do because of certain ingrained beliefs we have about the reliability of various cognitive processes, and if some of these beliefs are false, then we should revise the intuitions that depend on the false beliefs. We have the intuition that (ordinary) memory beliefs are (prima facie) justified, presumably because we have always taken memory to be generally reliable. If memory is *not* generally reliable, however, we should not put much confidence in its deliverances; though our intuitive epistemological principles license mnemonic belief, a better set of epistemological principles would not. It is likely that a true believer in clairvoyance, one whose intuitions are also generally in sympathy with external object foundationalism, would fail to have the "correct" intuition about the Norman case, but would intuitively judge Norman to be justified. The present approach allows us to specify what is wrong with that intuition: it depends on the false belief in the reliability of clairvoyance.

Old habits die hard, and it is no refutation of this general descriptive epistemological theory that our intuitions would remain—at least for some time—even if we were to change our minds about, for example, the reliability of memory or to temporarily suppose memory to be unreliable (see Goldman [1992a] for more on this score). My changing my mind about where the light source is does not affect the outputs of my visual system, which continues with its own assumption that things are lit from above. This is just informational encapsulation and is common of cognitive modules (nearly definitive of Fodor's conception of modularity). The general approach to descriptive epistemology sketched here will need to be supplemented by specific empirical proposals about the psychological mechanisms responsible for our epistemic intuitions and the ways in which and the extent to which these mechanisms might be (synchronically and diachronically) cognitively penetrable. Perhaps, for example, it is better to say that a subject will intuitively judge a belief to be justified if it is deemed to be the result of a process that the subject has historically deemed reliable, instead of one that the subject currently deems reliable.[23] The important point for the present purposes, however, is the content of the operative beliefs; it is beliefs about reliability, for example, that influence the intuitions.

Descriptive epistemology, thus construed, is actually a branch of cognitive psychology: it seeks to explain why we make the intuitive judgments we do, and it does so by describing the knowledge structures causally responsible for these judgments. It is therefore perhaps understandable that an epistemologist might seek merely to sketch enough of the descriptive theory to see that reliability is implicated and proceed on to the normative project without bothering with the details of exactly which beliefs about reliability (occurrent, long-held, both, etc.) need to be cited by the appropriate descriptive theory.[24]

23. The suggestion that ingrained beliefs are more important than current beliefs is consonant with the idea that epistemic intuitions are the result of a noninferential primal system, an idea I return to later.

24. If descriptive epistemology is really cognitive psychology, one might reasonably object that we should kick it out of the armchair and into the laboratory, where psychological matters are best studied. This is true, and it is good that some philosophers have begun practicing experimental philosophy for just this reason (e.g., Weinberg et. al 2001; Nichols and Knobe 2007). The field is still incipient as of this writing, however, and hasn't come close to addressing the questions I am asking about the causes of (certain)

In a similar vein, I think that we have intuitions about basicality,[25] and I think that these intuitions are due to our (long-standing) beliefs about what cognitive modules there are and which of these are noninferential and primal.[26] The reader will have noticed that, while I have been trying to capture intuitions to some extent, I have occasionally suggested ways in which we might go beyond these intuitions. Thus, like most epistemologists, I have been engaged in a project that is neither purely descriptive nor purely normative. The arguments of chapters 4 and 5 rested on certain empirical assumptions about the outputs of certain cognitive systems. For example, I claimed that while it is plausible to think that 'there's a conspecific in front of me' is an output of an existing perceptual system, it is doubtful that 'there's a sib in front of me' is. The epistemological status of such cases I take to be intuitively borderline; they are not the sort of cases we want to use as evidence for an epistemological theory. Instead, I suggested that *if* 'there's a sib in front of me' is not the output of a perceptual system, then we *ought* to deny that it is a perceptual belief. To the extent that we lack a settled conviction about whether this belief is the output of a perceptual module, I would predict that we lack a strong intuition about whether it is a perceptual belief.

At the beginning of the present chapter, on the other hand, I explicitly took the project at hand to be the descriptive epistemological task of capturing intuitions. The account of basicality offered there is easily amended to yield a rough approximation more clearly aimed at a descriptive epistemological project.

I want to introduce one new wrinkle before offering that theory, however. Just as we have long-held convictions about which processes are reliable and about what cognitive systems there are, we have ingrained assumptions, too, about how systems come into existence. And just as beliefs about the reliability of clairvoyance and the like may vary from person to person, and just as these differences might explain differences of intuition about Norman and the like, our beliefs about what system etiologies are normal may vary and thus may account for varying intuitions. Most of us, I take it, assume that learning and innateness are the only ways systems do in fact come about; these are the etiologies we would thus take to be "normal." Our intuitions about justifiedness frequently hinge on the system in question having what we would intuitively take to be an abnormal etiology. If, however, we were convinced (or, at least, had a long-standing conviction) that systems do frequently just pop into existence, that they often result from exposure to radiation, that God is prone to

---

of our epistemological intuitions. A more mature experimental philosophy might refute the psychological claims I am making here. This does not, of course, imply that these claims are groundless. The fact that I don't have statistics and thus can't report p-values does not indicate that I don't have evidence for the descriptive epistemology I endorse; I've been adducing evidence throughout this book. Social psychology is *a* source of evidence; it is not the only source of evidence.

25. Strictly speaking, I don't really think this is true, but the difference between it and what I really do think is true (discussed later, p. 157) won't matter for the present purposes.

26. The present claim requires that the folk have some background beliefs about primal systems, modules, classifications, and the like. I think this really is plausible, though of course they don't use anything like the terminology developed here. This is perhaps clearest in the case of perception. I argued in chapter 4 that ordinary language recognizes the perceptual output sense of 'look' and its ilk. More generally, I think that there is a folk concept of something like cognitive systems in the present sense, though I won't take the time to argue for that here. (The argument is laid out in Lyons 1999.)

implant cognitive systems in otherwise normal adults, that innate systems can none-theless come suddenly into action at a relatively advanced age, or the like, we would likely have different intuitions about such cases.

Thus, we can formulate a more explicitly descriptive theory, one that aims to capture intuitive judgments of justifiedness in terms of the attributor's beliefs:

> (B_D) *An attributor will judge S's belief B at t to be basic iff the attributor judges* B *to be* the output at t of one of S's cognitive systems that (i) is inferentially opaque, (ii) has a normal etiology, and (iii) does not base B on any doxastic inputs at t.[27]

The move from the descriptive epistemology offered by B_D to a normative episte-mology will be much like the one suggested before for simpler versions of reliabilism. We have the intuitions we do about basicality because of our convictions about the nature of the mind, in particular, about what noninferential primal systems there are. One way to improve on these intuitions is to correct whatever false beliefs we might have about which beliefs are or might be the outputs of noninferential primal sys-tems. Hence the original theory of basicality offered previously:

> (B) A belief B [really] is basic for S at t iff B is the output at t of one of S's cog-nitive systems that (i) is inferentially opaque, (ii) has resulted from learning and innate constraints, and (iii) does not base B on any doxastic inputs at t.

By taking the attributor out of the equation, we are once more talking about systems that *really are* inferentially opaque, and so on.

The present approach is to take intuitions seriously, though not as seriously as a purely descriptive epistemology would. Both Kitcher and Kornblith find the slavish adherence to pretheoretic intuitions objectionable and suggest that we abandon the descriptive project altogether in favor of some normative epistemological project, without concerning ourselves with capturing intuitions. Kitcher suggests a means-ends approach to normative epistemology: identify our epistemic goals and then endorse whatever belief-forming methods are most conducive to them. Kornblith offers a natural kinds approach: figure out which natural kind the term 'knowledge' refers to, and then see what properties the members of this kind have in common. Both approaches see epistemic intuitions as irrelevant to normative epistemology.

Adherence to intuitions need not be slavish, however. My own view is that a nor-mative theory can and perhaps should take epistemological intuitions seriously, even if we are willing—as we certainly should be—to revise or abandon some or even all of these intuitions. Though I don't want to be held hostage to naive intuitions about justification, I'm not ready to abandon the standard philosophical methodology of using consonance with pretheoretic intuitions as part of an argument for a philosoph-ical theory, at least in a normative discipline like epistemology. Were there independent

---

27. This is merely a rough approximation in that, as mentioned two paragraphs previously, current and long-held beliefs might differ, so that, for example, it is the attributor's current judgment that the belief is the output of a system that the attributor has historically believed to be opaque, and so forth, that determines the attributor's intuition about justifiedness.

access to justification itself (as there is to the mind itself for the philosophy of mind/philosophy of cognitive science), we might very well ignore our intuitions altogether, but it is very difficult to believe that this is the situation epistemologists are in.

A different argument for dismissing philosophical intuitions has been mounted by a skeptical wing of the experimental philosophy movement. Weinberg, Stich, and various colleagues (Weinberg et al. 2001; Swain et al. 2008) have amassed empirical evidence showing that philosophical intuitions vary according to such epistemically irrelevant features as socioeconomic status of the intuitor and the order in which various cases are presented. (One of their favorite stimuli is the Truetemp case, which, of course, has loomed large in this book!) This variation, they claim, undermines the status of philosophical intuitions as evidence for a philosophical theory, at least as evidence for a *normative* theory.[28] This is a challenging position, and an adequate response would take me too far afield. Let me just note that on the normative epistemology I endorse, (some) epistemological intuitions may turn out to be basic, and if they are reliably produced, they will be prima facie justified. To a rough approximation (I'll discuss evidence in more detail in chapter 7), I hold that this is enough to poise a belief to serve as evidence. If the intuition skeptics want to deny this, they will have to back this denial with normative epistemic principles that indicate that our intuitive beliefs are unjustified or that despite their being justified, they can't serve as evidence for an epistemological theory. Absent such an argument, I am not yet convinced that intuitions need to be abandoned wholesale, though I do think they need to be treated with a great deal of care and suspicion.[29]

The approach I am endorsing contrasts with both the natural kinds approach and the means-ends approach to normative epistemology. I want to try out a reflective equilibrium approach: start with the pretheoretical intuitions but be willing to modify those to better render them consistent with each other and, especially, with additional empirical information. It is this last component, the requirement that empirical information figure into the equilibrium, that distinguishes this approach from the standard conceptual analysis of the descriptive project. This empirical information may include psychophysical information about the reliability of various processes, cognitive neuroscientific information about the architectural details of cognitive systems, development information about their etiologies, and even social psychological information about the sources of our epistemological intuitions, as we will see in section 2.4 (though my treatment will be different from the experimental philosophy treatment).

Normative epistemology thus construed is not committed to any very robust understanding of justification *an sich*; it certainly need not bear the metaphysical encumbrance of justification as a natural kind. What makes the normative epistemological

---

28. Stich, at least, is quite happy to allow intuitions to serve as data for a descriptive epistemology but has serious doubts that we can ever get from a descriptive theory from a normative one without assuming that our intuitions are correct, despite the fact that large numbers of perfectly normal people have conflicting intuitions.

29. There is a kind of "epistemic circularity" here, in Alston's (1993) sense; he argues fairly convincingly that this kind of circularity (as opposed to "premise circularity") is not vicious. Any *complete* epistemological theory, turned to address the evidence for that theory, will either yield epistemic circularity or be self-undermining. I prefer the former.

principles superior to the descriptive epistemological principles is not that the former get at the truth about justification itself, while the latter gets at only what we think about justification (though who knows? maybe this is also true). What is superior about the normative principles is that, in contrast to the principles we in fact endorse, the normative principles are the ones we would endorse if fully informed about the descriptive features of the world.

I advocate a reflective equilibrium approach largely because it hasn't really been tried out in the context of a naturalistic epistemology; if it bears fruit, then it is worth pursuing further. In addition, however, the normative epistemology I defend, a type of inferentialist reliabilism, might receive independent support from a strictly means-ends approach: what we want, epistemically, is a lot of true beliefs, and thus we want to use processes that are genuinely reliable. But we have other epistemic goals as well, and among them is a certain kind of self-assurance in our beliefs, and thus we want to have grounds for the less obvious of these beliefs. Maybe we desire stability in our beliefs (Plato and Hume certainly did), and so we want, for those beliefs that are psychologically optional, that we have reasons on which to base them.

Obviously, this is the bare beginning of a sketch of a rapprochement between the two approaches to normative epistemology, and it is hampered in part by the fact that we don't have a canonical, exhaustive list of our epistemic goals. Nonetheless, if the results of the means-ends approach converge even roughly with the results I get from the reflective equilibrium approach (and I take it the foes of intuition endorse a reliabilist epistemology—what else could they?), this does much to recommend my view, for mine has the clear dialectical advantage of getting there without the whole-sale dismissal of intuition ab initio. Obviously, this is a dialectical virtue when one's chief opponents in substantive epistemological matters develop their contrary views largely or entirely to do justice to just those intuitions. It is also pretty clearly an epistemic virtue if one can meet each of the opponent's intuitive objections, individually, with a fairly unified response, rather than defining the rules of evidence so as to throw a blanket over these objections en masse. Everything else equal, the theory that actually handles the opponent's objections is better than one that rules them out of court. One would have to be *very* confident that philosophical intuitions have *zero* evidential contribution to proceed in that way.

Again, my main reason for adopting the reflective equilibrium approach is that it strikes me as promising, which is a consideration that is not independent of claims about the epistemic status of intuitions. This, however, brings us to the brink of a whole research program, and I can only gesture at some of the reasons for optimism. One reason I'm hopeful is that this approach starts with a whole (defeasible) epistemological apparatus at hand; the normative project will be genuinely *revisionist*, in the sense that it will revise an existing epistemology (the descriptive inferentialist reliabilist episte-mology I've been articulating so far), rather than starting from scratch. This will give us an epistemology that is conceptually rich, as well as empirically responsible.

2.2. Cognitive Science and Basicality

I have argued that our intuitions about which beliefs are basic depend in part on our background assumptions about which beliefs are the noninferential outputs of primal systems. These assumptions, of course, depend on assumptions about what primal systems there are. Similarly, our intuitions about which beliefs are perceptual beliefs depend on our background assumptions about which systems are perceptual systems and what kinds of beliefs they produce as output. The present theory allows us to explain why we have the intuitions we do and why at least some clashes of intuitions occur. Plantinga (2000), for example, seems to have the epistemic intuition that belief in God is basic; I myself do not. I would conjecture that this is because Plantinga also believes we have a "God module"—a "*sensus divinitatis*," as it is called in Calvinese—while I do not. Plantinga's God module is presumably conceived to be a noninferential primal system. If this really is the source of disagreement, then the present theory explains it. But the theory can do more than explain such disagreements about basicality; it can settle them, at least in principle. The disagreements need not be intractable. All that would be required to resolve the present dispute is sufficient empirical evidence for or against the existence of a God module.

Cognitive science investigates such questions as (1) what cognitive systems there are, (2) what kinds of outputs they produce, (3) what kinds of interlevel representations they produce (and whether these are introspectively accessible), (4) how these systems operate, and (5) how they come about. Questions (1) and (2) are mainly under the jurisdiction of cognitive neuroscience, (3) and (4) of cognitive neuroscience and cognitive psychology, and (5) of cognitive psychology, especially developmental psychology, as well as developmental neurobiology. All of these have an obvious bearing on the question of whether a given belief is or might feasibly be basic, that is, whether it might be the output of an inferentially opaque system, with a normal etiology, operating noninferentially.

Claims of basicality are easily abused. If I have some pet view but lack an argument for it, I can stymie interlocutors by simply insisting that the belief in question is basic. I might claim that premarital sex is immoral or that nature abhors a vacuum or that the principle of sufficient reason is true, and if these beliefs are challenged, resort to the claim that the beliefs in question are basic, a priori even. If challenged again, I might even aver that this belief about the basicality of the other belief is itself basic. Even so, a theory of basicality prevents such a situation from degenerating into a total impasse. Even if we do have basically justified beliefs about basicality, it by no means follows that we cannot apply the present theory of basicality to determine—at least in principle—whether these prima facie justified beliefs are ultima facie justified or, more important, to see whether they are true. If cognitive science reveals that we have no primal systems that produce moral beliefs as their outputs, then it follows that our moral beliefs are all nonbasic, any contrary intuitions notwithstanding.

It is often assumed in epistemology—perhaps on the authority of the Descartes of the *Meditations*—that belief in one's own existence is basic. I tend to think that the view he seems to endorse in the *Discourse*, that this belief is nonbasic, is more plausible. I suspect that things are as Descartes's most famous phrase suggests: my belief that I am thinking is evidence for my belief that I exist; I conclude the latter from the former. In any case, we could, in principle, determine whether belief in one's own existence is (ever) basic by determining whether we have any primal systems that noninferentially produce 'I exist' as outputs.

Lehrer (1990a, 1997) has argued that basic beliefs would have to involve a kind of "epistemic surd"; if a belief is genuinely basic, then it is ungrounded and so must have the character of a brute and dogmatic insistence. Thus basicality and justification don't fit comfortably together. "Any explanation of why our basic beliefs are justified would become the basis of an argument to the conclusion that they are justified, and such an argument would render the justification of the beliefs in question non-basic" (1997, pp. 60–61). Similarly, BonJour (e.g., 1985) famously argued that any argument for belief B's being basic (B has F and anything with F is likely to be true) was ipso facto an argument for B, which meant that B wasn't basic after all. There are several well-known problems with this style of argument, the most salient of which is that it is one thing to argue for some belief's basicality and quite another to argue for the belief itself. Basicality is not even sufficient for justification (on my view, a basic belief must also be reliably formed to be prima facie justified, and it must be undefeated to be ultima facie justified), let alone *truth*. And of course my *having* an argument for B is no threat to B's basicality; it's only my *needing* an argument for B that makes B nonbasic.

Nonetheless, some antifoundationalist suspicions are somewhat warranted; there does seem to be something brute, dogmatic, even "surdish" about an epistemologist's insistence that some class of beliefs is basic, and then defending this claim by holding that this higher order belief, that the members of class C are basic, is itself basic. This ceases to be a problem, however, if we have a solution to the delineation problem. It is possible, even if unlikely, that some beliefs about basicality are themselves basic. It would not follow from this that there couldn't be any independent, empirical evidence for or against basicality. A neuroscientist might give me some compelling evidence for thinking that my belief that Fred is upset with me is the noninferential output of a primal system. This is not yet evidence for thinking that Fred really is upset with me, so it clearly does not interfere with the basicality of the first-order belief. Nor would it preclude the basicality of a higher order belief that this first-order belief was basic. I might now have two justifications for this higher order belief: a basic intuition about the basicality of the first-order belief and a long inferential justification, including the testimony of the neuroscientist and premises that include a theory of basicality.

I have been allowing for the sake of argument that we might have intuitions about basicality. I doubt that this is true if 'intuition' is understood in the historical sense of a basic a priori belief; instead, I expect that our intuitions, narrowly construed, are about justifiedness, rather than basicality per se. It is much more likely that our beliefs about basicality are inferentially justified on the basis of these basic beliefs about justifiedness. Here is how I suspect it goes: we have some primal system that noninferentially produces as outputs beliefs of the form 'S is justified in believing that p'; such beliefs therefore are basic. When we note that S has no doxastic evidence for p, we justifiedly infer that the belief that p was basic. This would make beliefs about basicality at least typically inferential.[30]

This same system might produce basic beliefs about nonactual cases if it operates like the hypothetical reasoning system mentioned in section 1.2. That is, when

---

30. I am anticipating what might be called a particularist (Chisholm 1982b) psychology of epistemic judgments, rather than a methodist one. The methodist possibility is that, instead of or in addition to particular beliefs about justifiedness, we have primal systems that noninferentially produce general beliefs about justification (e.g., that it requires reliability, or that it doesn't, or what have you).

fed hypothetical case descriptions as inputs, the system returns beliefs about conditional justifiedness: for instance, an agent in such conditions would be justified. When fed beliefs about purportedly actual situations, however, it produces unconditional attributions of justifiedness: the agent is justified. Thus, the very same system might produce my basic belief that Normina is (i.e., would be) justified in her perceptual beliefs, and my nonbasic belief that Ed was justified a minute ago in believing that there was a pencil on his desk. The former belief resulted from the noninferential operation of this system, and the latter belief resulted from the inferential operation of the system, taking such beliefs as 'Ed formed the visual belief that there was a pencil on the desk, in such-and-such lighting conditions' as inputs.

If this is right, then we have two ways of arriving at the nonbasic belief that some other belief B is basic: (i) form the basic belief that B is justified, note that the agent had no doxastic evidence for B, and infer that B was noninferentially justified or (ii) determine that B is the noninferential output of a primal system and infer from that (and the present theory of basicality) that B is basic.

The epistemology I am endorsing here might turn out to be self-undermining. That is, it might be that empirical investigation determines that we have no noninferential primal systems that output either general beliefs about justification or particular beliefs about justifiedness. If we lack any basic beliefs about justification, it is hard to see how we could have any justified nonbasic beliefs about it—this is just an application of Hume's 'no ought from is' principle. Such an empirical finding would indicate that if the present epistemology is correct, we couldn't be justified in thinking it was correct. Though there is nothing contradictory about such a result, it seems sufficiently undesirable that we might reasonably take it as a refutation of my theory.

Similarly, the theory might turn out to have undesirably skeptical consequences. We might determine that there are precious few primal systems that operate noninferentially and consequently precious few basic beliefs. It might be reasonable to conclude from this that my theory of basicality yields unacceptably few basic beliefs, that it leads to a skepticism far more implausible than the denial of the theory.

The threat of self-undermining and the threat of skepticism are real enough to count the present theory as being, to some interesting extent, empirically refutable.[31] But being empirically refutable in principle is, I think, more a virtue than a vice for a theory, so the mere possibility of such a refutation, without any indication that it is likely, doesn't trouble me. One reason this theory is empirically refutable is that it relies on the cognitive scientific concept of cognitive systems and makes justification contingent on certain empirically determined facts about such systems.

Many proponents of naturalized epistemology have claimed that empirical findings in cognitive science can have direct relevance to epistemological questions. For most such epistemologists, cognitive psychology is the empirical discipline of choice. The role I ascribe to modules, to cognitive systems, makes cognitive neuroscience one of the most decisive disciplines. The most compelling evidence for distinctness

31. I take it, for roughly Quinean/Duhemian reasons, that empirical refutability comes in degrees, so any claims about empirical refutability should be read with the tacit rider 'to some interesting extent'.

of systems, for independent operation, will always come from lesion studies and the inferences supported by findings of double dissociations (Lyons 2001, 2003). However, many of the cognitive capacities of concern to us are distinctively human, and certain tentative conclusions about system boundaries can be drawn on the basis of indirect evidence supplied by cognitive psychology, evolutionary psychology, and neuroimaging studies.[32]

Not all epistemological theories with similar-sounding commitments make anything like testable claims. Sosa (1991), for example, claims that justification (or "aptness," as he calls it, reserving 'justification' for something else) is determined by the reliability of the responsible faculty. But he says very little about what a faculty is supposed to be or how to individuate them. One gets the sense that Sosa posits a distinct faculty for every distinct competence (indeed, his later work [2007] seems to move away from faculties and focus on competencies instead), but he offers no means of distinguishing or counting either faculties or competencies. He claims (1991) that I have a distinct faculty responsible for my belief that I exist. It is hard to see what might count as evidence for this view. If he means by 'faculty' anything like what I mean by system, then the claim is exceedingly doubtful from an empirical perspective.

2.3. Illustration: Why My Philosophy Is More God-Friendly than Plantinga's

A concrete illustration of the present view might be helpful. To this end, I want to contrast a certain epistemology of religious belief that one could extract from the view endorsed here with the well-known epistemology of religious belief recently defended by Alvin Plantinga (2000). Plantinga notoriously argues that belief in God is basic. More precisely, he argues that if God exists, then belief in God is very likely basic (and prima facie justified), though if God does not exist, then belief in God is most likely not basic. Plantinga claims that if theism is in fact true, then it is quite probable that we are designed to noninferentially believe in God and that such a belief process is both reliable and aimed at the truth, conditions that are more or less sufficient for basicality on his view.[33] If God does not exist, then in all likelihood the process satisfies neither the design requirement nor the reliability requirement (Plantinga 2000).

I differ from Plantinga in three crucial respects: one epistemological, one psychological, and a third methodological. First, I have a different theory of basicality, one that does not impose a teleological requirement. Second, I doubt that we have a *sensus divinitatis*, if this is supposed to be some robust psychological structure and not just an orotund characterization of a mere capacity. I think that people do have more or less intuitive beliefs in the existence of God, so, in a trivial sense those who

---

32. I think of neuroimaging studies as offering indirect evidence simply because neuroimaging alone does not discriminate causal antecedents from causal consequents.

33. For a more detailed account of Plantinga's theory of basicality, see pp. 128–29. Plantinga prefers the phrase 'properly basic', by which he means basic and warranted.

have such beliefs do have the capacity to form a more or less intuitive belief in God.[34] If a cognitive faculty is merely a capacity, and there are no robust constraints on what count as distinct capacities, then of course we have a God faculty. But this fact would have no epistemological implications—on my view, anyway—concerning the status of belief in God. It doesn't begin to follow from our having a capacity to form the belief that God exists that we have a God *module*, a system that specializes in producing beliefs about God.

Finally, when it comes to trying to ascertain whether a given belief is indeed basic, I favor turning to the empirical disciplines to discover which (if any) of the agent's cognitive systems is/are responsible for the belief and what the synchronic and diachronic features of those systems are. To figure out whether we do have a God module, we can do far more than make a priori guesses conditional on God's existence or nonexistence (or invoke the authority of Calvin, who was hardly renowned as a cognitive neuroscientist). We can empirically discover (at least in principle) where these beliefs come from.

It may be true that if God (or a certain kind of God) exists, the probability of our having a *sensus divinitatis* is fairly high. However, there does not seem to be much, if any, empirical support for the claim that we have a system that specializes in producing beliefs about God.[35] Instead, it is likely that something in the neighborhood of one of the hypotheses now taken seriously in the psychology of religion will turn out to be true. Perhaps our belief in gods results from our taking a teleological stance to nonartifacts (Kelemen 1999, 2003). Perhaps it results from the operation of predator-detection systems or more general intentional agent mechanisms (Atran 2002). Probably culture-guided learning affects the outputs of these systems, determining that the resulting belief is that Yahweh created this lovely mountain vista (rather than that Omecihuatl or Ilúvatar or the Flying Spaghetti Monster did). There are a number of other possibilities concerning the origin of intuitive religious belief, and I won't try to enumerate them. I do, however, want to point out (a) that this is an empirical issue and (b) that which hypothesis turns out to be correct will determine which, if any, beliefs about God, gods, or the supernatural more generally turn out to be basic.

When I say that I doubt that we have a God module, what I mean to deny is that we have a cognitive module that specializes in producing beliefs about God. I also doubt the weaker claim that we have a module that specializes in producing beliefs about supernatural agencies more generally. Beliefs about the numinous are most likely the outputs of systems that do something else, something more directly connected to inclusive fitness. Would it follow from this that beliefs about the gods are nonbasic? That would depend on which epistemology is correct.

Suppose, to anchor the discussion, that our more or less intuitive beliefs about the communicative purposes of divine agencies result from the operation of our

34. As mentioned before, the historical sense of 'intuition' only applies to beliefs that are both basic and a priori. I don't want to include either assumption right here, hence the 'more or less' hedge.

35. Some scientists have spoken of a "God module." The term, however, is surely aimed more at grabbing attention than at careful description. Ramachandran et al.'s (1997) study, for instance, made no effort whatsoever to establish any claims of specialization; the researchers were not claiming that there is a *system* for religious experience in the sense that there is a system for face recognition.

theory of mind mechanisms (Bering 2004). Just as these mechanisms yield beliefs about the mental states of conspecifics, they yield beliefs about the mental states of supernatural entities, in particular, beliefs of the form 'someone is trying to tell me something'. There is nothing about my theory of basicality that precludes such beliefs from being basic. If our theory of mind mechanisms are noninferential primal systems, as seems plausible, their outputs will be basic, even when these outputs are about the communicative intentions of supernatural beings.[36]

Plantinga will have a more difficult time here in view of his teleological requirement. The theory of mind module is probably a truth-aimed adaptation, but Plantinga's view seems to require more. Religious belief per se might be a spandrel; that is, there may have been selection *of* religious belief, rather than selection *for* it (Atran 2002; Kelemen 1999), because, though itself not fitness conducive, it piggybacked on something that was fitness conducive. In such an event, religious belief would not satisfy Plantinga's teleological requirement. Even if religious belief is an adaptation, it may be for some purpose other than truth, something like social cohesion (Wilson 1998), perhaps by serving a moral regulatory function (Bering 2004). Again, such belief would violate Plantinga's teleological requirement, though it may still satisfy my requirements for basicality. In that sense, my view is more God-friendly than Plantinga's.

These teleological worries are substantial even if God exists. Plantinga thinks that if theism is true, then it is very likely that our belief in God is produced by reliable truth-aimed processes. But this is at least in part because he builds a lot into theism: "How could we make sense of the idea that theism is true but belief in God doesn't have warrant? We'd have to suppose (1) that there is such a person as God, who has created us in his image and has created us in such a way that our chief end and good is knowledge of him, and (2) that belief in God...has no warrant" (2000, p. 189). Certainly, such a robust conception of theism (replete with what amounts to the claim that God cares whether we believe in him) seems to be quite conducive to thinking that our religious beliefs are truth-aimed. Work the notion of theism just a bit more, and we'll have a view that does not merely render plausible the claim that belief in God is warranted, but actually entails it. A more bare-bones theism, however, which merely claims the existence of some Prime Mover or the like, has little to say about whether religious beliefs are aimed at truth or at something else or at nothing at all.

The differences between my view and Plantinga's are magnified when we consider the possibility that God does not exist. Plantinga thinks our more or less intuitive religious beliefs are the result of a highly specialized God module, a *sensus divinitatis*. If God does not exist, then there probably is no such faculty; it would almost certainly not be truth-aimed. It would decidedly not be *successfully* truth-aimed: because it does nothing but produce beliefs about God, the faculty would be perfectly unreliable. Hence its outputs would be neither justified nor, probably, even basic.

On my view, however, the nonexistence of God makes no difference vis-à-vis the basicality of religious beliefs, and it *might* not make any difference to the justifiedness

---

36. If this is true, it is an important empirical discovery, not part of our commonsense theory of mind—not part of mine at least. The fact that such a hypothesis is not part of my long-established commonsense view of the mind may explain why I don't have the intuition that belief in God is basic.

of such beliefs either. Basic beliefs are prima facie justified if they are reliably produced, and the religious outputs of the theory of mind module might count as reliably
produced, even if God does not exist. Obviously the module itself could easily be
generally reliable, despite its production of the occasional false religious belief. One
could try to make a virtue of the generality problem and claim that all the outputs of
the module therefore count as reliably produced. This would be illegitimate, but it
would be equally illegitimate to claim that belief in God cannot be the result of a reliable process, on the grounds that the belief in question is false. I don't have a solution
to the generality problem to offer, but a reasonable solution will have to leave room for
false beliefs that are nonetheless reliably produced. So depending on how the generality problem is solved, belief in God might be basic and justified on my theory, even if
God does not exist.

Here, then, is another sense in which my philosophy is more God-friendly than
Plantinga's. If God does not exist, then on Plantinga's view, beliefs about God are
probably not basic and almost certainly not basically justified. On my view, they might
still very well be both. Plantinga makes a certain psychological assumption, which,
in conjunction with his epistemology and if true, implies that noninferential belief in
God is probably prima facie justified if God exists and probably not otherwise. I have
made a psychological assumption, which, in conjunction with my epistemology and if
true, implies that noninferential belief in God is probably prima facie justified if God
exists and quite likely still prima facie justified even if God doesn't exist.

So far, I have been glossing over an important problem for both my and Plantinga's
epistemologies of religion. I have been presuming that the relevant module is a primal system. But this alone is insufficient for basicality; the system must also operate
noninferentially. Though I suspect that the theory of mind module sometimes does, I
also suspect that sometimes it does not. Return to Plantinga's view for a moment. He
claims that lovely mountain vistas and the like serve as inputs to the *sensus divinitatis*. Yet this leaves a crucial question unanswered. These may be the *distal* inputs, but
we need to know what the *proximal* inputs are. If they are beliefs, for example, 'there's
a lovely mountain vista', then the output beliefs, for example, 'God made that', would
have to be nonbasic. Plantinga skirts this issue by claiming, in effect, that since I don't
normally consciously dwell on the belief that there's a lovely mountain vista, the
belief that God made this isn't inferentially dependent on it (2000, p. 175). But as I
have argued in section 1.1, my visually initiated belief that my sister is in front of me
is epistemically based on my belief that Jane is my sister, even if I don't consciously
dwell on the latter. The analogous situation holds for both the *sensus divinitatis* and
the theory of mind module. Perhaps our mental state ascription modules are integrated
with perceptual systems in such a way that often the former takes nondoxastic outputs
from the latter as its inputs, to yield beliefs like 'Susan looks angry'. But the broader
use of the module, to attribute goals to inanimate objects or to conclude from a sudden
lightning strike that some divine power is trying to warn me, may very well require
doxastic inputs. This is why I described the relevant religious beliefs as "more or less"
intuitive or noninferential; they may not be basic, but they might be pretty close.

To explain how close, I need to recall an earlier discussion and anticipate a later
one. Plantinga seems to think that the only way to serve his religious agenda is to
ensure that the religious beliefs come out to be basic. Another way, however, is to claim

merely that the *sensus divinitatis* produces basic *inferences* (pp. 142, 171*ff.*). The epistemic significance of basic inferences is addressed in the next chapter, but for now we can simply note this much. If the nature of the responsible cognitive systems can determine which beliefs are in need of inferential support and which are not, perhaps the nature of the responsible inferential system can determine what can be directly (i.e., without auxiliary premises) inferred from what. The fact that it is a reliable inferential primal system that takes my beliefs about mountain vistas as inputs and yields beliefs about God as outputs may be enough to secure the legitimacy of the inference from 'there's a lovely mountain vista' to 'God made that'. What the reformed epistemology movement wants is for belief in God to be prima facie justified independently of the traditional theistic arguments. Making belief in God come out to be basic is only one of the possible ways to ensure this.

My own purposes, of course, are not religious but epistemological, and here it is especially important to distinguish the possibility that belief in God is basic from the possibility that belief in God, though nonbasic, is justifiable independently of the traditional arguments. Belief in God is intended merely to play an illustrative role here. Consequently, I won't make any effort to substantiate the operative cognitive scientific assumptions. My concern is less with the epistemic status of religious belief per se than with the more general point about the epistemological implications of various cognitive scientific theses.

Nonetheless, it bears repeating that the present discussion only concerns prima facie justification. The problem of evil and the like may serve as a rebutting defeater for religious beliefs, and the conclusions of evolutionary psychology of religion may serve as undercutting defeaters.[37] In fact, the very psychological assumptions from which I have just argued that belief in God might be basic (or nearly so) could serve as undercutting defeaters for any belief in God that results from those mechanisms. If I have reason to think that my spontaneous religious beliefs are merely the result of an overactive mental state ascription system, then I have no reason to retain those religious beliefs—provided I don't have any other justification for them. Of course, this does not imply that ordinary agents, who are unaware of the origins of their religious beliefs, are unjustified, for they don't possess the undercutting defeaters.

2.4. Reflective Equilibrium and Etiological Constraints

I have been examining one important way in which we might transcend our intuitions about justifiedness and endorse better epistemic principles than those that merely get the intuitions right. The strategy has been to see what putative features of beliefs lead us to attribute to them a particular epistemic status, and then reserve that epistemic status for beliefs that really do have those features, whether we intuitively thought they had that status or not. Another important way of transcending our intuitions is to look at those features that we intuitively though tacitly think are epistemically important and try to determine whether we are rationally, as well as intuitively, committed

---

37. A rebutting defeater for *p*, in Pollock's (1986) terminology, is a reason for thinking that *p* is false, while an undercutting defeater for *p* is a reason for thinking that one's reason for believing *p* isn't a good one.

to their importance. Though the approach so far has been mostly particularist, epistemic principles can also be criticized on methodist grounds. Irrespective of their ability to get the cases right, some may be better (or at least worse) than others.

I want to briefly consider one example. An important component of a descriptive or even quasi-descriptive epistemological theory is the presumed etiology of the system that produces the relevant belief. We take Nyrmoon to be justified, while we take Norman not to be. The cases can be described in such a way that the only potentially relevant difference is the presumed etiology of the responsible system; Nyrmoon's clairvoyance system is the result of a normal developmental trajectory, while Norman's has just come out of nowhere. In addition, just as our assumptions about which processes are reliable and which primal systems there are are subject to experimental test, we might also modify our intuitions if they result from what turns out to be a mistaken assumption about which etiologies are in fact normal. If cognitive systems do indeed come suddenly into existence late in life, if neurosurgery becomes commonplace (or turns out to have been all along), perhaps we should modify our standard intuitions on the clairvoyance-type cases.

There is another, somewhat more radical, departure from our intuitions that I want to consider, though perhaps not unreservedly endorse. One might quite reasonably think that there is something unprincipled about our etiological requirement and insist that this constraint therefore be dropped from a normative epistemological theory. Just as we replace or augment the epistemic principles we do endorse with those that we would endorse if we were fully informed about the descriptive features of the world, we might replace, modify, or abandon those that seem unprincipled, unmotivated, and unduly idiosyncratic.

The etiological constraint is in this respect quite different from some of the other features relevant to our epistemic intuitions. There is nothing arbitrary or idiosyncratic about requiring reliability for justified belief; we do, of course, want our beliefs to be true, and the use of reliable processes is conducive to that epistemic goal. Similarly, there is nothing unprincipled about the very idea of a basic-nonbasic belief distinction. We wouldn't, on pain of circularity, want to require inferential support for every belief, yet there seems to be something unduly licentious about not requiring any arguments for any beliefs. So it is reasonable for our epistemology to count some beliefs, but not all, as basic.

Again, I am pursuing a reflective equilibrium approach to normative epistemology rather than a means-ends approach (though what I have said in the previous paragraph is compatible with both). If our sole criterion for endorsing certain epistemic principles over their competitors were goal-conduciveness, any choice of normative principles would have to answer pretty directly to these ends. To endorse any set of epistemic principles, we would have to argue that the preferred principles are more conducive to our epistemic goals than the rejected principles. This is notoriously difficult.[38] My approach is different. Though I don't want to endorse principles that

---

38. For one thing, believing only truths is more conducive to our epistemic goals than accepting the results of reliable processes. An internalist would reject the 'believe only truths' principle on the grounds that it is not the kind of principle an agent could follow—it is not "reason-guiding" (Pollock 1986). Of course, reliabilists do not and cannot require that epistemic principles be reason-guiding in this sense. Thus the ordinary motivation for rejecting the 'believe only truths' rule is blocked for the reliabilist.

clash with means-ends considerations, not every endorsed principle has to justify its inclusion in the finished theory by its conduciveness to epistemic ends. Thus it is uncertain whether the etiological constraint, which I think is indispensable to a descriptive epistemology, earns its keep in a normative epistemology.

Thus, I want to leave open the possibility that we simply drop the etiological constraint from our normative epistemology. Thus, even though we have the intuitions that Norman and Truetemp are unjustified, perhaps an improved epistemology would count them as justified. There is, I think, even a bit of intuitive pull behind such a view, despite our intuitions about the particular cases. Though I have the intuition that Norman and Truetemp are unjustified, it nonetheless seems to me that there is an important sense in which what they ought to do is to maintain their beliefs. And this 'ought' seems to be an epistemic one.

It is tempting to explain the intuitive ambivalence here by insisting that Norman is justified in his belief that the president is in New York (Schmitt 1992); one might even try to mitigate the counterintuitive nature of this claim by conceding that Norman is unjustified in any metabelief to the effect that the first-order belief is justified. Such a move, however, strikes me as inadequate. The reason is that I have a similar kind of intuitive ambivalence regarding demon world cases, and a parallel response seems implausible in these cases. Agents in the demon world intuitively seem to me to be justified, even though I also think there is a sense in which they really shouldn't rely on perception (or what passes for it in their world). A normative reliabilist epistemology should surely claim that demon worlders shouldn't maintain their putatively perceptual beliefs.

In the clairvoyance case and the demon world case, we have an intuition of justifiedness, which may conflict with what a normative epistemology would eventually endorse. Norman is unjustified, in the sense of 'justified' that typically concerns epistemologists, though he may be justified in some other sense of the term. The demon victim is justified, in the sense of 'justified' that typically concerns epistemologists, though he may be unjustified in some other sense of the term. Epistemologists are typically concerned primarily with the descriptive project, so the claim is that Norman is unjustified in the descriptive sense of the term. Perhaps, however, Norman is justified in the sense of 'justified' invoked by the normative project, though unjustified in the descriptive sense. If our normative epistemology counts as an improvement over our descriptive epistemology, it would not be much of a stretch to say that the sense in which Norman is justified is superior to the sense in which he is unjustified. He is unjustified in an intuitive sense, but he is justified in a different, *better*, sense of 'justified'. The reverse holds for the demon victims.

Again, the discussion of the possibility of rejecting the etiological constraint is intended more as an illustration of the general approach to normative epistemology than as the articulation of substantive doctrine. *If* the etiological constraint is, in fact, unprincipled, then we might well consider omitting it from a developed normative epistemology, despite its considerable role in accounting for the intuitions that are the concern of descriptive epistemology.

7

Basic and Nonbasic Beliefs
in a Reliabilist Epistemology

I have offered what I hope is an adequate theory of basicality and tried to use this theory to solve certain notorious problems for reliabilism. To recap, I have argued for a kind of inferentialist reliabilism, which explicitly marks a distinction between basic and nonbasic beliefs, reliability being sufficient for the prima facie justification of basic beliefs but not of nonbasic beliefs. A commitment to the existence of basic beliefs is more credible in the context of a theory that also insists that some beliefs are nonbasic. What looked to be objections to the claim that any beliefs were basic, or to the claim that reliability is sufficient for the prima facie justification of some beliefs, begin to look like objections to the claim that some particular belief is basic. Likewise, resistance to the idea that beliefs might be justified though ungrounded turns out mostly to be resistance to the idea that some particular beliefs—like Norman's belief that the president is in New York—might be justified though ungrounded.

Using perceptual belief as a representative case, I argued that the basic beliefs are those that are the outputs of a certain kind of operation of a certain kind of cognitive system, in particular, an inferentially opaque cognitive system, which results from learning and / or innate developmental processes, where the system is not basing its outputs on any doxastic inputs.

A theory of basicality is, however, only part of a full-blown epistemology, and it is likely that claims about the basicality of certain beliefs are hard to evaluate in the absence of a more general epistemological theory, in particular, a theory about the justification conditions for nonbasic beliefs. Although basicality has been the primary concern here, I want to survey some possibilities concerning the justification of the nonbasic beliefs and the overarching theory that results. With something more like a full epistemological theory in hand, I want to examine the larger epistemological implications.

1. Toward a Theory of Justification

The kind of reliabilism I endorse is explicitly committed to the claim that some beliefs are nonbasic. Thus it is explicitly only basic beliefs that can be justified though ungrounded. The reliabilist element of the theory does much for the plausibility of the commitment to justified but ungrounded beliefs. Though these beliefs lack evidential justifiers, they don't lack justifiers, for reliability serves as the nonevidential justifier for these beliefs. Although I have argued that basic beliefs are ungrounded, I insist that nonbasic beliefs must have grounds in order to be justified. A nonbasic belief, after all, just is one that must be evidentially justified if it is to be justified.

It would be nice, to put it mildly, to have at least a sketch of the justificatory conditions on nonbasic beliefs. The preceding discussion of basic beliefs paves the way for what I think is a fairly plausible account of evidential justification in a reliabilist framework. It is to that account that I now turn.

1.1. Evidential Justification

The very ideas of evidential justification and reliabilism may seem to be somewhat at odds with each other, and it is fortunate for reliabilism that such appearance is merely a sociological artifact and not some central implication of the theory itself. Reliabilists have typically been more concerned with the nonevidential justifiers than with the evidential justifiers, but there is nothing standing in the way of a reliabilist theory of justification that allows for the formulation of a relatively sophisticated theory of evidential requirements. Insisting that some beliefs are nonbasic goes some short way in this direction, but what we will really need is a nonevidential theory of evidential justification, that is, a theory of what it is in virtue of which something is evidence for something else.

I argued in chapter 3 that only beliefs can serve as justifying evidence for beliefs, but this is clearly only a very small part of a full theory of evidential justification. A reliabilist will impose some sort of reliability requirement on evidential justification as well: for the belief that q to be evidentially justified on the basis of the belief that p, p must be a reliable indicator of q, or the process involved in inferring q from p must be a reliable (or perhaps conditionally reliable) one, or the like. Of present importance is not which of these reliability requirements should be imposed, but the question whether any additional requirements should be imposed. An initially obvious response on behalf of the reliabilist is the straightforward claim that no other conditions are necessary. We have already seen, for example, that Alston (1988) is explicit in claiming that the ground's being a reliable indicator of the truth of the belief in question is sufficient for the justification of that belief. He thus endorses what we might call a straight reliability theory of evidential justification:

> (SRT): S's belief that p is evidentially justified on the basis of g iff (1) S's belief that p is based on g and (2) the appropriate reliability connection obtains between g and p.

I formulate SRT a little vaguely so that we can focus on a sufficiently general view and avoid issues tangential to the present purposes. Thus, even though I don't believe that nondoxastic grounds can be justifying grounds, SRT is written to be compatible with the possibility that g is nondoxastic. Similarly, I require only that "the appropriate reliability connection obtains" in order to include various different reliabilist proposals under SRT. Alston, for example, endorses a reliable indicator theory and thus holds that the appropriate connection is a matter of conditional probabilities, but one could endorse a process reliabilist version of SRT. Finally, a doxastic ground presumably must be justified in order to evidentially justify another belief; this fact could either be built into the notion of an appropriate reliability connection or added as an additional requirement; I omit it here merely to minimize clutter.

Problems with SRT have been addressed already, in both chapter 3 and chapter 5. To take up where the earlier discussion left off, a crippling problem for proposals like Alston's is that at least some evidence is clearly belief-dependent evidence: the ability of the ground to evidentially justify the target belief depends on the agent's other beliefs. More precisely, for some e, e serves as (justifying) evidence for the belief or proposition h only because the believer also (justifiedly) believes that e is evidence for h, that the probability of $h \mid e$ is sufficiently high, or the like. My knowledge (or belief) that the solution turned pink in the presence of phenolphthalein does not serve as justifying evidence for the claim that the solution was alkaline—not for me at least—unless I also know or am justified in believing that bases but not acids turn pink in phenolphthalein solutions.

Thus, I think it is inescapable that some evidence is belief-dependent. That is, some things are evidence for other things, only in virtue of the agent's having certain additional beliefs. The question remains whether any evidence is belief-independent, that is, whether any evidential relations hold independently of the agent's believing they hold. At the opposite extreme from SRT is the view that a ground justifies a belief only if the agent justifiedly believes that the ground is evidence for that belief (or that it implies, or probabilifies, etc., the belief in question). Call this belief about the connection between the ground and the justificandum belief an *evidential belief*. (I am not concerned here with precisely what content the evidential belief should have but with the general role evidential beliefs should play.) So the proposal being scouted here is that a belief is evidentially justified only if the agent has a justified evidential belief. Fumerton endorses a restricted version of this claim; his Principle of Inferential Justification (PIJ) (1985, 1995) holds that a ground can inferentially justify a target belief (this is evidential justification where the ground is a belief) only if the agent justifiedly believes that the former makes the latter probable. Although I don't want to endorse this view, I do want to endorse something vaguely similar, and it is important to see what the problems for this view are—and are not.

One initial worry for Fumerton's PIJ is that it seems to court regress, but Fumerton solves this problem by insisting that some justification is noninferential. Since inferential justification requires justified evidential beliefs, this solution to the regress argument requires that some evidential beliefs be themselves noninferentially justified, that is, basic. (If evidential belief b_1 is nonbasic, it must be inferentially justified, which would require the justification of another evidential belief, b_2, etc.) Fumerton's account of noninferential justification is a bit obscure, but I read him as endorsing a kind of experientialism. He claims that we are directly acquainted with certain facts (e.g., about our own mental states), and this is what justifies the noninferentially justified beliefs. Though he is not explicit about it, it is plausible to take this acquaintance to serve an evidential, rather than a nonevidential, role.[1] If so, then his Principle of Inferential Justification is not about evidential justification in general, for on the view I'm attributing to Fumerton, *some* evidential justification—namely, inferential justification—requires justified evidential beliefs, while *other* evidential justification—namely, noninferential justification—is made possible by the relation of direct acquaintance. All justified beliefs on this view are evidentially justified, but only those whose evidential justifiers are beliefs count as inferentially justified, and it is only here that evidential beliefs are required.

A more general Principle of Evidential Justification (PEJ) holds that no ground evidentially justifies a belief unless the agent justifiedly believes that the ground is evidence for the belief. In many ways, I think that PEJ is more attractive than PIJ. For one thing, it offers a unified account of evidential justification. For another, it does so without invoking any mysterious notions of acquaintance, which, on Fumerton's view, must include direct acquaintance with facts about evidential relations or probabilities.[2] A proponent of PEJ would avoid the regress problem in the obvious way, by denying that all justified beliefs are evidentially justified. Such a view would need to posit basic beliefs about evidential relations, but this is not necessarily a problem; it is presumably a weaker requirement than requiring direct acquaintance with these evidential relations, whatever exactly that is. On my own view, at least, the apparent lack of any plausible candidate grounds for evidential beliefs ("intellectual experiences," direct acquaintance, and the like) is no argument against either the basicality or the justifiedness of these evidential beliefs. Evidential beliefs need only be the outputs of a noninferential primal system, which they plausibly are. The Principle of Evidential Justification is inconsistent with the claim that basic beliefs are nonetheless evidentially justified, but it is compatible with the kind of foundationalism I am endorsing.

This suggests what I will call an intellectualist theory of evidential justification:[3]

(IT): S's belief that p is evidentially justified on the basis of g iff (1) S's belief that p is based on g, (2) the appropriate reliability connection obtains between g and p, and (3) S is justified in believing that g is evidence for p (or that g probabilifies p, etc.).

Although I don't think that IT is true, I think it is a step in the right direction, and it points out some interesting possibilities concerning evidential justification. IT, it

1. On Fumerton's view, every justified belief ultimately depends on acquaintance. If this requirement were not mandated by a commitment to the Grounds Principle, he would probably simply do without it. The notion of acquaintance is a troublesome one; he insists repeatedly that acquaintance is sui generis, which explains why he has little to say about it, but he clearly recognizes that his readers will not be very happy with his claim that he knows the relation of acquaintance by acquaintance. Fumerton's task would be considerably easier and his view considerably clearer if he were to reject the Grounds Principle, for he could then simply make acquaintance an optional nonevidential justifier.

2. Fumerton thus departs from standard versions of experientialism by allowing nonmental facts, or acquaintance with them, to serve as grounds for beliefs as well. These evidential relations are presumably nonmental.

3. Because of its close affinities to a view Pollock (1986) calls "the intellectualist model."

should be noted, is intended to find a place in a more general theory of justification, hence the promissory reference to justified belief in clause (3).

However, (3) needs special comment; as stated, it is silent on important questions concerning the justificatory status of the evidential belief. Theories according to which the epistemic status of a belief is determined by the causal history of that belief are primarily theories of *ex post* justification (Goldman 1979): justification that attaches to a belief token that is already, occurrently, held. Sometimes, however, we want to discuss the epistemic status a proposition has for some person, whether she believes it or not, or how justified she is in some nonoccurrent belief. This is *ex ante* justification. Now a question arises: in order for, say, *modus ponens* to result in justified inferential belief, must I occurrently believe and be *ex post* justified in believing that *modus ponens* is valid, or might I merely dispositionally believe and be *ex ante* justified in believing so? The former alternative seems far too restrictive. Not only does it require a great deal of cognitive and conceptual sophistication on the part of the agent but it also requires that higher level beliefs actually be explicitly formed, and this is something that even those who favor a highly intellectualist theory of justification are likely to reject.

The latter alternative, however, opens up some interesting possibilities. For example, if we insist that a ground for a belief must be occurrent,[4] then an agent inferring q from 'p' and '$p \supset q$' might have a belief that is grounded on 'p' and '$p \supset q$' in accordance with *modus ponens*, without belief in the validity of *modus ponens* actually being one of the grounds for the belief that q. The subject's justification for believing that q might nonetheless depend on her justification for thinking that *modus ponens* is valid. The proponent of IT could thus distinguish three different kinds of epistemic dependence:

(1) *negative*: S's belief that p depends negatively on S's not believing that q iff S's believing that q (or being justified in believing that q) would serve as a defeater for S's belief that p.

(2) *inferential*: p depends inferentially on q iff p is based on q.

(3) *positive but noninferential*: p depends positively but noninferentially on q iff p is justified only if q is, and the belief that p is not based on the belief that q.

The proposal on the table is that evidentially justified beliefs depend positively but noninferentially on beliefs about evidential relations.

As tempting as such a view is, it is too weak. Suppose I am *ex ante* justified in believing that it is bases that turn phenolphthalein solution pink, in the sense that if I thought about it, I would be able to recall some mnemonic I learned several years ago. At the moment, however, I do not recall the mnemonic, nor token even implicitly the belief that bases turn the solution pink, but merely infer alkalinity from the pinkness of the solution. The belief is justifi*able*, perhaps, but it is not justifi*ed*. Mere *ex ante* justification of evidential beliefs (even in conjunction with reliability, etc.) is thus insufficient for evidential justification.

---

4. In earlier chapters, I endorsed a causal theory of basing, which requires that grounds be occurrent, though it does not require that they be conscious.

Nor would a return to the occurrent/*ex post* reading help matters, for IT is too strong whichever way we read condition (3). Even on the nonoccurrent/*ex ante* reading, condition (3) requires too much cognitive sophistication on the part of the agent. A cognizer might be able to justifiedly *use modus ponens* without being able to justifiedly *believe modus ponens*, perhaps (a) because the processes responsible for use are different, perhaps more reliable, than those responsible for belief or perhaps (b) because the subject doesn't have the conceptual sophistication to believe *modus ponens*; it might lack concepts like implication, evidence, probabilification, and the like. Certainly a cognizer ought to be capable of having *some* justified inferential beliefs without having justified higher order beliefs about evidence and the like.

The intellectualist theory of evidential justification won't work; we need something less intellectualist. Though Descartes may seem an unlikely source of inspiration for *less* intellectualist theories, the theory of evidential justification I want to endorse is actually a roughly Cartesian one.

Descartes ([1637a, 1641] 1985) divided knowledge into intuition, which is the direct, immediate perception of truth, and deduction, which is the indirect perception of truth by means of an argument that is formed by chaining together intuitions. The crucial point is that for an argument to deliver knowledge, Descartes required each step in the argument to be intuitive: "intuition is required... for any train of reasoning whatever. Take for example, the inference that 2 plus 2 equals 3 plus 1: not only must we intuitively perceive that 2 plus 2 make 4, and that 3 plus 1 make 4, but also that the original proposition follows necessarily from the other two" (1985, pp. 14–15). In a longer proof, where the connection between the premises and the final conclusion is not intuitively perceived, the proof must be decomposable into steps, the connections between which are intuitively perceived.[5]

Descartes, of course, was concerned with knowledge—*scientia*, in fact—and not only was he an infallibilist (on the standard readings, anyway) but a rationalist. That is, he thought that for something to justify a belief, it must conclusively establish the truth of that belief and must do so a priori. My concerns are with fallible justification, and this is not something I assume must be a priori. Given these differences, perhaps basicality could play the role here that intuition played for Descartes. One proposal in the Cartesian spirit would be to endorse IT, with the additional requirement that the inference be decomposable into inferences for each of which the agent has a justified, *basic*, evidential belief. This, however, only exacerbates one of the problems with IT, making justification too difficult to come by. A better approach is to employ a broad conception of intuition, such that in addition to intuitive *beliefs*, there are also some intuitive *inferences* as well. In chapter 6 I introduced the notion of a basic inference. We can define a basic inference as one that does not require a corresponding evidential belief; I now suggest that a basic inference is one that results from the inferential operation of a primal system (a nonbasic inference is any other inference). This account of basic inferences obviously fits nicely with the theory of basic beliefs I have been defending. Putting this together with the Cartesian proposal, we get something like the following: some inferences are basic and some are nonbasic; basic inferences do not require the presence of evidential beliefs to

5. See Owen (1999) for a fuller discussion.

yield justification, though the evidential relations involved in nonbasic inferences are belief-dependent.

This leads us to a Cartesian theory of evidential justification:

(CT): S's belief that p is evidentially justified on the basis of g iff (1) S's belief that p is based on g, (2) the appropriate reliability connection obtains between g and p, and (3) either (a) S is justified in believing that g is evidence for p (or that g probabilifies p, etc.), or (b) S's inference from g to p is a basic inference, that is, is the result of the inferential operation of one of S's primal systems.

To avoid the problems that made IT too weak, I think we need to read (3a) as requiring occurrent, *ex post* justified belief. But because we also have clause (3b), this won't result in CT's being too strong. CT allows basic inferences to yield belief-independent evidence. This significantly reduces the amount of cognitive sophistication necessary for having justified nonbasic beliefs. A simple cognizer might lack all concepts of evidence, probability, and the like but still have justified nonbasic as well as basic beliefs, provided that these nonbasic beliefs are arrived at by way of basic inferences. Without some vaguely evidential concepts, nonbasic inferences would not result in justified belief, but this wouldn't undermine the epistemological efficacy of inference in general, even in the absence of evidential concepts, for basic inferences would still be capable of yielding inferential justification. Of course, (3a) would be applied recursively; if the relevant evidential belief were nonbasic, then the agent would have to believe it on the basis of a basic inference or have yet another evidential belief. There are limits to how sophisticated an inference might be while still yielding justification for ordinary cognizers, but this seems to be the right result.

Suppose, for example, that I infer q from p and '$p \supset q$', in accordance with *modus ponens*. My being justified in believing that q does not require that I actually believe that *modus ponens* is valid, so long as this inference is basic for me, so long as this use of *modus ponens* constituted a basic inference, perhaps, as I suggest, because the inference is the work of a primal system (my believing that *modus ponens* is *not* valid may serve as a defeater, of course). For cognizers like us, the inference from 'it turned the solution pink' to 'it has a high pH' is never a basic inference, but the conclusion might nonetheless be justified if the cognizer is justified in believing, presumably on the basis of memory or the like, that turning the solution pink indicates high pH.

To be epistemologically relevant, an evidential belief needs to be occurrent, but it need not be consciously dwelt on. That is, it needs to be tokened at the time of the inference; it cannot merely be some wildly dispositional belief, like your belief that Thomas Aquinas never woke up naked in a zoo. But many mental states can be occurrent without being conscious. This, presumably, is the status of my edge-detector firings. Though I lack conscious awareness of them, they are representing edges at certain times and not at others. To be *ex post* justified, a belief must be occurrent, but it does not, I think, need to be conscious; certainly there is little reason for a reliabilist to insist on that. So I want to at least allow the possibility that the relevant evidential beliefs are sometimes tokened unconsciously but are epistemically efficacious even then. Because it is occurrently tokened, the evidential belief can serve as an actual ground, and not merely a positive but noninferential factor. To play this role, the evidential belief may need to be more than merely occurrent; it might need also to be accessible in a way edge detections are not, though I think this accessibility should be understood in such a way as to allow accessibility in the requisite sense without the belief's being consciously dwelt on.[6]

The concept of basic inference is an important one, one that might be used to solve various other epistemological problems. The concept is intuitive enough; it is just that few epistemologists offer an explicit theory of which inferences are those for which the agent needs a corresponding evidential belief and which inferences are not. Not only does the distinction between basic and nonbasic inference solve Lewis Carroll's regress but it does so in a way that provides for principled claims about which inferences can yield justification for unsophisticated cognizers. It also might ease certain worries about basicality, allowing us to get the kind of mileage we hoped to get from claims about basic beliefs out of corresponding claims about basic inference (recall the discussion of religious epistemology in chapter 6, 2.3).

The distinction between basic and nonbasic inference also paves the way for a response to an important objection to naturalistic projects in epistemology. BonJour (1994) argues that there could not be justified belief whose content is not restricted to immediate experience, unless some beliefs were justified a priori. His argument is that a belief that is not directly observational must (if not already a priori) be based on direct observations, but for this to yield justification, the agent must be justified in believing the corresponding conditional. But since this conditional itself can hardly be directly observed, it must, on pain of regress, be a priori justified or owe its justification ultimately to a conditional that is. The obvious response to this argument is to deny that the agent must be justified in believing the corresponding conditional, but it is hard to make good on such a claim without some distinction between basic and nonbasic inferences. With such a distinction independently argued, the answer to BonJour is straightforward: his argument gives us no reason to think that *all* beliefs that go beyond immediate experience must involve nonbasic inferences.

CT is incompatible with evidence essentialism; by endorsing CT, I am denying that evidential relations hold necessarily. I think it is not a necessary truth that p is evidence for 'p or q' but, rather, it is a fact about us and a consequence of our contingent cognitive makeup. We humans find *modus ponens* much more obviously valid than we do *modus tollens* (Rips and Marcus 1977), but it could have been the other way around, had we been constructed differently. Perhaps, roughly in the spirit of Rips (1983), *modus ponens* is a basic inference for us but *modus tollens* is not (or at least not for that 43 percent of the subject pool who didn't recognize its validity). The theory of basicality already endorsed implies that which propositions of logic count as axiomatic for us and which merely as theorems (i.e., which are basic and which are nonbasic) is a contingent matter of our cognitive architecture. Just as there seems nothing problematic about a creature for whom the Pythagorean theorem is basic but

6. Nothing I say here precludes the agent's having an evidential belief corresponding to a basic inference; however, in such a case it is primarily the basicality of the inference that makes the ground a justifying ground; the evidential belief is at most an overdeterminer.

for whom *modus ponens* is not, there is nothing obviously wrong with the possibility of a creature for whom the move from 'this right triangle has a side of 6 cm and a hypotenuse of 10 cm' to 'the other side is 8 cm' is so obvious in itself that nothing further is needed by way of justification for this inference. For this very same creature, however, the move from p and '$p \supset q$' to q might be quite unjustified, on a par with my inference from the solution turning pink to it being alkaline. On reflection, it is hard to see why one might claim that *any* evidential relations hold necessarily, let alone that all do. It seems rather doubtful that anything is necessarily evidence for anything else, but only evidence to a class of cognizers that are equipped to use it as evidence.

In chapter 3, I pointed out that such nonessentialist theories were unlikely to appeal to experientialists; since the external factor is doing most of the work, there is little reason to view the epistemological relevance as particularly *evidential*. Is there any reason to think that what I have offered here is a theory of evidential justification, rather than an account of why evidence is unnecessary? I think what makes the basic and nonbasic inference relations evidential relations, and not merely nonevidential justificatory relations, is the indispensable role of justified input beliefs. I argued in chapter 3 that all evidential justification is a matter of transmission, rather than generation, of justification. Even if that has been unconvincing, it seems clear that all transmission is evidential. If the justifier needs to be itself justified in order to confer justification, then the relation in question really does seem to be an evidential one; otherwise, the justifiedness requirement is mysterious.

1.2. Defeat

The discussion to this point has focused on prima facie justification, but if a full theory of justification is to be given, an account of defeat will also be needed. Prima facie justification is my main concern, however, and I have little to add to existing discussions of defeat. The theory of defeat I endorse is a fairly standard one, and I don't intend to give it a very vigorous defense; it is largely to tie up loose ends that I even espouse any particular theory of defeat. It is my hope, though I won't pursue the details, that the consequences to be drawn from this theory of defeat would apply to another theory of defeat as well, should that turn out to be superior.

Earlier, in chapter 5, we encountered Goldman's alternative reliable process view of defeat.

> (ARP): S's belief that p is defeated iff there is available to S an alternative reliable process, the use of which, in addition to or instead of the one actually used, would have resulted in S's not believing that p.

There I mentioned that the account would have to be modified to accommodate defeater defeaters. Provided that this can be done, I think that something like ARP offers an attractive reliabilist theory of defeat.

Now ARP appeals to availability, and it is far from clear just what this amounts to. Is a process available to S if S doesn't know that it's available? Should a process count as available if S doesn't know that the process is reliable? Justifiedly believing that my speedometer is malfunctioning, I make fairly reliable (though in this case slightly inaccurate) vestibular/kinesthetic guesses about how fast I am driving.

Unbeknownst to me, my speedometer is working fine again, and were I to take its deliverances seriously, I would change my mind about my speed and slow down. Are my kinesthetic beliefs defeated or not? In this and similar cases, I think our intuitions are unclear as to whether a process is relevantly available. Correspondingly, however, our intuitions are unclear as to whether the given belief's prima facie justification is defeated. So the vagueness surrounding the notion of availability might actually be a virtue of ARP, since it matches that of our concept of defeat.

Another potential virtue of ARP is that it keeps with the original spirit of relia-bilism. It is tempting to think that the very notion of defeat is an evidentialist notion and one to which reliabilism cannot consistently help itself. Though I have taken pains to show that reliabilism can provide a theory of evidential justification, relia-bilism is not an evidentialist theory; justification is primarily a matter of reliability rather than evidence; evidential relations merely constitute a particular kind of reli-ability connection. Welding ARP to a generic reliabilism yields a thoroughgoingly reliabilist theory of ultima facie justification. The overarching injunction is just to use the most reliable process available.

Finally, and this is my primary concern in this section, ARP specifies an impor-tant epistemic role for experiential states, even if these states are evidentially irrele-vant. This is quite likely to be true of any adequate reliabilist theory of defeat, though I will state the argument here in terms of ARP.

In chapter 2, I registered the familiar complaint that there is no room in a dox-astic epistemology for experiential states. This leads to the famous isolation objec-tion; nothing in my belief set need indicate whether I have a headache or not, and on a doxastic theory, my actually having a headache or not cannot be relevant to the justification of the belief that I have a headache. It might seem, however, that similar problems arise for my view. I have denied that nondoxastic experiential states can serve as evidential justifiers for beliefs, and for exactly parallel reasons, they must be incapable of serving as evidential defeaters as well. So provided that my belief that I do have a headache is the result of a reliable process, that belief would have to be justified, despite the glaringly obvious fact that I don't have a headache!

Though I have denied that experiential states play an evidential role, this does not require me to deny that they play an *epistemic* role. The nonevidentialist discon-nection of justification from evidence allows experiences to be epistemically signifi-cant, though nonevidentially. I offered a nonevidentialist account in chapter 4 of the epistemic significance of looks. I held that the experientialist is right in thinking that looks are epistemically relevant but wrong in thinking of said looks as nondoxastic experiential states. The current worries present another way in which experientialism almost gets things right. My having a headache is relevant to the epistemic status of my belief that I don't have a headache, but not evidentially, as would be, for instance, the belief that I've just been hit in the head. Rather, it is significant in the way that the room's being conspicuously full of people is relevant to my belief that the room is empty. If I use induction to arrive at the belief that the room is empty, when it's conspicuously not, the use of vision or some other reliable process would result in my not believing that the room is empty. Presumably, this is part of what is meant by marking the fullness of the room as conspicuous. So my belief that the room is empty is prima facie justified in virtue of the reliability of induction, but the belief is defeated in accordance with ARP. The belief is (ultima facie) unjustified because there is an available alternative reliable process, which, if used in addition to the one actually used, would have resulted in my not believing the room was empty.

Similarly, some inductive process might confer prima facie justification on my belief that I don't have a headache, despite the glaringly obvious fact that I do have a headache. The glaring obviousness of this fact consists in there being a highly reliable, highly available, alternative process of introspection, which, if used, would have resulted in my firmly believing that I do have a headache. So the belief that I don't have a headache is prima facie justified, but defeated and thus not ultima facie justified. This diagnosis is bolstered by the fact that if my introspective processes were damaged to the point of unreliability, what it would be epistemically appropriate for me to do is to rely on the inferentially produced (but false) belief after all. That is, the inductively formed belief that I don't have a headache would be prima facie justified and, since undefeated, justified outright.

This account of the epistemic role of experiential states handles the inverse case quite nicely and in an exactly parallel manner. Consider my inductively formed belief that I do have a headache when in fact I don't. The same story can be retold with minor modifications: though I may have good inductive reasons for thinking I have a headache, there is an alternative reliable process available to me, introspection, the use of which would result in my not believing that I have a headache. The experientialist, on the face of it at least, will have to see a deep asymmetry between this false-positive case and the preceding false-negative case, for here, there seems to be no experiential state to serve as a defeater. Presumably the experientialist will want to claim that the absence of the experiential state serves as negative evidence, but it is not obvious that this claim is just a simple extension of the basic experientialist position. Do absences of experiences have propositional or nonpropositional content? Do they stand in causal relations to the beliefs they justify? The nonexperientialist treatment of the role of experiential states, in terms of introspection and alternative available processes, strikes me as far preferable.

Experiential states are typically reliably introspectible, and this suits them to an important epistemological role, especially regarding defeat. Experiential states—and not just beliefs about them—can be epistemologically significant even if nonevidentially and thus not in the way that experientialists think. The nonevidentialist does not have to deny the epistemological significance of looks, even where "looks" are construed as experiential states, though the nonevidentialist will disagree with the experientialist regarding the exact nature of this significance. However, it is not the existence of the nondoxastic states all by themselves that has epistemic import. If I were incapable of introspecting my experiential states—or very bad at it—they would be nothing to me. Their epistemic significance for me derives from the fact that my introspective processes are reliable.

Finally, though I have argued that my zombie counterpart has justified beliefs without any experiential states, the present view could accommodate the intuition that *I* may not be justified in perceptual beliefs were *I* to be missing the corresponding experience. Just as the conspicuous absence of a headache serves as a defeater for my belief that I have a headache, my lack of any experiential state may serve as a defeater for some putatively perceptual belief of mine. This, however, is only because of what I know and justifiedly believe about perceptual processes and only because my introspection processes are reliable; it is not because there is any kind of general experiential requirement on justified perceptual belief. You and I might not be—ultima facie—justified in experienceless perceptual beliefs, but the lack of experiences need not pose any epistemic problem for zombies. Unlike us, zombies have terribly unreliable introspective processes (they believe themselves to have a host of experiential states, which, by definition, they lack), and they therefore lack the alternative reliable process and hence the defeaters that a normal adult human would possess in a case of spontaneous perceptual belief without experiential states.

1.3. Outline of a Theory

All the components are in place; they can now be put together to yield a sketch of a general theory of justification. It is a reliabilist theory, though a reliabilist theory that takes nonbasicality and evidential justification seriously. It does this without, I think, sacrificing the basic reliabilist spirit.

Reliability is necessary and sufficient for the prima facie justification of basic beliefs, and a basic belief is a belief that is the noninferential output of a primal system. Reliability is necessary but not sufficient for the justification of all other, nonbasic, beliefs. In addition to the reliability requirement, a nonbasic belief must be the result of either a basic inference from justified premise beliefs (a basic inference, again, being one where a primal system bases its outputs on one or more of the agent's beliefs) or a nonbasic inference where the agent believes justifiedly (*ex post*) that the premises are evidence for (or probabilify, etc.) the conclusion. Add to this an alternative reliable process theory of defeat, and we have a general theory of justification.

A foundationalist-structured theory of justification needs to offer accounts of (1) basic beliefs, (2) basic inferences, and (3) nonbasic inferences. To characterize justification recursively, we will need (4) a standard closure clause. Because (1) through (4) will be concerned with prima facie justification, we will also require (5) a theory of defeat, accompanied by (6) a reminder of the relation between defeat and ultima facie justification.

Thus, we have the following:

(1) If S's belief that p is the result of the noninferential operation of a primal system, and the relevant process is reliable, then the belief that p is prima facie justified.[7]

(2) If S's belief that p is the result of the inferential operation of a primal system Σ, where
  (i) Σ bases the belief that p on the input beliefs that $q_1 \ldots q_n$,
  (ii) the process resulting in the belief that p is conditionally reliable, and
  (iii) S is prima facie justified in each of $q_1 \ldots q_n$, then the belief that p is prima facie justified.

---

7. I am requiring that the relevant process be reliable rather than that the responsible system be. This allows for the possibility of individuating relevant processes (e.g., vision in bright lighting conditions) more finely than systems. The generality problem looms, of course, but I cannot address it here.

(3) If S's belief that p is the result of an inferential process where
   (i) the belief that p is based on the input beliefs that $q_1 \ldots q_n$,
   (ii) the process resulting in the belief that p is conditionally reliable,
   (iii) S is prima facie justified in each of $q_1 \ldots q_n$, and
   (iv) S is prima facie justified in believing that $q_1 \ldots q_n$ are evidence for p (or imply p or reliably indicate p, etc.), then the belief that p is prima facie justified.

(4) No other beliefs are prima facie justified.

(5) If any of the prima facie justified beliefs mentioned in (1)–(3) is such that there is an alternative reliable process available to S, the use of which, in addition to or instead of the process actually used, would have resulted in S's not having that belief, then that belief, as well as any belief epistemically dependent on it, is defeated.

(6) A belief is (ultima facie) justified iff it is prima facie justified and not defeated.

2. Internalism and Externalism

In discussing these epistemological views with others, I have frequently been accused of endorsing a hybrid internalist-externalist theory (though this interpretation isn't typically intended as an accusation). I want to resist this interpretation of my position. Though I do impose requirements for justification that externalists do not normally impose, the theory I defend is a far cry from either standard internalist theories or standard internalist-externalist hybrids.

There is nothing like a consensus among epistemologists about what exactly internalism and externalism are, and I won't try to canvass the alternative formulations, but a central and recurrent theme is "cognitive access," either to justification itself (i.e., the justificatory status of the belief) or to the justifiers (i.e., whatever the factors are that make a belief justified).

A kind of internalism that requires access to justification itself implies a "JJ Principle" (so-called because it parallels the famous KK Principle): If S is justified in believing that p, then S is (*ex ante*) justified in believing that S is justified in believing that p. Certainly nothing like such a principle follows from the present account. In part, this is due to the reliability requirement but in part because an agent cannot tell by mere reflection whether a given belief is basic. To know whether a given belief is basic, one would have to know at least the following:

- which system produced the belief
- whether the system is inferentially opaque
- whether the system was operating inferentially
- what the causal history of the system was

Not all of these can be known on the basis of introspection, or mere reflection. I don't deny that most of us have a fairly good idea, most of the time, whether a given belief is the noninferential output of a primal system and thus whether a given belief is basic. In a similar vein, I think we have a fairly good idea, most of the time, whether a given belief is a perceptual belief and even whether a given cognitive process is generally reliable. But internalism requires more than this; our having a fairly good idea most of the time is not enough to make basicality accessible in the relevant sense.

Suppose, then, that I have some cognitively spontaneous belief for which I have no independent evidence. Such a belief is justified only if it is basic, but since I do not have the necessary access to the basicality of the belief, I do not have the necessary access to the justificatory status of this belief. Analogous considerations apply to my knowing on the basis of introspection whether a given inference is basic. In this sense, my view implies that justification is not internally accessible in the requisite sense.

The second main type of internalism holds that the justifiers need to be accessible, even if justification itself does not. It is common to distinguish different varieties of internalism by citing different senses or degrees of accessibility (Alston 1988), but we can also take up a distinction that has been in play throughout this book and cite different senses of 'justifier'. "Evidential internalism" would hold that if belief B is justified for S, then S has access to the evidential justifiers for B, while "nonevidential factor internalism" would hold that if belief B is justified for S, then S has access to the nonevidential justifiers for B.

A coherentist, for example, will typically endorse evidential internalism: beliefs—the standard relata of the coherence relation—are accessible. She may or may not endorse nonevidential factor internalism, however, depending on whether she takes the coherence relation itself to be accessible. It is not obvious that it is (Kornblith 1989). Even a proponent of nonevidential factor internalism need not endorse the aforementioned brand of internalism that adopts the JJ Principle. Alston (1988) usefully distinguishes between the accessibility of a justifier and the accessibility of the fact that it is a justifier. One might hold that coherence is accessible for any normal agent, without holding that the truth of coherentism is as well. I might know on the basis of mere reflection that my beliefs cohere, without knowing that coherence is sufficient for justification.

Again, the theory I have been endorsing does not imply anything like nonevidential factor internalism, and this is for the reasons already given. The relevant factors on my view are causal, etiological, and architectural facts that are not accessible on any natural sense of the term. Whether it implies evidential internalism depends on exactly what we take evidential internalism to be. Evidential internalism holds that if belief B is justified for S, then S has access to the evidential justifiers for B. On the straightforward reading, this is trivially true, for it claims merely that if belief B is justified for S, then *if* B has evidential justifiers, then S has access to them. It is part of the definition of evidential justifiers that they are accessible in some relevant sense, so there could not be anything contentious about evidential internalism, thus construed. Evidential internalism is only contentious if read in such a way that it implies the Grounds Principle, as holding that if belief B justified for S, then B has evidential justifiers and S has access to them.

Obviously, I will accept evidential internalism on this straightforward reading and reject it on this contentious reading. Is this a significant concession to internalism? Is it enough of one to make my view a partially internalist view? I don't think it is.

Internalism is first and foremost the view that if an agent is justified in a belief, then there is *something* accessible to the agent that is relevant to the justification of that belief. Since I hold that there are basic beliefs, that basic beliefs are ungrounded, and that some basic beliefs are justified, I hold that there are instances of justified belief where there is *nothing* accessible to the agent that is particularly relevant to the justification of the belief. In fact, though I have repeatedly stated that some beliefs are nonbasic, the intended claim is merely that some *possible* beliefs are nonbasic; there need not be any actual nonbasic beliefs. I think we normal adult humans do have nonbasic beliefs, but this is only because we have both nonprimal systems and inferential primal systems. A creature whose cognitive architecture consisted entirely of noninferential primal systems, on the other hand, would be one all of whose beliefs would be basic. Such a creature might have many justified beliefs, all of which were ungrounded and none of which was accompanied by anything accessible and relevant to justification.

Thus, I think that in order to count as a genuine form of *internalism*, the evidential internalist's claim must be read as asserting that if belief B is justified for S, then B has evidential justifiers and S has access to them. The difference between this claim and the version I endorse is, of course, the Grounds Principle, and the omission of this principle from my view is a crucial feature of the theory. It is his insistence on the Grounds Principle that makes Alston's (1988) view an internalist hybrid. Though he denies the JJ Principle and nonevidential factor internalism, Alston insists that every justified belief has a ground, which must be accessible in the relevant sense. Alston is explicitly committed to the claim that where there's justification, there's something accessible that's relevant to the justification.

I do require of any *nonbasic* beliefs that the agent have some (doxastic) ground that serves to evidentially justify that belief. I even require of some (possible) nonbasic beliefs that the agent has a metabelief about the status of the evidence on which that belief is based. These grounds and metabeliefs would have to be accessible to the agent, and so an accessibility requirement does fall out of my theory of justification, even though only for a certain species of nonbasic beliefs. One might argue that this makes my view a partially internalist one after all. I think this trivializes the notion of internalism, but I have no desire to argue over necessary and sufficient conditions for philosophical *ism*s. What matters is not what a theory must assert to count as internalist (for who could care about that?) but what general considerations drive the requirements imposed by the theory. What motivates my view is not the blanket assumption that there must be something accessible to the agent; rather, it is that certain specific *kinds* of reliable processes are required for the justification of certain kinds of beliefs. Just as ARP harmonizes with the basic spirit of reliabilism in requiring that the most reliable available process be used, my inferential requirements on nonbasic beliefs are a way of adding specific reliability requirements on beliefs, not a way of imposing nonreliabilist requirements.

Thus, even if the theory I have endorsed is a partially internalist theory in the very weak sense of imposing an internally accessible constraint on *some* beliefs, this constraint is not motivated by anything like the standard internalist concerns. It really matters that traditional internalists place a constraint on *all* beliefs, while I only place a vaguely similar constraint on *some* beliefs. Alston thinks there is something right about the internalists' general principles; I think there is something right about the internalists' intuitions about particular cases. However, I think the internalists have mistaken what that something is; consequently, all the distinctively internalist principles that have been derived from these intuitions about the particular cases are false. The particular cases show not that justification requires some kind of accessibility but merely that some beliefs can't be justified unless they result from a reliable inferential process.

3. The Problem(s) of the External World

Ever since Descartes, *the* problem for epistemology has been the problem of the external world. For most of the subsequent history of the problem, the solution was assumed to proceed along MSF lines. Given a highly restricted set of basic beliefs, a set consisting of beliefs about present experiential states and a few a priori principles, how could we infer from this a whole external world? Reid anticipated a different line of approach, which was forgotten again until the twentieth century: endorse EOF instead of MSF, and the problem doesn't arise. At least, the problem doesn't arise in its traditional form, for the traditional form of the problem presupposes MSF. The problem of the external world is traditionally posed as the problem of justifiably inferring the existence of external objects from a small, Cartesian basis of beliefs about one's current mental states. This particular problem obviously does not arise for the EOFist, but a pair of similar problems does: that of explaining which beliefs are basic and that of explaining how these basic beliefs manage to be justified.

These are problems I have tried to solve here. My solution to the delineation problem is that the basic beliefs are those that result from the noninferential operation of primal systems; since primal systems do sometimes noninferentially produce beliefs about physical objects, this is how it is possible for us to have basic beliefs about physical objects. My solution to the source problem is that the nature of the belief-producing system determines what the epistemic requirements on a belief are going to be and that reliability is sufficient for the justification of basic beliefs. Taken together, these solutions to the delineation problem and the source problem constitute a solution to the problem of the external world.

Such a statement immediately sounds quite immodest, but I think it's not. There are, in fact, at least two different problems that might be thought of as "the" problem of the external world, only one of which do I claim to offer a solution to.

The *metaphysical problem of the external world* is the question of whether an external world exists. The *epistemological problem of the external world* is that of explaining whether and how we might have justified beliefs or knowledge about such a world. Any reader who is not sure whether an external world exists and is reading this book in search of arguments for an external world is sure to be disappointed, for I have not attempted to solve this metaphysical problem, and I would be surprised if I have accidentally succeeded. For obvious reasons, however, such readers are likely to be exceedingly rare. Instead, I have tried to offer a solution to the epistemological problem of the external world: the problem of explaining how justified beliefs about the external world could be justified, in the face of the Cartesian predicament. I do claim to have a solution to this problem, but so does anyone who has an epistemological theory to offer.

Still, having a solution to the epistemological problem of the external world is no trivial matter, and having a decent solution is harder still. My solution to this problem of the external world is successful only insofar as (a) the overarching epistemology developed here is a plausible epistemology, and (b) this epistemology really does account for the possibility of justified beliefs about external objects.

Working out an epistemology is difficult and honest toil, but it can seem more like theft if the distinction between metaphysical and epistemological questions is not kept quite clear. Just as I noted in chapter 1 that metaphysical solutions to epistemological problems are inappropriate, the converse is also true: epistemological solutions to metaphysical problems are doomed to failure. It might seem as if the view defended here offers an unacceptably facile solution to some genuine long-standing problems in philosophy, not just the problem of the external world, but the problem of other minds and an analogous problem concerning the existence of God.

Before turning to these traditional topics, it might help to look at a fresher one, the problem of animal minds.[8] People who spend enough time training animals eventually come to form cognitively spontaneous judgments, attributing certain beliefs and desires to the animal. But are they right to do so? Do nonhuman animals really possess a belief-desire psychology, or is this just anthropomorphizing on the part of the trainers? Suppose we were to investigate the cognitive neuroscience of animal trainers and find that these putatively anthropomorphic beliefs resulted from a standard theory of mind module that satisfied the conditions I have already laid down for producing basic beliefs. So the trainer's belief, that JoJo believes she has a biscuit coming, is basic. Congratulations, by studying humans, we've answered the question of whether nonhuman animals have a belief-desire psychology, right? Of course not. We have—at most—settled the question of whether and how people are justified in attributing beliefs to animals. But justified beliefs are notoriously capable of being false, and basic beliefs need not even be justified, let alone true. This, as we saw previously, is a key element of a response to a famous coherentist objection to foundationalism. To answer the epistemological question is not necessarily even to have begun to answer the metaphysical question.

In fact, because the theory endorsed here is a version of reliabilism, our answers to the epistemological questions will always rest on assumptions about answers to some metaphysical questions (though perhaps not always the exactly corresponding metaphysical question). That is, our claim that the members of some class of beliefs are typically justified will hinge on a working assumption about the reliability of the responsible process, which in turn hinges on a working assumption about the underlying metaphysics, the truth-values of the beliefs that process produces. Adopting these working assumptions is acceptable in the general case of the epistemological problem of the external world precisely because we are not trying to solve the metaphysical problem of the external world, not, at least, with our epistemological theory. Epistemologists are not likely to be very badly misled by this, because very few of us take the metaphysical question of the external world very seriously, though we do take the epistemological question quite seriously. In doing epistemology, we are not trying to get convinced that there is an external world but, rather, trying to understand how knowledge of it is possible.[9] In the case of animal beliefs, on the other hand, the

---

8. Thanks to Colin Allen for this example and for bringing this sort of objection to my attention.

9. This is a contingent sociological fact and one that has not always been true. It is likely that a majority of philosophers over the bulk of the history of the discipline have been more concerned with

metaphysical question is more pressing for most of us than the epistemological question, and we are likely to mistake claims in this neighborhood as answers to those questions we cared more about.

The more general problem of other minds is more like the problem of the external world in this respect. In fact, it may be even easier here to see that the questions are primarily epistemological, rather than metaphysical. Most of us are quite satisfied that other human minds do exist and merely want to know how our beliefs about the mental states of others can be justified or count as knowledge. Thus, the suggestions I have made in earlier chapters regarding the justification of third-person mental state attributions are not likely to seem like an epistemologist trying to pull a fast one. Because most of us are not really very worried about the metaphysical problem of other minds, we aren't likely to mistake epistemological claims for metaphysical claims in this area.

These considerations apply to the reformed epistemology movement, where the most pressing questions seem to be the metaphysical questions. The topic of religious belief is thus more like that of animal minds than of other human minds. If the reformed epistemologist's claims about the basicality of belief in God strike us as hollow, cheap, or somehow evasive, that is probably because we were seeking an answer to the metaphysical question, not the epistemological question.[10] If you're sure that God exists (or if you *don't care* whether God exists) and want to understand how ordinary people can be justified in believing God exists, then reformed epistemology is for you. If, however, you are trying to figure out whether God exists, then you should read Aquinas, not Alston; Paley, rather than Plantinga.

The distinction between the epistemological and metaphysical problems of the external world may be blurred by the fact that to give a good answer to the metaphysical question about x just is to show that there is some good reason to believe in x. Though metaphysics is about truth and epistemology about justification, and though these two are different, to *answer* a metaphysical question adequately is to show that some belief is justified. Thus one might argue that the metaphysical–epistemological distinction, though sound in theory, breaks down in practical application.

Such reasoning is flawed, however. To answer the metaphysical question of the external world is to provide a good argument whose conclusion is that an external world exists. To answer the epistemological question of the external world is to provide a good explanation whose explanandum is that we are justified in believing in external objects. The propositions arrived at are different: one is about the world, one about justification; and the status of these propositions is different: one is a conclusion, the other an explanandum. *Perhaps* it is true that to give a good answer to a

---

the metaphysical question than with the epistemological one. In fact, one early (and to some extent still lingering) source of resistance to reliabilism was that it could not give a non-question-begging solution to traditional skeptical problems about the external world. This is true, however, only if we view these skeptical problems as raising the metaphysical problem of the external world, rather than the epistemological problem.

10. Plantinga (2000) does, of course, note this distinction, but for some reason he prefers to use the Kantian *cum* eighteenth-century German legal philosophy terminology of '*de jure*' and '*de facto*' instead of the more transparent terminology used here.

metaphysical question about *x* is to show that there are good reasons for believing in *x*, but these good reasons need not be revealed *as being* good reasons. Nor need they be reasons possessed by anyone.

It is essential to distinguish the objective existence of evidence for *p* from some particular agent's evidence for *p*. There are proofs in mathematics that have yet to be discovered; there is thus in some objective, disembodied sense evidence for certain truths, even though perhaps no one is currently justified in believing them; no one possesses or appreciates this evidence. Suppose that Descartes's proof of the external world had been sound; it still would not have begun to answer the question of how the ordinary person is justified in believing in corporeal objects, since the proof Descartes offered was presumably not a mere elaboration of common sense. What counts as evidence in this disembodied sense for the proposition that an external world exists need not have much or anything to do with what accounts for the justification of particular belief tokens about the external world.

Though I don't want to commit to this view, one might think that the best objective evidence for the external world is, as Locke and Russell have suggested, some kind of inference to the best explanation. If we suppose that bodies are real and mind-independent and pretty much the way our best science describes them as being, this offers a cogent and comprehensive account of the data, where the data in question are introspectible mental events and their properties and relations.[11] What would give these mental events and their properties this special status as data for the existence of a material world is not that they have some higher epistemic status than beliefs about external objects; I doubt that they do. Introspective beliefs are no more basic than perceptual beliefs, and it is not obvious that they are more highly justified. Rather, what would make the introspective beliefs capable of serving as data is their epistemic independence from and relevance to belief in an external world. This independence is symmetric, but the relevance probably is not. We could just as well turn around and use claims about tables and chairs as evidence for claims about how we are appeared to, if only anyone could figure out how a plausible argument might go.

All of this would be compatible with the epistemology I have been defending here. Even if there exists somewhere in Plato's heaven a good abductive reason for thinking that there are genuinely external objects, it does not follow from this that any particular person's beliefs about external objects are abductively justified. Post-Gettier epistemology has been concerned with the conditions under which *S* is justified in believing that *p* at *t*, and for this, the disembodied evidence of the Lockean or Cartesian sort is simply not relevant. These offer answers to the metaphysical question of the external world, not the epistemological question. So providing a solution to the metaphysical problem of the external world does not entail providing a solution to the epistemological problem of the external world, any more than providing a solution to the epistemological problem of the external world entails providing a solution to the metaphysical problem of the external world.

---

11. It is difficult to know whether we could have any good reason to think that this is the best of the competing explanations, without making question-begging assumptions about the existence and nature of the external world. Since I'm not endorsing this solution to the metaphysical problem here, I won't worry about this.

A more promising case of abductive solutions to metaphysical problems concerns the question of other minds. As a realist in the philosophy of mind, I think that the explanatory successes of mentalistic cognitive science give us good reason to affirm the existence of mental states. Surely, however, this does not commit us to an abductivist epistemology of mental state attribution. The abductive evidence is only available to those who are familiar with the cognitive scientific data and only argues for the existence of mentality in general, not particular mental state tokens held by agents whom cognitive science has never investigated.

In a conflation of proof and evidence seldom seen outside creationist anti-evolution tracts, Kant famously complained of philosophy's failure concerning the problem of the external world: "It still remains a scandal to philosophy and to human reason in general that the existence of things outside us...must be accepted merely *on faith*, and that if anyone thinks good to doubt their existence, we are unable to counter his doubts by any satisfactory proof" ([1781] 1929, p. 34n). If an air of immodesty necessarily accompanies any claim to a solution to the metaphysical problem of the external world, it is perhaps because there are in fact two different metaphysical problems of the external world: one is to provide some evidence for the claim that there is an external world; the other is to *prove* that there is an external world. Even if a roughly Lockean approach will solve the first problem, it is clear that it falls far short of *proof*. It is almost certain that the existence of an external world cannot be proved, in the usual philosophical or mathematical sense of 'proof'. We can counter someone's doubts, though not with a proof, and not the doubts of someone who rejects the possibility of nondemonstrative evidence. I see nothing particularly scandalous about that.

But again, the metaphysical problem was only part of Descartes's problem, and not, in my view, the more interesting part. The interesting problem is that even if we, as theorists, allow that there is an external world, a particular agent cannot seem to know this or be justified in believing it, for she can't seem to know or be justified in believing that she's neither dreaming nor deceived by an evil demon and thus has no grounds for inferring perceptual beliefs from appearance beliefs. The dream and demon scenarios illustrate just how badly appearance might fail to match reality. If some primacy of experience thesis (p. 9) is true, and if basing perceptual beliefs on experiences requires having some reason to think that appearances are not in this particular case misleading, then we are indeed in grave epistemological trouble.

I have offered the outline of an epistemological theory that rejects the primacy of experience thesis, thus explaining how justified perceptual belief is possible, even for an agent who cannot mount any evidence whatsoever against the dream or demon hypotheses. I hope that I have done so in a way that makes this rejection seem plausible and not a mere stopgap measure to avoid skepticism. I have tried to ensure that the solution is somewhat principled by embedding it in a larger epistemology that:

- solves an important class of problems for standard versions of reliabilism, without resorting to an internalist theory,
- explains the epistemic role of nondoxastic experiential states without raising Sellarsian worries,
- provides a principled means of distinguishing perceptual and nonperceptual beliefs,

- provides a principled means of distinguishing basic from nonbasic beliefs,
- draws an important distinction between basic and nonbasic *inference*, which allows us to articulate a theory of evidential, nonbasic justification, while avoiding Carroll's regress, and
- allows for principled, independent, empirical tests of various claims about the basicality of particular beliefs and particular inferences.

The project is far from complete, but I hope that this much is enough to show the promise of a nonevidentialist reliabilism that still finds a place for inference and therefore evidence.

REFERENCES

Alston, W. P. (1988). An internalist externalism. *Synthese* 74, 265–83.

———. (1991). *Perceiving God*. Ithaca, NY: Cornell University Press.

———. (1993). *The reliability of sense perception*. Ithaca, NY: Cornell University Press.

———. (2002). Sellars and the myth of the given. *Philosophy and Phenomenological Research* 65, 69–86.

Atran, S. (2002). *In gods we trust*. Oxford: Oxford University Press.

Audi, R. (1988). *Belief, justification, and knowledge*. Belmont, CA: Wadsworth.

———. (1998). *Epistemology: A contemporary introduction to the theory of knowledge*. New York: Routledge.

Bartlett, F. C. (1932). *Remembering*. Cambridge: Cambridge University Press.

Bering, J. M. (2004). The evolutionary history of an illusion: Religious causal beliefs in children and adults. In B. Ellis & D. Bjorklund, eds., *Origins of the social mind: Evolutionary psychology and child development*. New York: Guilford.

Berkeley, G. ([1709] 1975). *Essay toward a new theory of vision*. In M. R. Ayers, ed., *George Berkeley: Philosophical works, including the works on vision*. London: Dent.

———. ([1710] 1975). *Treatise concerning the principles of human knowledge*. In M. R. Ayers, ed., *George Berkeley: Philosophical works, including the works on vision*. London: Dent.

———. ([1713] 1975). *Three dialogues between Hylas and Philonous*. In M. R. Ayers, ed., *George Berkeley: Philosophical works, including the works on vision*. London: Dent.

Biederman, I. (1990). Higher-level vision. In D. N. Osherson, S. M. Kosslyn, & J. M Hollerbach, eds., *An invitation to cognitive science, vol. 2: Visual cognition and action*. Cambridge, MA: MIT Press.

———. (1995). Visual object recognition. In S. M. Kosslyn & D. N. Osherson, eds., *An invitation to cognitive science, vol. 2: Visual cognition and action*, 2nd ed. Cambridge, MA: MIT Press.

Block, N. (1995a). The mind as the software of the brain. In E. E. Smith & D. N. Osherson, eds., *An invitation to cognitive science*, vol. *3: Thinking*, 2nd ed. Cambridge, MA: MIT Press.

———. (1995b). On a confusion about a function of consciousness. *Behavioral and Brain Sciences* 18, 227–87.

BonJour, L. (1978). Can empirical knowledge have a foundation? *American Philosophical Quarterly* 15, 1–13.

———. (1980). Externalist theories of empirical knowledge. *Midwest Studies in Philosophy* 5, 53–73.

———. (1985). *The structure of empirical knowledge*. Cambridge: Harvard University Press.

———. (1994). Against naturalized epistemology. In P. A. French, T. E. Uehling, & H. K. Wettstein, eds., *Midwest studies in philosophy, vol. 19: Naturalism*. Minneapolis: University of Minnesota Press.

———. (1999). The dialectic of foundationalism and coherentism. In J. Greco & E. Sosa, eds., *The Blackwell guide to epistemology*. Malden, MA: Blackwell.

———. (2001). Toward a defense of empirical foundationalism. In M. DePaul, ed., *Resurrecting old-fashioned foundationalism*. Lanham, MD: Rowman and Littlefield.

———. (2002). *Epistemology: Classical problems and contemporary responses*. Lanham, MD: Rowman and Littlefield.

Brandom, R. B. (1994). *Making it explicit: Reasoning, representing, and discursive commitment*. Cambridge, MA: Harvard University Press.

Brewer, B. (1999). *Perception and reason*. Oxford: Oxford University Press.

Carroll, L. (1895). What the tortoise said to Achilles. *Mind* 4, 278–80.

Chalmers, D. J. (1996). *The conscious mind*. Oxford: Oxford University Press.

Champene, A. R. (2003). The possibility of basic beliefs. M.A. thesis, University of Arkansas.

Charness, N., E. M. Reingold, M. Pomplun, & D. M. Stampe (2001).The perceptual aspect of skilled performance in chess: Evidence from eye movements. *Memory and Cognition* 29, 1146–52.

Chisholm, R. (1957). *Perceiving*. Ithaca, NY: Cornell University Press.

———. (1966). *Theory of knowledge*. Englewood Cliffs, NJ: Prentice Hall.

———. (1977). *Theory of knowledge*, 2nd ed. Englewood Cliffs, NJ: Prentice Hall.

———. (1982a). The foundation of empirical statements. In *The foundations of knowing*. Minneapolis: University of Minnesota Press.

———. (1982b). *The foundations of knowing*. Minneapolis: University of Minnesota Press.

———. (1989). *Theory of knowledge*, 3rd ed. Englewood Cliffs, NJ: Prentice Hall.

Churchland, P. M. (1979). *Scientific realism and the plasticity of mind*. Cambridge: Cambridge University Press.

———. (1985). Reduction, qualia, and the direct introspection of brain states. *Journal of Philosophy* 82 (1), 8–28.

———. (1988). Perceptual plasticity and theory neutrality: A reply to Jerry Fodor. *Philosophy of Science* 55, 167–87.

Clark, A. (1993). *Sensory qualities*. Oxford: Clarendon.

Coady, C. A. J. (1992). *Testimony: A philosophical study*. Oxford: Oxford University Press.

Conant, R., & J. T. Collins (1998). *Reptiles and amphibians: Eastern Central North America*. Boston: Houghton Mifflin.

Conee, E., & R. Feldman (2004). *Evidentialism: Essays in epistemology*. Oxford: Oxford University Press.

———. (2005). Some virtues of evidentialism. Presented at the American Philosophical Association, Central Division, meetings.

Crick, F. H. C., & C. Koch (1990). Towards a neurobiological theory of consciousness. *Seminars in the Neurosciences* 2, 263–75.

Cummins, R., J. Blackmon, D. Byrd, P. Poirer, M. Roth, & G. Schwarz (2001). Systematicity and the cognition of structured domains. *Journal of Philosophy*, 98, 167–85.

Davidson, D. (1986). A coherence theory of truth and knowledge. In E. Lepore, ed., *Truth and interpretation: Perspectives on the philosophy of Donald Davidson.* New York: Blackwell.

———. (1987). Knowing one's own mind. *Proceedings and Addresses of the APA* 61, 441–58.

de Groot, A. D. (1966). Perception and memory versus thought. In B. Kleinmuntz, ed., *Problem solving research, methods and theory.* New York: Wiley.

DePaul, M., ed. (2001). *Resurrecting old-fashioned foundationalism.* Lanham, MD: Rowman and Littlefield.

Descartes, R. ([1637a] 1985). *Discourse on the method.* In J. Cottingham, R. Stoothoff, & D. Murdoch, trans., *The philosophical writings of Descartes.* Cambridge: Cambridge University Press.

———. ([1637b] 1985). *Optics.* In J. Cottingham, R. Stoothoff, & D. Murdoch, trans., *The philosophical writings of Descartes.* Cambridge: Cambridge University Press.

———. ([1641] 1985). *Meditations on first philosophy.* In J. Cottingham, R. Stoothoff, & D. Murdoch, trans., *The philosophical writings of Descartes.* Cambridge: Cambridge University Press.

———. ([1644] 1985). *Principles of philosophy.* In J. Cottingham, R. Stoothoff, & D. Murdoch, trans., *The philosophical writings of Descartes.* Cambridge: Cambridge University Press.

De Soto, C. B., M. London, & M. S. Handel (1965). Social reasoning and spatial paralogic. *Journal of Personality and Social Psychology* 2, 513–21.

Duncan, L. (1982). *Chapters: My growth as a writer.* Boston: Little, Brown.

Elman, J. L., E. A. Bates, M. H. Johnson, A. Karmiloff-Smith, D. Parisi, & K. Plunkett (1996). *Rethinking innateness: A connectionist perspective on development.* Cambridge, MA: MIT Press.

Farah, M. J. (1990). *Visual agnosia.* Cambridge, MA: MIT Press.

Feldman, R. (1988). Having evidence. In D. F. Austin, ed., *Philosophical analysis.* Dordrecht: Kluwer.

———. (2003). *Epistemology.* Upper Saddle River, NJ: Prentice Hall.

Feldman, R., & E. Conee (1985). Evidentialism. *Philosophical Studies* 48, 15–34.

Felleman, D. J., & Van Essen, D. C. (1991). Distributed hierarchical processing in primate cerebral cortex. *Cerebral Cortex* 1, 1–47.

Field, H. H. (1978). Mental representation. *Erkenntnis* 13, 9–61.

Fodor, J. A. (1978). Propositional attitudes. *Monist* 61, 501–23.

———. (1983). *The modularity of mind.* Cambridge, MA: MIT Press.

———. (1984). Observation reconsidered. *Philosophy of Science* 51, 22–43.

———. (1987). Modules, frames, fridgeons, sleeping dogs, and the music of the spheres. In J. Garfield, ed., *Modularity in knowledge representation and natural-language understanding.* Cambridge, MA: MIT Press.

———. (1988). A reply to Churchland's "Perceptual plasticity and theory neutrality." *Philosophy of Science* 55, 188–94.

———. (2003). *Hume variations.* Oxford: Oxford University Press.

Fodor, J. A., & B. McLaughlin (1990). Connectionism and the problem of systematicity: Why Smolensky's solution doesn't work. *Cognition* 35, 183–204.

Fodor, J. A., & Z. W. Pylyshyn (1988). Connectionism and cognitive architecture: A critical analysis. *Cognition* 28, 3–71.

Fricker, E. (1994). Against gullibility. In B. K. Matilal & A. Chakrabarti, eds., *Knowing from words.* Dordrecht: Kluwer.

Fumerton, R. A. (1985). *Metaphysical and epistemological problems of perception*. Lincoln: University of Nebraska Press.

———. (1995). *Metaepistemology and skepticism*. Lanham, MD: Rowman and Littlefield.

———. (2001). Classical foundationalism. In M. DePaul, ed., *Resurrecting old-fashioned foundationalism*. Lanham, MD: Rowman and Littlefield.

Gibson, J. J. (1966). *The senses considered as perceptual systems*. Boston: Houghton Mifflin.

Goldman, A. H. (1988). *Empirical knowledge*. Berkeley: University of California Press.

Goldman, A. I. (1979). What is justified belief? In George Pappas, ed., *Justification and knowledge*. Dordrecht: Reidel.

———. (1986). *Epistemology and cognition*. Cambridge: Harvard University Press.

———. (1992a). Epistemic folkways and scientific epistemology. In *Liaisons*. Cambridge, MA: MIT Press.

———. (1992b). In defense of the simulation theory. *Mind and Language* 7, 104–119.

———. (1992c). *Liaisons*. Cambridge, MA: MIT Press.

———. (2006). *Simulating minds*. Oxford: Oxford University Press.

Goldstone, R. L. (1998). Perceptual learning. *Annual Review of Psychology* 49, 585–612.

Goodale, M. A., & A. D. Milner (1992). Separate visual pathways for perception and action. *Trends in Neurosciences* 15, 20–25.

———. (2004). *Sight unseen: An exploration of conscious and unconscious vision*. Oxford: Oxford University Press.

Gordon, R. M. (1986). Folk psychology as simulation. *Mind and Language* 1, 158–71.

Gould, S., & R. Lewontin (1979). The spandrels of San Marco and the Panglossian paradigm: A critique of the adaptationist programme. *Proceedings of the Royal Society of London* 205, 281–288.

Greco, J. (2000). *Putting skeptics in their place*. Cambridge: Cambridge University Press.

Gupta, A. (2006). *Empiricism and experience*. Oxford: Oxford University Press.

Haack, S. (1993). *Evidence and inquiry: Toward reconstruction in epistemology*. Oxford: Blackwell.

Harman, G. (1973). *Thought*. Princeton, NJ: Princeton University Press.

Harnish, R. M. (2002). *Minds, brains, computers*. Malden, MA: Blackwell.

Harris, P. (1992). From simulation to folk psychology: The case for development. *Mind and Language* 7, 120–44.

Helmholtz, H. von (1962). *A treatise on physiological optics*. J. P. C. Southall, ed. and trans. New York: Dover.

Hoffman, D. D. (1998). *Visual intelligence*. New York: Norton.

Huemer, M. (2001). *Skepticism and the veil of perception*. Lanham, MD: Rowman and Littlefield.

Hume, D. ([1739] 1978). *A treatise of human nature*. P. H. Nidditch, ed. Oxford: Oxford University Press.

Jolicoeur, P., M. A. Gluck, & S. M. Kosslyn (1984). Pictures and names: Making the connection. *Cognitive Psychology* 16, 243–75.

Kant, I. ([1781] 1929). *Critique of pure reason*. N. K. Smith, trans. New York: St. Martin's Press.

Kaplan, D. (1989). Demonstratives. In J. Almog, J. Perry, & H. Wettstein, eds., *Themes from Kaplan*. Oxford: Oxford University Press.

Kelemen, D. (1999). Beliefs about purpose: On the origin of teleological thought. In M. Corballis & S. Lea, eds. *The descent of mind*. Oxford: Oxford University Press.

———. (2003). Are children "intuitive theists"? Reasoning about purpose and design in nature. *Psychological Science* 15, 295–301.

Kelly, S. D. (1999). What do we see (when we do)? *Philosophical Topics* 27, 107–28.

Kitcher, P. (1992). The naturalists return. *Philosophical Review* 101, 53–114.

Knauff, M., T. Fangmeier, C. C. Ruff, & P. N. Johnson-Laird (2003). Reasoning, models, and images: Behavioral measures and cortical activity. *Journal of Cognitive Neuroscience* 15, 559–73.

Korcz, K. A. (1997). Recent work on the basing relation. *American Philosophical Quarterly* 34, 171–91.

———. (2000). The causal-doxastic theory of the basing relation. *Canadian Journal of Philosophy* 30, 525–50.

Kornblith, H. (1989). The unattainability of coherence. In J. Bender, ed., *The current state of the coherence theory*. Dordrecht: Kluwer.

———. (2002). *Knowledge and its place in nature*. Oxford: Oxford University Press.

Kosslyn, S. M. (1994). *Image and brain: The resolution of the imagery debate*. Cambridge, MA: MIT Press.

Kosslyn, S. M., W. L. Thompson, I. J. Kim, & N. M. Alpert (1995). Topographical representations of mental images in primary visual cortex. *Nature* 378, 496–98.

Kvanvig, J. L. (2003a). Coherentist theories of justification. *The Stanford Encyclopedia of Philosophy* (Winter 2003). Available at http://plato.stanford.edu/archives/win2003/entries/justep-coherence/.

———. (2003b). Justification and proper basing. In E. Olsson, ed., *The epistemology of Keith Lehrer*. Dordrecht: Kluwer.

Kvanvig, J. L., & W. D. Riggs (1992). Can a coherence theory appeal to appearance states? *Philosophical Studies* 67, 197–217.

Lackey, J. (2003). A minimal expression of non-reductionism in the epistemology of testimony. *Noûs* 37, 706–23.

Lashley, K. S. (1929). *Brain mechanisms and intelligence: A quantitative study of injury to the brain*. Chicago: University of Chicago Press.

Lehrer, K. (1974). *Knowledge*. Oxford: Clarendon.

———. (1989). *Thomas Reid*. London: Routledge.

———. (1990a). Chisholm, Reid, and the problem of the epistemic surd. *Philosophical Studies* 60, 39–45.

———. (1990b). *Theory of knowledge*. New York: Routledge.

———. (1997). *Self-trust: A study of reason, knowledge, and autonomy*. Oxford: Oxford University Press.

Locke, J. ([1690] 1975). *An essay concerning human understanding*. P. H. Nidditch, ed. Oxford: Oxford University Press.

Loftus, E. F., & J. C. Palmer (1974). Reconstruction of automobile destruction: An example of the interaction between language and memory. *Journal of Verbal Learning and Verbal Behavior* 13, 585–89.

Lyons, J. C. (1997). Testimony, induction, and folk psychology. *Australasian Journal of Philosophy* 75 (2), 163–78.

———. (1999). Epistemological consequences of a faculty psychology. Ph.D. diss., University of Arizona.

———. (2001). Carving the mind at its (not necessarily modular) joints. *British Journal for the Philosophy of Science* 52, 277–302.

———. (2003). Lesion studies, spared performance, and cognitive systems. *Cortex* 39, 145–47.

———. (2005). Clades, Capgras, and perceptual kinds. *Philosophical Topics* 33, 185–206.

Marr, D. (1982). *Vision*. London: Allen and Unwin.

Marsolek, C. J. (1999). Dissociable neural subsystems underlie abstract and specific object recognition. *Psychological Science* 10, 111–18.

McClelland, J. L. (1981). Retrieving general and specific knowledge from stored knowledge of specifics. *Proceedings of the Third Annual Conference of the Cognitive Science Society*, Berkeley, CA, 170–72.

McDowell, J. (1994). *Mind and world*. Cambridge, MA: Harvard University Press.

McGurk, H., & J. Macdonald (1976). Hearing lips and seeing voices. *Nature* 264, 746–48.

Millikan, R. G. (1984). *Language, thought, and other biological categories*. Cambridge, MA: MIT Press.

Moscovitch, M., G. Winocur, & M. Behrmann (1997). What is special about face recognition? Nineteen experiments on a person with visual object agnosia and dyslexia but normal face recognition. *Journal of Cognitive Neuroscience* 9, 555–604.

Nichols, S., & J. Knobe (2007). Moral responsibility and determinism: The cognitive science of folk intuitions. *Noûs* 41, 663–85.

Owen, D. (1999). *Hume's reason*. Oxford: Oxford University Press.

Peacocke, C. (1983). *Sense and content*. Oxford: Oxford University Press.

Peterson, M. A., & G. Rhodes, eds. (2003). *Perception of faces, objects and scenes: Analytic and holistic processes*. Oxford: Oxford University Press.

Plantinga, A. (1983). Reason and belief in God. In A. Plantinga & N. Wolterstorff, eds., *Faith and rationality*. Notre Dame, IN: University of Notre Dame Press.

———. (1993). *Warrant and proper function*. New York: Oxford University Press.

———. (2000). *Warranted Christian belief*. New York: Oxford University Press.

———. (2001). Direct acquaintance? In M. DePaul, ed., *Resurrecting old-fashioned foundationalism*. Lanham, MD: Rowman and Littlefield.

Pollock, J. L. (1986). *Contemporary theories of knowledge*. Savage, MD: Rowman and Littlefield.

———. (2001). Nondoxastic foundationalism. In M. DePaul, ed., *Resurrecting old-fashioned foundationalism*. Lanham, MD: Rowman and Littlefield.

Pollock, J. L., & J. L. Cruz (1999). *Contemporary theories of knowledge*, 2nd ed. Lanham, MD: Rowman and Littlefield.

Pryor, J. (2000). The skeptic and the dogmatist. *Noûs* 34, 517–49.

———. (2004). A defense of immediate non-inferential justification. In M. Steup & E. Sosa, eds., *Contemporary debates in epistemology*. Malden, MA: Blackwell.

Pust, J. (2000). *Intuitions as evidence*. New York: Routledge.

Putnam, H. (1975). The meaning of 'meaning'. In K Gunderson, ed., *Minnesota studies in the philosophy of science, vol. 7: Language, mind, and knowledge*. Minneapolis: University of Minnesota Press.

Pylyshyn, Z. W. (1984). *Computation and cognition*. Cambridge, MA: MIT Press.

Quinton, A. (1966). The foundations of knowledge. In B. Williams & A. Montefiore, eds., *British analytical philosophy*. London: Routledge & Kegan Paul.

Radeau, M. (1994). Auditory-visual spatial interaction and modularity. *Cahiers de Psychologie Cognitive* 13 (1), 3–51.

Ramachandran, V. S., W. S. Hirstein, K. C. Armel, E. Tecoma, & V. Iragui-Madoz (1997). The neural basis of religious experience. Society for Neuroscience Conference presentation, October 1997.

Ratliff, F. (1965). *Mach bands: Quantitative studies on neural networks in the retina*. San Francisco: Holden-Day.

Reid, T. ([1764] 1997). *An inquiry into the human mind on the principles of common sense*. D. Brooks, ed. Edinburgh: Edinburgh University Press.

———. ([1785] 1967). *Essays on the intellectual powers of man*. In *Philosophical works*. W. Hamilton, ed. Hildesheim: Georg Olms Verlagsbuchhandlung.

Reynolds, S. L. (1991). Knowing how to believe with justification. *Philosophical Studies* 64, 273–92.

Rips, L. J. (1983). Cognitive processes in propositional reasoning. *Psychological Review* 90, 38–71.

Rips, L. J., & S. L. Marcus (1977). Supposition and the analysis of conditional sentences. In M. Just & P. Carpenter, eds., *Cognitive processes in comprehension*. Hillsdale, NJ: Lawrence Erlbaum.

Roediger, H. L., & K. B. McDermott (1995). Creating false memories: Remembering words not presented in lists. *Journal of Experimental Psychology: Learning, Memory, & Cognition* 21, 803–14.

Rueckl, J. G., K. R. Cave, & S. M. Kosslyn (1989). Why are "what" and "where" processed by separate cortical visual systems? A computational investigation. *Journal of Cognitive Neuroscience* 1, 171–86.

Russell, B. ([1912] 1997). *The problems of philosophy*. New York: Oxford University Press.

Schmitt, F. F. (1992). *Knowledge and belief*. London: Routledge.

Schiffer, S. (1987). *Remnants of meaning*. Cambridge, MA: MIT Press.

Sellars, W. (1956). Empiricism and the philosophy of mind. In H. Feigl & M. Scriven, eds., *Minnesota studies in the philosophy of science*, vol. 1. Minneapolis: University of Minnesota Press.

Senor, T. D. (1995). Harman, negative coherentism, and the problem of ongoing justification. *Philosophia* 24, 271–94.

Shepard, R. N., & J. Metzler (1971). Mental rotation of 3-dimensional objects. *Science* 171, 701–3.

Shin, S. J. (1994). *The logical status of diagrams*. Cambridge: Cambridge University Press.

Siegel, S. (2006). Which properties are represented in perception? In T. Gendler & J. Hawthorne, eds., *Perceptual experience*. Oxford: Oxford University Press.

Siewert, C. P. (1998). *The significance of consciousness*. Princeton, NJ: Princeton University Press.

Sosa, E. (1980). The raft and the pyramid: Coherence vs. foundations in the theory of knowledge. In P. A. French, T. E. Uehling, & H. K. Wettstein, eds., *Midwest studies in philosophy, vol. 5: Studies in epistemology*. Minneapolis: University of Minnesota Press.

———. (1991). Reliabilism and intellectual virtue. In *Knowledge in perspective*. Cambridge: Cambridge University Press.

———. (1993). Proper functionalism and virtue epistemology. *Noûs* 27, 51–65.

———. (2007). *A virtue epistemology: Apt belief and reflective knowledge*, vol. 1. Oxford: Oxford University Press.

Spillmann, L. (1994). The Hermann grid illusion: A tool for studying human perceptive field organization. *Perception* 23, 691–708.

Steup, M. (1996). *An introduction to contemporary epistemology*. Upper Saddle River, NJ: Prentice Hall.

———. (2000). Unrestricted foundationalism and the Sellarsian dilemma. *Grazer Philosophische Studien* 60, 75–98.

Swain, S., J. Alexander, & J. Weinberg (2008). The instability of philosophical intuitions: Running hot and cold on Truetemp. *Philosophy and Phenomenological Research* 76, 138–55.

Tanaka, J. W., & M. Taylor (1991). Object categories and expertise: Is the basic level in the eye of the beholder? *Cognitive Psychology* 23, 457–82.

Teuber, H. L. (1968). Alteration of perception and memory in man: Reflection on methods. In L. Weiskrantz, ed., *Analysis of behavioral change*. New York: Harper and Row.

Titchener, E. B. (1926). *A text-book of psychology*. New York: Macmillan.

Tye, M. (1995). A representationalist theory of pains and their phenomenal character. In J. Tomberlin, ed., *Philosophical perspectives* 9. Northridge, CA: Ridgeview.

Ullman, S. (1979). *The interpretation of visual motion.* Cambridge, MA: MIT Press.

Ungerleider, L. G., & M. Mishkin (1982). Two cortical visual systems. In D. J. Ingle, M. A. Goodale, & R. J. W. Mansfield, eds., *Analysis of visual behavior.* Cambridge, MA: MIT Press.

van Cleve, J. (1985). Epistemic supervience and the circle of belief. *Monist* 62, 90–104.

————. (2002). Thomas Reid's geometry of visibles. *Philosophical Review* 111, 373–416.

Weinberg, J., S. Nichols, & S. Stich (2001). Normativity and epistemic intuitions. *Philosophical Topics* 29, 429–60.

Wiesel, T. N., & D. H. Hubel (1963). Single-cell responses in striate cortex of kittens deprived of vision in one eye. *Journal of Neurophysiology* 26, 1002–17.

Wilson, E. O. (1998). *Consilience.* New York: Knopf.

Wynn, M. K. (1992). Evidence against empiricist accounts of the origins of numerical knowledge. *Mind and Language* 7, 315–32.

Yaffee, G. (2002). Reconsidering Reid's geometry of visibles. *Philosophical Quarterly* 52, 602–20.

INDEX

195